TRIBES OF THE HILL

꧁꧂

TRIBES
ON
THE HILL

꧁꧂

J. McIVER WEATHERFORD

RAWSON, WADE PUBLISHERS, INC.
New York

Library of Congress Cataloging in Publication Data
Weatherford, J. McIver.
 Tribes on the Hill.

 Bibliography: p.
 Includes index.
 1. United States. Congress. 2. Political anthropol-
ogy. I. Title.
JK1051.W38   328.73   81-40277
ISBN 0-89256-180-7   AACR2

Copyright © 1981 by J. McIver Weatherford
All rights reserved
Published simultaneously in Canada by
McClelland and Stewart, Ltd.
Composition by American-Stratford Graphic Services, Inc.
Brattleboro, Vermont
Printed and bound by R. R. Donnelley & Sons Co.,
Crawfordsville, Indiana

Designed by Jacques Chazaud

ACKNOWLEDGMENTS

The writing of a book is rarely a solitary venture; particularly in the field of anthropology, the results usually depend upon the sustained cooperation of a number of people.

Over the past decade it has been to my great benefit to work with the political anthropologist Marc J. Swartz on research projects in Europe, Africa, and the United States. His influence undoubtedly shows in many places in this manuscript where he is not specifically cited. Much of my ethnographic training also stems from F. G. Bailey. As an anthropologist from Great Britain, he helped me to see the politics of my own society as an object of exotic study. Aside from the general debt I owe to both these anthropologists, I am particularly appreciative of the guidance they offered me in the present project. Other anthropologists who played a role in helping to develop the ideas of the book are Kevin Avruch, Peter Black, Paul Bohannan, Eleanor Gerber, Evelyn Jacob, Priscilla Reining, and Carol Stack.

In the Washington community, I was greatly assisted by Rochelle Jones, who shared her journalistic insights with me. Both she and Peter Woll encouraged and helped me on the basis of their own experiences as writers of political books.

Dan Davis acted as one of those special friends every writer needs—someone who knows the subject matter intimately and also has a firm grasp on the subtleties of the English language. In a similar fashion, Z. I. Giralso shared her historical skills with me in researching the long history of this tribe.

A great deal of anthropological research is done around the campfire, the Capitol Hill equivalent being the lunch or dinner table. Consequently, I spent more time sitting at the American Café than on the floor of the Senate and more time dining at La Brasserie than listening to committee hearings. Gabriel Aubovin and Raymond Campet of La Brasserie made my life "in the bush" far more bearable with their outstanding food and warm friendship. Many of those dinner hours were spent with John and Nancy Neubauer, who provided much-needed counteropinions and sincere encouragement.

The greatest debt of all is owed to my first editor, Walker Pearce. Despite her dogged disagreement, she never waivered in her support. Her wealth of knowledge and her enthusiasm saved me from abandoning the project on several occasions.

Credit or blame for the spelling goes to Walker Pearce Maybank, who checked such matters with an accuracy that put me to shame. Roy Pearce Maybank assisted in the research and proved invaluable in gaining access to some of the seemingly impenetrable offices of senators. Special appreciation goes to R. Roy Pearce and Margery Walker Pearce, who bought the typewriter and contributed in many very tangible ways.

My early work in Congress was made possible by the American Association for the Advancement of Science and by the Society for Research in Child Development. While acknowledging my debt to these organizations and to Richard Scribner and Eileen Blumenthal, in particular, they should not be held responsible for the results. Their early financial assistance, however, makes it possible for me to say that no taxpayer's money was used for this research, which some politician might otherwise attack as a waste and as qualifying for a Golden Fleece Award.

Special gratitude is owed to John Glenn and to his staff. Even though this book in no way represents a study of him and even though he does not agree with everything in it, it was in working as an assistant to him that many of the ideas originated. His encouragement throughout the project and his occasional skepticism both helped to improve the content. In order to protect his and Annie Glenn's privacy, nothing in the book is written to reflect upon them, but their encouragement is appreciated.

Many of the people who work on Capitol Hill and who assisted me should remain nameless out of respect for their own careers. Particular thanks, however, go to Diane Lifsey, Edward Furtek, and Catherine Prendergast, who read the manuscript and supplied valuable suggestions.

Joyce Howser and Patty Dinwiddie assisted with the typing under adverse circumstances, and my sincere appreciation goes to them both.

*Dedicated
with Love and Appreciation
to*

*Alfred Gregg Weatherford
and
Anna Ruth Grooms Weatherford*

◆§◈

CONTENTS

CONCLUSION

TRIBES OF THE HILL

1

❦❦❦

On a Hill Faraway

IKE TIMBUKTU, SODOM, and Babylon, the City of Washington shimmers on the edge of reality, more a state of mind
than a physical place. Its blurred pastiche of scandal, power,
and money in inconceivably enormous sums combines to paint
a larger than life scene that provokes awe, comedy, and dread.
As some site lost in time and space and enshrouded in the fogs of
myth, Washington evokes sensations more like a convulsive
shudder from the primal memory than rational understanding.
In its surreal dimensions, the city and its culture float just beyond the grasp of the rest of the world.

Twentieth-century Americans are not the first to feel that
deep bewilderment at life on the Potomac. The settlement of
Jamestown, Virginia, had barely appeared in the New World
when the hapless Henry Fleet stumbled into and nearly lost his
life in the complex alliances, chiefly rivalries, and monopoly economics of the Washington area. Wandering into the site of the
present national capital, which was at the time the Conoy Indian trading center of Nacochtanke, Fleet arrived in 1623
searching for beaver furs. Unknown to Fleet, the Chief of Nacochtanke claimed a monopoly on the trade and was struggling
to protect it from the Chief of Patawomeke farther downriver.

Fearing that Fleet was allied with the Patawomeke, the Chief of Nacochtanke ordered his capture. When it became apparent that Fleet represented an even larger and potentially more dangerous tribe of Europeans, he ordered Fleet imprisoned for life. The chief could not afford to let these new people know the details of his lucrative trade and possibly threaten it as the Patawomeke chief had done.

For five years Fleet remained a captive, but one with a "trustee" status that allowed him to get to know something about the life of the Conoy. In due course, however, he took advantage of his casual imprisonment to escape. Once out of the Conoy's hands, Fleet did exactly what the old chief had feared: he sailed off to England and procured financial backing for a major trading expedition up the Potomac to this new "strange and populous nation."

Despite Fleet's lengthy sojourn on the Potomac, he never really grasped the subtleties of politics there. When he returned with his new ship, the Nacochtanke chief, by now resigned to sharing some of the wealth with the newcomers, demanded "a present" in exchange for permission to trade. Fleet refused, sailed on past Nacochtanke, and set to trading directly with the Indians. To his dismay, he found that his new trading partners demanded even higher levels of tribute from him. Fleet was trapped between the firm demand of the Indians upriver and the squadron of canoes sent in pursuit by the Nacochtanke chief. He managed once again to escape with his life, but in explaining the situation to his backers, Fleet penned the first example of restrained bureaucratic reportage from the Potomac. As he described the attacks, the Conoy "did seek to withdraw me from having commerce with the other Indians . . . because they knew that our trade might hinder their benefit."

Fleet's repeated failures to deal effectively with the political system on the Potomac in the 1620s is not unlike the difficulty any outsider to the area would experience in the 1980s. The tangled web of chiefly rivalries, the conflicting demands of turf, the strange language and customs, and the exchange of "presents" are all just as important and yet no less difficult to understand today.

The continuities between life in the Conoy town of Nacochtanke and modern life on Capitol Hill, however, may not be immediately apparent. In the intervening centuries, the new residents have done everything seemingly imaginable to plaster over the old culture. The name "Nacochtanke" has long since been Latinized into Anacostia, a division of Washington, while the closest survival of the "Patawomeke" is the crisp, Anglicized Potomac. The highest mound in the area was rechristened Capitol Hill after the high point in Rome where the great temple of Jupiter Optimus Maximus stood. Instead of a temple to the Roman god, however, the new settlers built on it a temple to democracy, the United States Capitol. To match the majesty of this new Rome of the Americas, the little Goose Creek at the bottom of the hill was renamed the Tiber, but in due time it had to be covered to make room for the expanding edifices of the Byzantine bureaucracy.

Since the time of Fleet, the new residents on the Potomac have waged a steady campaign to hide the older history, or prehistory as they like to think of it, by emphasizing a mythical genealogy that connects the City of Washington to London and Paris and back to the classical civilizations of Rome and Athens. Within their ten square miles, they tried to recreate all the marvels of the classical world, erecting the most eclectic collection of architecture known to archeology. Down from the Greco-Roman Capitol stands the world's largest masonry obelisk, built in pharaonic style to honor the founder of the country. Flanking it are a Roman temple dedicated to Thomas Jefferson and a Greek temple commemorating Abraham Lincoln, complete with a massive statue of the President seated like Zeus ready to confer judgment on the mortals below. In addition to the Georgian country mansion blown up to American size for a home of the current President, the surrounding hills of the city, like those of Rome, hold architectural wonders from the Old World. A Romanesque-Byzantine cathedral stares at the Capitol from the northeast, while a Gothic one stares from the northwest. Of the Seven Wonders of the Ancient World, Washington has copied two: the great lighthouse of Alexandria, Egypt, now located in Alexandria, Virginia; and the tomb of King Mausolus of Halicarnassus, now found on 16th Street, N.W. Directly across from the Senate chamber stands a replica of the great Triumphal

Arch of the emperor Constantine, now used as the entrance to Union Train Station, the inside of which is a recreation of the Baths of Diocletian, complete with twenty-five-ton statues of the gods of fire and electricity.

More a predecessor to Disneyland than a successor to Rome, Washington emphasizes the facade over the contents, appearance over reality. The same trait appears in the organization of the government that its buildings house. The division of the federal government into the executive, judicial, and legislative branches traces its origins back through *L'Esprit des lois* of Montesquieu to *The Politics* of Aristotle. The Constitution itself derived from the Magna Carta, the common-law traditions of the Germanic tribes, and Roman legal theory. The House of Representatives combines the British House of Commons with the Athenian Assembly, and in choosing a title for the upper House of Congress, the founding fathers bypassed the aristocratic part of the British Parliament to borrow the name of the Senate of republican Rome.

Yet, if we scratch the surface of the facade of these neoclassical designs, we find in Washington a rhythm of life far different from that of the Old World. A number of these features would be as readily recognizable to the old Chief of Nacochtanke as they are to the modern congressman. When the House of Representatives, for example, sits down to do real business, it meets in "caucus," a word which, despite its Latin resonance, came from the Algonquin language, signifying the tribal councils that influenced early settlers' ideas of democracy. Similarly, the United States Senate, despite its Roman name, is organized not at all like the patrician families of Rome which it frequently mimics, but instead like the formal organization of the League of the Iroquois with which the Conoy Indians were allied. The League and its Congress of Sachems represented the fifty permanent groups, or sachemships, of the five Indian nations within it. As in the Senate, each of the tribes of the League had an equal voice, no matter how large or small their population. Like the modern Congress, the League had its Doorkeeper and Assistant Doorkeeper, as well as the Keeper of the Wampum who recorded the laws of the nation in wampum belts.

The extensive parallels between various Indian institutions

and the modern American government reach deep into the political process. In the inner core of political life in the twentieth century, politics, that ancient brand of face-to-face interaction, is not far removed from what it was four or five centuries ago. The Chief of Nacochtanke building a monopoly over the fur trade and trying to outmaneuver his rival chiefs sounds strikingly similar to the persistent disputes between the House and the Senate for control over the flow of government revenues. The many-layered network of relations existing among contemporary politicians, bureaucrats, lobbyists, and journalists parallels some of those among various chiefs, clans, villagers, and tribes encountered by Fleet in 1623. A senator presiding over a dispute between competing bureaucrats for administration of the same government project is not unlike an Indian chief arbitrating between the conflicting demands of rival clans over the same cornfield, each side complete with a battery of witnesses and complex historical precedents for their defense.

Like the native politicians before them, modern congressmen also clothe their political activities in the awesomeness of ritual and ceremony, filled with fetishes and an esoteric argot. The initiation of a new brave into the ranks of manhood, and his rising to give his first oration before the caucus of his seniors, are not far removed from the initiation of a freshman congressman and the delivery of his maiden speech. The make-up and careful attention to dress, the right arrangement of authority-evoking colors, and most imposing coiffure are no less important to the twentieth-century politician before the television camera than to the brave before his clansmen.

WHERE THE MASTODONS ROAM

Any understanding of Washington and its continuity with the past begins with the geographical and historical setting of the city. Washington is a gift of the last Ice Age. Its present importance in America owes more to that time and to the mastodons who roamed the area 20,000 years ago than it does to the politics of Athens and Rome. Before we can unravel congressional politics in the back room, or a funding feud between clans, or even a congressional sex scandal, we need to know

something about the Ice Age that made possible the rise of Nacochtanke and its evolution into the modern city of Washington.

The great ice sheets of the Wisconsin period never quite
reached the present site of Washington, but as the glaciers from
that time slowly melted and withdrew toward the Arctic, they
carved up the face of North America in a peculiar way. Washington and the whole of the Potomac River valley were left in
position to influence greatly the movements of large game animals, including mammoths, caribou, and mastodons as they
migrated across the North American plate.

As its name implies, the North American plate is largely a
huge, flat plain of land; but flanking it on both sides are the thin
mountain ridges of the Appalachians in the East and the
Rockies in the West. Just beyond these mountains lie ribbons of
coastal plain on both the Atlantic and the Pacific sides of the
continent. Even though the great interior plain is a fertile grass-
land, it is the coastal plains that harbor the greatest abundance
and diversity of life forms, including the thickest populations of
humans on the continent. Being warmed by ocean currents, the
coastal areas were not as thickly iced as the northern interior of
the continent during the Ice Ages. The richer vegetation of the
coast lured caribou, wild pigs, and squirrels into the area. Following them lurked their predators, the wolves, foxes, and bears.
The expanding food sources also attracted the appetites of
mammoths and mastodons, ever in search of more fuel for their
gargantuan frames. And on the heels of the mastodons came
their predators, humans.

In those early migrations of mastodons and humans, the Potomac River valley and the area around Washington, in particular, developed a special role. Originating high in the Appala-
chian Mountains, the Potomac River approximates a natural
corridor linking the coastal plain of the Atlantic seaboard with
the Ohio and Mississippi River valleys and thereby with the
vast interior of the North American continent. Thus, 20,000
years ago the Potomac emerged as a primary east-west route
connecting two major ecological zones.

The river valley may have been an advantage to mastodons
or humans travelling east to west, but rivers are also barriers to

travel up and down the coastal plain. Near the coast, the rivers are much too wide to cross as they fan out and empty into the Atlantic. Yet, in the narrow headwaters of the rivers steep mountains intervene between each river. The easiest place to cross those rivers is roughly in the middle, down the Fall Line that separates the mountainous regions from the very flat coast.

The point at which the Fall Line crosses the Potomac River is the present site of Washington, D.C., making it the prehistoric crossroads at the junction of east-west and north-south routes. Washington was then the natural spot at which a mastodon ambling up from South Carolina to Ohio would cross the path of another mastodon on his way from Maine to Arkansas. For the early Indian who may have tired of following these beasts on their long treks, the area around Washington became a good spot at which to hang around and wait for another migrating mastodon. In between mastodons, the area furnished enough diversity in plants, fish, and smaller game to keep the hunter and family well fed.

The exact date at which the first village was founded in the District of Columbia lies lost in prehistory, but it probably occurred early in the Archaic period, about 8,000 years ago, at roughly the same time that Jericho in the Middle East was being established. As the Indians settled in the area, they found that it had more to offer than the profligate flora and fauna on its surface. In particular, it was a large source of steatite, commonly called soapstone. From this malleable but durable material the early residents manufactured ornate bowls, tobacco pipes, and diverse tools that helped them to capture the smaller, more agile animals, to trap the large quantities of fish in the river, and eventually to till the soil and raise crops. One of the largest steatite quarries in the East stood about two and a half miles up Connecticut Avenue from the present location of the White House. Scattered around the quarry the Indians built small manufacturing shops, where the stone was worked and carved before being traded. Relics from this period constantly surface in the twentieth century as growth in the Washington area accelerates: as recently as 1975, in digging for President Gerald Ford's swimming pool on the White House grounds, relics from these earlier civilizations emerged.

Gradually, as the population around the site grew and its importance as a crossroads increased to include manufacturing and trade, the Washington site began to prosper. About a thousand years before Christ the East Coast began the era of Indian history known as the Woodland period. About the time that Alexander the Great left Macedonia to conquer Persia, the Indians of the area began manufacturing pottery; and by the time of Julius Caesar, the Washington Indians learned to cultivate maize corn from their neighbors in classical Mexico. Their knowledge of growing corn paved the way for the cultivation of squash, beans, gourds, and other domestic crops from the Mexican highlands. Combined with the earlier manufacturing, fishing, and hunting of the area, life around Washington reached a level of civilization roughly analogous to that of the Celts, Angles, and Saxons of northern Europe. The typical Indian from Washington in the millennium before Columbus would probably have felt much more at home in the court of King Arthur or Charlemagne than he would among the Hollywood images of Cochise or Sitting Bull from the Great Plains and the Southwest.

Throughout this new surge of civilization, Washington remained a focal and crossing point for the new Indian cultures as much as it had been for the mastodons and Paleo-Indians of the earlier era. It was at this point that three major language families of North America came together; these were the Iroquoian to the North, Algonquin to the East, and Siouan to the West. Further south were the Muskogean languages of the Creeks and other Civilized Nations. Politically, Washington was a transition zone separating and unifying the Iroquois League to the north, the Five Civilized Nations to the south, and the Siouan tribes to the plains.

Because the Potomac area was so thickly populated, the first European colonists were unable to settle it, being forced into more remote and inhospitable areas such as Jamestown where fewer Indians lived. The first European resident in the area did not arrive until almost a century after the major Indian centers of the Mayas, Aztecs, and Incas had already fallen to European invaders. Here the slow conquest of the Indian nations of North America by English invaders is in contrast to the rapid conquest

of Central and South America by the Spanish. The conquista-
dores entered their domains with small armies, which marched
straight to regional and national capitals, conquering the Indians with superior European arms and the awe-inspiring horse.
The Spanish then set about erecting new settlements on the
ruins of the old ones. The English, however, first entered North
America in small enclaves of colonists. Once established, these
colonies slowly expanded with new immigrants. The conquest
of the Indians owed more to the new epidemic diseases introduced by the Europeans than to their superior cannons and
muskets. As the Indians slowly succumbed to the poxes and
fevers carried by the English, they became easy targets for the
colonial expansion. In this way, Indian settlements such as the
Potomac River valley and the Iroquois, Creek, and Cherokee
nations suffered decades of strangulation and atrophy before
the English moved in for the final kill.

Just how great a change occurred in the area is evident if we
compare the characterization of Washington in 1800 as a "ma-
larial swamp" with the description given by Henry Fleet in the
1620s:

This place without all question is the most pleasant and
healthful in all this country, and most convenient for habita-
tion, the air temperate in summer and not violent in winter.
It aboundeth in all manner of fish. . . . And as for deer, buffa-
loes, bears, turkey, the woods do swarm with them, and the
soil is exceedingly fertile.

The land was nominally granted to one George Thompson in
the mid-seventeenth century under the authority of the English
king, Charles II, but it was to take another hundred years before
the white occupation became a fact with the final expulsion of
the Indians. During this century of conquest the area around
Washington experienced profound ecological changes.

The Indians, lacking beasts of burden, travelled by footpath,
or, when they had cargoes of furs or crops to be transported,
carried them by canoe. But the first Europeans brought horses
and eventually oxen-pulled carts and wagons to transport
goods. The footpaths were widened to accommodate the new

transports, while the firm ground trod by generations of human feet became ruts and bogs under the hoofs of the oxen and wheels of the heavy carts and carriages. In the rain the ruts turned to mud, which proved a favorite wallowing spot for the other European animal, the pig. As the English established their villages of Alexandria and Georgetown, more oxen, horses, pigs, carts, carriages, and people came into the area. By the time the site was chosen as the national capital of the United States, it was nearly drowning in a pigsty of soupy mud that became a breeding ground for mosquitoes and another European import, malaria.

It was this diseased and decaying place that George Washington and the founding fathers "discovered" as a suitable site on which to build a national government. From his work travelling around the area as a land surveyor and officer during the French-Indian and Revolutionary wars, George Washington in fact had rediscovered what the Indians had known before him and the mastodons before them. Commanding troops at the headwaters of the Potomac River, the general realized that the river was the best connection to the inland Ohio River system.

The new technology of the European invaders with their railroads and canals finally bypassed the Potomac River as the prairie corridor to the West; but in the meantime, the banks of the Potomac had been selected for the new national capital. The first proposal to locate the capital on the Potomac originated in the Continental Congress of 1783; but it was not until 1790, after the Constitutional Convention, that Congress under the new presidency of George Washington finally decided on the exact spot. This new designation of the area was not so much a radical departure for the site as a return to the regional status it had known under the Woodland Indians. Even as capital of the thirteen small seaboard colonies, Washington was little more than a secondary regional center, ranking behind most state capitals in importance. From here it would grow into a major national, continental, and, eventually, international center: the gradual evolution from its original status as a mastodon crossroads, through a major Indian center, to eventual position as a national capital, shows the modern role of Washington as a clear and almost linear extension of the role it had already played for several thousand years.

Thus, the importance of the city did not spring fully grown from the perspicacity of George Washington, Pierre L'Enfant, and the founding fathers. It was more hindsight than foresight that pointed out to them the significance of the area. Like cities as varied as Peking, Rome, Cuzco, and Jerusalem, Washington has a precise history, which seems to continue of its own accord regardless of who happens to occupy, control, or conquer it. The present name of the site may have originated in the eighteenth century, but its historical role stretches back millennia in time. The current inhabitants of Washington are but the latest in a long succession of residents to build atop and benefit from the previous civilization, but the present inhabitants are still bound by the same geography, climate, and environment.

In laying out their capital, however, the new residents did not see themselves as the inheritors of an Indian civilization. That their own prosperity derived from their continued cultivation of the Indian crops of tobacco, cotton, and corn, as well as the fact that they took over the Indian fur trade, was of little significance to them. The new residents arrived to build the new Rome, not a new Nacochtanke. And in the rush to build the new city, all remnants of the past were buried. As the archeologists Robert Humphrey and Mary E. Chambers put it: "The tragedy of unchecked urban development and suburban sprawl have eradicated every trace of nearly all these remarkably archaeological sites. The remains of the implement shops, soapstone quarry, and fishing villages . . . now lie below buildings, houses, and roads."

Most of that archeological history is forever lost to us. As future centuries unfold, we may find an occasional Indian remnant irrevocably smashed beneath tons of marble and concrete in the building of the downtown bureaucracy, or possibly a few steatite pots dredged from the mud of the Potomac. For the most part, however, the civilization has been permanently destroyed, ground into gravel for the sidewalks of Washington, dug out for the subway system and underground garages, flattened for roads, and excavated for swimming pools and sewer pipes. But even what little we know of it helps to place Washington within the appropriate historical context, showing that it is as much shaped by, as the shaper of, its environment. It is this history of the physical place of Washington that we should bear in mind as we approach the modern city and its inhabitants. The background of mastodons and Ice Age, of prairie corridor and Fall Line, and of Paleo-Indians is more important to our analysis than the intellectual milieu of Enlightenment ideas, Anglo-Saxon jurisprudence, or the political ideals of classical Greece.

EXPLORING THE CONGRESSIONAL CATACOMBS

Today, the two highest points in Washington are the twin spires of the Washington Monument and the Capitol dome. By law, no structure may surpass the height of these edifices. Looking only loosely like a bloated Temple of Jupiter, the Capitol perches atop Capitol Hill with its wings extended, ready to swoop down on the bureaucratic fortresses below.

By growing up in America we feel that we *know* what the Congress is like. We see pictures of the Capitol in the newspapers; the monuments and postcard vistas of Washington slip through our fingers when we drop a coin into a vending machine, and they cross our tongue when we stamp a letter. Every night the inside and outside of the Capitol intrude into our living rooms with yet another televised report from the lawn of the Capitol or a snippet from a congressional hearing room. At some point in our lives, most of us have hurried through the marble halls either on a school tour or with our own kids in tow as we plod through an educational family vacation. And it seems that every year in school we waded through one more book on American history, civics, or political science.

Congress is a familiar theme. But this time, let us try to look at Congress with some of the same novel detachment with which we would look at the Paleo-Indians who used to live around Washington or the early Algonquins who fished the Potomac and hunted on Capitol Hill. Let us approach the Capitol building the same way that we would Tutankhamen's tomb, an Aztec pyramid, or the hut of a New Guinea hunter. Putting away as many preconceived notions as possible, perhaps we can find something new that will help us to understand what goes on inside the Capitol.

Viewed from afar, the most striking characteristics of the Capitol are its huge size, its sheer whiteness, and its precise symmetry. The massive facade implies a neat, systematic arrangement of activity and organization within its perfect curves and pure parallels. The two identical wings of the building stretch out in pristine symmetry to house the two equal chambers of Congress, exactly as specified in the Constitution—two bodies united by the imposing majesty of one of the largest domes in the world.

As we move closer to the building, its architectural features become somewhat distorted. That dome looms precariously and a bit too large over the sides of the building, and the massive steps do not fit the human scale; only energetic tourists exhibit the stamina to climb them. Underneath the steps are smaller doors and even hidden driveways large enough for limousines to enter and discharge passengers who are screened from the gaze of outsiders. Upon entering the building, confusion abounds. The formal symmetry of the outside is not reflected in the interior. Large passageways go nowhere, merely connecting a door into the building with another door leading out of the building on the other side. The side halls are more like mazes linking one room after another, with an endless progression of odd names and ornate but empty lobbies. There are statues, paintings, busts, and murals in a pastiche of history. George Washington sits with Neptune and Mercury. King Kamehameha of Hawaii reaches out, almost goosing General Lee with his spear. Will Rogers seems to be telling a joke to Father Serra, founder of the California missions, and Pocahontas is being baptized in front of the Magna Carta. Richard Nixon stares out of the window ignoring John C. Calhoun, while down the hall Neil Armstrong steps out of his moon ship, narrowly missing a Carolina parrot and a plow.

Windows open onto blank walls. Cavernous rooms obviously built for some specific purpose now stand neglected, while small cubicles seem jammed with people and papers. Like a Victorian home that has been added to and remodeled through the years, the interior of the Capitol is a jumble of styles and history. Since the cornerstone was laid on September 18, 1793, by George Washington, the building has been built and rebuilt, added to and burned, rebuilt and extended, so much so that the cornerstone was buried in the mass and subsequent searches for it have all failed. A new wing was appended here, a new facade there, a larger dome, a more imposing front. Care was taken to preserve the external symmetry, but at the great expense of internal continuity. Walking through the halls and rooms of the Capitol, one might wonder if this were not in fact the attic of the Smithsonian Institution rather than a national legislature.

The facade of Congress and its interior seem to be two separate and unconnected spheres. But if we follow our archeological instincts down into the basement, we find ourselves in a third and totally different layer in the physical layout of Congress. Between plain walls and waterpipes is a busy world bustling, not with tourists and school classes, but with congressmen trying to get past the carts of dining-room linen, staffers racing past refrigerators to attend a committee hearing, and senators taking time out for a cigarette before bounding upstairs to meet with the waiting visitors from Peoria.

Through unmarked miles of catacombs, we can wander around the real corridors of power. This underground world has its own television and recording studios, cafeterias and snack bars, which bear no resemblance to the formal dining rooms above. There are barbershops and beauty salons, newsstands and tobacco kiosks, stationery shops and computers, banks and travel bureaus. The underground complex houses a virtual hidden city, connecting not just various parts of the Capitol building itself but nearby office buildings, the Library of Congress, and massive underground parking garages. The complex of tunnels and underground chambers is large enough to necessitate three miniature subway lines exclusively for the use of legislators and staffers in the Capitol complex. With few signs pointing the way, and few doors marked by name to hint at what is behind them, the underground complex may be initially more confusing than the one above ground, but there is a familiarity to what goes on underneath. It feels much more like a suburban

shopping mall or a large high school than the marble colon-
naded passageways of the Capitol above.

To the inhabitants of the Hill, this underground complex is a
much easier place in which to maneuver. Just as villagers anywhere in the world know the back paths between City Hall and
the church, the denizens of the Capitol know how to leave one
office and pop up at the correct committee room without ever
going above ground. They avoid the great ceremonial hall connecting the House of Representatives with the Senate; they de-
tour beneath the massive rotunda and all the statues.

The tripartite division of the Capitol into its formal facade, a
chaotic interior, and underground catacombs mirrors the three
cultural levels of congressional action. The simplified exterior of
Congress as ordained in the Constitution and outlined in civic
texts is the public appearance, which Congress only halfheart-
edly tries to maintain before its skeptical public. Behind this facade appear the semi-public arenas of power politics, seniority,
and redoubtable chairmen—the complex and dizzying view of
politics presented in the daily newspapers and nightly news.
Underlying both of these versions of Congress operates the unmarked underground, which despite its initial appearance of
chaos turns out to be a reasonably simple way of getting things
done. These cultural catacombs house what the political analysts Rochelle Jones and Peter Woll have dubbed "the private
world of Congress," which is so often alluded to in political discussions, but so rarely explained.

Much of the difficulty in discussing these nether regions of
Congress arises from the lack of names for their parts. The visitor to the above-ground part of Congress finds a catalogue of
names for the exterior and interior of the building, and these
names correspond with pieces of the social organization of Congress. The Senate Wing and the House Wing enclose the Senate
chamber and the House chamber. They are in turn surrounded
by the Foreign Relations Committee, Statuary Hall, the Senate
Lobby, Office of the Doorkeeper, and so forth, down to the
smaller rooms, which suffice with numbers instead of names.
Each of these names represents a physical space; but more important, it designates a social entity or institutional actor as

well. It becomes very easy to blur this distinction between people and rooms, as when a journalist reports that "it was decided in the Appropriations Committee Room," "by a vote on the Senate floor," or "meeting in the caucus room. . . ." The social and spatial underground of Congress is much more difficult to discuss simply. Without names, the spaces can only be referred to obliquely in such phrases as "meeting behind closed doors," "in a rash of back-room negotiations," or "in the bowels of Congress. . . ." Sometimes the activity may be assigned to "the Cloakroom," as an amorphous catchall space in which happens whatever it is that the reporter cannot explain.

This type of analysis accentuates some parts of the congressional structure while leaving equally important parts quite vague. The Caucus, the Committee, and the Conference all become concrete actors as firm and real as the marble and oak paneling in the rooms with the same names. Yet the equally important activities of the back room, the underground corridor, or some unnamed group of people can only be alluded to in somewhat sinister terms. One of the main purposes of this analysis is to figure out what these other units of action are and to give them names. Our investigation is here concerned less with the caucuses and committees of the formal congressional organization than with the entities to which names will be applied as we encounter them. The book contains no flow chart of "How a Bill Becomes a Law," no diagram of "The Organization of Our Congress," no chapter on "The Way Government Works." Much of that formalized information is simply unnecessary to our task, as it is often superfluous to politics. The explanatory path through those vertiginous mazes of diagrams and organization charts has lost and killed many an otherwise admirable explanation of Congress; any reader who has survived high-school civics lessons can attest that the results often generate more confusion than clarification.

As an example of what happens when too much energy is spent on the formal organization, we can look at the problems with one of the best books ever written on Congress, Woodrow Wilson's *Congressional Government*. In the 1880s, Wilson wrote this as his doctoral dissertation at Princeton University, and later published it as a best-selling political book. In it he said:

Like a vast picture thronged with figures of equal prominence and crowded with elaborate and obtrusive details, Congress is hard to see satisfactorily and appreciatively at a single view and from a single stand-point. Its complicated forms and diversified structure confuse the vision, and conceal the system which underlies its composition.

Despite this accurate and still true picture of congressional confusion, Wilson went ahead trying to make sense of the facade rather than the "system which underlies its composition." This congressional underground was particularly hard for Woodrow Wilson to see because he stayed several hundred miles away in New Jersey and never bothered to observe personally the Congress he was trying to explain. Wilson preferred not to get bogged down in those elaborate details that obscure the vision. In the politically safe and intellectually pure climate of academe, his sterling logic and graceful prose could soar above cold fact and tarnished reality. Not surprisingly, three decades later when he took office as President, he experienced difficulty managing Congress. The task of getting the Treaty of Versailles through all those elaborate and obtrusive details proved too great for him.

As difficult as it was for Wilson to explain the formal organization of Congress a century ago, that facade is even more complex today. The congressional framework houses 435 representatives, 100 senators, 5 delegates, the Vice President of the United States, and 25,000 staffers. Nearly thirty caucuses represent not just the two major parties but every special-interest group from steel and coal to tourism and mushrooms. As of 1980, 379 committees, subcommittees, boards, and formal coalitions claimed some bailiwick, and each had its own chairman, from three to three dozen members, up to 200 employees, and budgets as large as $5 million. Paralleling these, the party structures have their own officers, committees, rooms, and staff, among them the Majority and Minority leaders, as well as all the Whips and Assistant Whips in each chamber. Then come the fifty state delegations, each headed by its respective dean or chairman, and behind them another layer of units, varying from the Democratic Study Group and the Wednesday Club to the almost farcical Chowder and Marching Band or the old Board of Education. These in turn are augmented by staff organizations, press assistants' clubs, and staff officers such as the Doorkeeper, Sergeant at Arms, Secretary, Architect, Chaplains, and Parliamentarians, each organization with its own staff.

The list could quite literally fill a volume, and it does indeed take a whole volume of the *Congressional Directory* just to list all the entities and titles that make up the formal structure of Congress. Unless we avoid that tangled web, we may find ourselves in an Escher drawing in which stairs going up end at their own beginning and fish merge into fowl. This Alice in Wonderland world numbs the senses and atrophies the mind as the things we look at get "curiouser and curiouser." Attempting to avoid the trap that ensnared Wilson and so many other congressional analysts, we will approach Congress as an anthropological endeavor. Like Margaret Mead explaining the Samoans or Bronislaw Malinowski untangling Trobriand Island culture, we can look at Congress in the full glory of its strangeness. In so doing, we can use the native concepts of committee, caucus, or seniority when they help in the explanation, but if necessary we can also pull in new ones.

THE ANTHROPOLOGICAL PERSPECTIVE

The task confronting any observer of Congress—whether journalist, academic, voter, or even spy—resembles that of an anthropologist stumbling into the middle of a tribal village. The natives do bizarre things and speak in strange ways. They arrange themselves in an amorphous web of clans, phratries, sibs, moieties, and lineages. As soon as sense can be made of these, the observer must decipher the morass of age grades, women's clubs, men's huts, elders' councils, and warrior groups. Taboos must be separated from courtesies, myths from history, and sacred objects from tools and from garbage. The anthropologist sifts and sorts, codifies and reduces this information to find some simpler, coherent theme in the culture, some underlying principle of human organization.

Throughout the process the observer must try to combat his own as well as the native's ethnocentrism. This temptation toward ethnocentrism is all the greater in a society with the un-precedented technological achievements of twentieth-century America. Even though we have been the first nation in the history of the world to fly to the moon or develop computers, that does not mean that our culture and society are unique. While granting that American society has produced a technology of unprecedented scope, it does not necessarily follow that Americans have built a social or political organization which is so vastly different from that of other peoples.

Whereas the technological range of human tools and machines seems extraordinarily diverse, the behavioral repertoire of humans appears remarkably circumscribed and repetitive. Each society organizes its institutions with different accents and rhythms, but the gamut of behavior remains the same. Particularly in the political sphere, human history seems a constant repetition of a very few behavioral themes. The amassing of power, the exercise of that power, and the losing of power show great similarities, no matter whether the society in question is a hunting band of only two dozen or a mighty nation of 200 million members. In the scale of human history, it has been hardly more than a blink of an eye since mankind settled into permanent villages and formed institutions such as the Roman Empire or the American Congress. It is not then surprising to find the same kinds of behavior among a congressional committee gathered in front of a television camera as we would among a group of tribal elders gathered before the tribe. Both sets of people share a common human history stretching back across millions of years. The full range of human political behavior shows no signs of being different today, on the dawn of the twenty-first century, than it did three thousand years ago in ancient Greece. We have certainly not invented any new form of government in the intervening centuries that was not already known and described by the Greek philosophers.

The tribal origins of all of these forms are still evident in our political vocabulary today. The very word "Congress" comes from the Latin *con* and *gradi,* meaning to go or walk together, and is related to the Latin word *grex* or flock, which is preserved in the related words "congregate" and "gregarious." And the "Senate" is derived from the Latin, meaning a council of elders, as related to other words, such as "senior" and "senility." A *senate* was much the same in Latin as a *caucus* was in the Algonquin language. The continuity between the modern Congress and earlier political forms is greater than etymological trivia. Just as words preserve within them forgotten and obsolete meanings, so, too, our political institutions preserve within themselves long-forgotten residues from our common tribal ancestry. Our modern institutions may broadcast themselves via television and radio rather than by drum beating and smoke signals, and they may record themselves on the printed page rather than by pictographs or wampum, but the underlying process of political activity remains fairly constant.

Seen in this light, there is nothing outrageous and certainly nothing invidious in comparing the American Congress with an East African baraza, with the Senate of Rome, or with a tribal council in New Guinea. On the very spot where the House Appropriations Committee meets to divvy up a $600 billion annual budget, it is quite possible that a group of Indians gathered to distribute the day's fish harvest or to divide a mastodon. The process differed in the scope of its results, but not necessarily in the way the results were decided. Under the same ancient tree where a congressman pauses to tape a short television interview for the evening news, it is possible that an Indian chief once addressed his own supporters in preparation for a battle, hunt, or trading expedition.

This book approaches the United States Congress from such a comparative perspective, looking past the facade to see just what goes on in Congress, and how it both resembles and differs from political behavior around the world. Anthropology is basically a two-pronged science: one branch is archeology and the study of the material culture left behind by previous societies. The outlines of the archeological history of Washington have been mentioned already. The other branch of anthropology is ethnology, the study and description of the living institutions of humankind—literally the study of *ethnos,* a people or cultural group, and of their *ethos,* or character and institutions. The ethnological approach that taught us so much about Zulu warriors, Indian castes, Aztec sacrifice, and Samoan sexuality can also be used to probe modern American institutions.

In using the anthropological approach, we seek to answer the same three basic questions of ethnography asked of any community, tribe, or institution: What do these people do? How do they do it? And why do they do it that way? Every academic discipline has its core of variables. Economists examine cost, demand, input, and resources; demographers look at birth, death, and migration; sociologists deal with the social factors of age, class, education, and occupation. But anthropology relies more on a central set of questions. There are historical variables and psychological variables. Anthropology focuses on culture, yet culture is not a specific set of variables. Instead, it is the unique configuration which all of these and other factors assume when combined. Anthropology mixes psychology, political science, history, economics, linguistics, and any other sources of information as they appear relevant. Anthropology offers a perspective, a point of view, a way of seeing the world. It looks at money as well as morals, at the present and the past, at the lies as well as the truths, depending on the importance any one of these has for the people being studied.

The anthropological approach differs in another fundamental way from that of other sciences. Even though all modern sciences rely on and demand careful observation in accumulating their data, anthropology alone of the sciences adds to this the requirement of participation. If a handful of scientists were taken to study a football game, each would approach it differently. An economist would look at money: how much do spectators pay, how much does the equipment cost, what is the salary of the players, how much profit or loss is sustained? A physicist would present a whole different set of observations and questions about the velocity of the ball, the impact of a tackle, or the traction of the turf. A sociologist might look at the education and backgrounds of the players as compared to the spectators. A statistician would calculate probabilities of winning or losing. The psychologist would question the motives of the players and the audience, relating them to cognitive processes, primal needs, and wish fulfillments; while the historian would document the game's origin.

An anthropologist would join the team. Only after playing the game, not just once but over a long period of time, would he (or she) then formulate questions and try to answer them. An observer may know all the rules of the game, all the statistics of the players, and even the latest locker-room gossip, but for the anthropologist the crucial organizing experience for this information would be the playing of the game—the thud of a block, the excitement of victory, the embarrassment of a fumble. These and all the other experiences forming a personal, subjective perspective would then be combined with the objective facts and figures of observation to produce a rounded, whole description—an ethnography.

So an anthropological study is always at least in part an "insider's account," and to this extent it shares in the approach of journalism and the interpretive analysis of literature. At the same time, however, anthropology is a science of human behavior, and all of these insider views must be placed in comparative terms, which relate that behavior to the other societies and institutions known to the human family.

PART I

❦

CLIMBING THE POWER PYRAMID

In the folklore of Washington, Congress operates as a body of 535 equals in which some are more equal than others. The disparities in rank are often compared to a feudal pyramid, forming a neat hierarchy from the multitude of peasants at the bottom to the ruling monarch at the top. The question of who occupies the top levels provokes endless rounds of debate among the political pundits in residence as professional Hill-watchers. The problem with this feudalistic scheme is that the power pyramid of Congress, like all government creations, arises from the work of a committee of political architects and is never completely stable. For a while the pyramid slopes too steeply on one side, then on the other. The top is overly decorated by one generation of builders, who are removed completely by the next. Sometimes the pyramid of power looks like a squat mastaba tapering off into a thin Gothic spire in the center; then it becomes a bulging mound, with no clearly differentiated top at all. Occasionally, an apex sits squarely atop the structure, but at other times a flock of gargoyles clusters loosely about the zenith, appearing more ornamental than functional.

This constantly changing power pyramid occupies the subject of the three chapters in Part I. Beginning at the base, with the incoming classes of freshmen legislators, we work our way up the protean edifice toward the heights of congressional power. Viewed in this manner, the flexible hierarchy of Congress appears more similar to that of an Amazon tribe or the political organization in highland New Guinea than it does to the feudal stability of medieval Europe. The long climb upward depends more on the individual initiative, skill, and plain luck of the politician than on any logical sequence of simple seniority. Yet the hallowed principle of seniority still plays a significant, if not determining, part in the process.

2

✽❦✽

Coming of Age in Congress
(or Fortunate Senex!)

M ANY TRIBES ATTACK, torture, and kill Western missionaries, explorers, traders, and anthropologists, but few
have been as consistently bold or ferocious as the Shavante of
central Brazil. Not only have they killed their share of priests and
settlers, but they have also attacked the Brazilian Air Force
planes with bows, arrows, and war clubs. On at least one occasion, a well-aimed war club made a direct hit on a low-flying
airplane. This display of bravado makes the Shavante one of the
last Indian tribes still resisting European conquest nearly half a
millennium after Christopher Columbus's discovery of the New
World. Four hundred years after the fall of the Aztec and Inca
empires and a century after the conquest of the North American
tribes, the Shavante, using only the most primitive technology,
continue to resist the white man.

Wandering through the jungle and among the many rivers
and tributaries of the Amazon, the Shavante have remained
self-sufficient for centuries. To outsiders, they appear as almost
stereotypic of the best or the worst of primitive life. Their brave
resistance to the outside world and their resourceful use of the
jungle without exploiting it place them somewhere near Rous-
seau's noble savage. Yet their pugnacity and strict code of war-

fare resurrects the brutal savage in Thomas Hobbes's war of all against all. Even the other Indians rank the Shavante as savage, and white settlers, miners, and traders still prefer to shoot at them first and ask questions later.

How could these people with their very simple tools and weapons survive intact for so long and have the confidence to attack airplanes with nothing more than a war club? The answer appears to lie less in their weapons and technology than in their social organization. This came to light in the work of an English anthropologist, David Maybury-Lewis, who managed to befriend and study a group of Shavante. Working with the part of the Shavante called the Akwe, Maybury-Lewis found that in their daily life they followed a routine that was not very dramatic but certainly impressive in its resourcefulness. They lead a traditional existence, fishing the many rivers, hunting the deer, peccary, tapir, and jaguar of the area, as well as growing some corn, beans, and pumpkins. In many ways their life is similar to that of the Indians around Washington a thousand years ago. Rather than trading for Western goods, the Shavante depend more on the immediate offerings of the environment. Piranha teeth are used for cutting hair and other tasks for which a westerner might use a razor blade or scissors. Needles are made from small bones and used to sew hides or feathers. Baskets are made from bark, and the tribe can survive on the march for days making tools as needed, living from the roots, fruits, nuts, and honey they know how to find and harvest.

But the ferocity of the Shavante warriors does not come naturally even to such a tribe; instead, it must be inculcated into young men in much the same way that Western men must go through basic training to become soldiers. For the Shavante male, this military training begins early and remains a focal point of activity throughout his life. The social mechanism at the center of this organization is the system of age sets dividing the male population into three major groups: boys, young men, and elders. A boy enters this system when he leaves his mother's hut and is initiated into the bachelor hut with other boys of his age. The important transition is marked by the boy's receipt of his first and only piece of standard clothing—a penis sheath. This small cone of palmito bark is placed over the head of his penis as a protective covering and as an elongation of his masculinity. Except for the biological demands of urinating and having sexual relations, it is never removed without great embarrassment.

While living in the bachelor's hut, the boys learn the skills of Shavante manhood. They practice singing and dancing the ceremonies that are a permanent part of Shavante life, and they work on their hunting and fighting talents. Inside the hut, under the supervision of their elders, the boys make masks and other body ornaments for use in the various rituals on their way to full adult status. Perhaps even more important than these manual skills, the boys learn the social skills of living and working together as a team. They get to know one another and practice the cooperation that is so necessary to hunting and fighting together as men. All along the way their elders guide them, watch over them, and judge their progress.

Once the elders determine that the boys can cope with the duties of manhood, the youngsters are put through another series of initiations, and emerge as young men. A young man carries a war club, marries, and sits at a special young men's council fire at the center of the village. When one group leaves the bachelor's hut for the council fire, another group of children moves into the hut as the new cohort of boys. Leaving the bachelor's hut and assuming a seat at the council fire begins a period of great bravado, as the young men ostentatiously display their newly acquired manhood. They compete on the hunt and in battle with the bow and battle club. They compete in body ornamentation, making decorations and painting themselves; and they learn the finer nuances of oratory, practicing at night making speeches before their peers and by extension to anyone else within earshot. These years are passed in a pageant of masculine ostentation; but as the young men mature, the competitiveness and show decrease as they assume positions of real power in the tribal community. Only then do the survivors of this period begin the transition into the final age grade of the elders.

As heads of families and as experienced hunters and warriors, the elders sit around their own campfire separate from that of the young men. At the end of each day, they convene to discuss the important issues of when to move to a new camp, how to settle a dispute, how to fight and when, and other matters of relevance to the whole community. As these men grow older and their age mates begin dying off, the survivors assume a position of personal respect based on their advanced age and demonstrated abilities as group leaders and organizers.

The Shavante system is but one of the many formal age structures used by societies throughout the world as a primary organizing factor in assigning duties and responsibilities, as well as rights and privileges. Along with gender, division of roles by age seems to be universal. In East Africa an even more complex system of age grades is used, while in traditional Europe men were divided into apprentices, journeymen, and masters roughly paralleling the Shavante system. Human beings have probably been using some form of that system since the first caveman survived long enough to have gray hair. It would be startling to discover that the United States Congress was exempt from this tested human principle. Even though congressmen do not sit around council fires, practice war songs, or wear penis sheaths, they do share some fundamental similarities with the Shavante.

THE BACHELOR HUT

Just as Shavante men are always known by the name of the cohort with whom they spent their formative years in the bachelor hut, congressmen are always known by the name of the cohort with whom they spent their formative years in the Longworth Building. Because a new class moves into the Longworth every two years, the groups are designated by their year of election, as in "the class of '80" or "the class of '46." Only exceptionally large classes, such as the Roosevelt Landslide of 1932 or the Watergate Babies of 1974, get their own name. Each class strives to be unique so that it can earn a permanent name, but with fifty separate classes in each century, it is hard for more than a few to stand out. In the 97th Congress, which opened in January 1981, nearly four dozen members survived from the Watergate class, but only Senator Jennings Randolph of West Virginia remained from that historic Roosevelt class of '32 half a century ago.

How many of the class of '80 or '82 will survive as long as Randolph is unknown, but what is certain is that they begin their terms in the Longworth Building much as the classes before them. Looking like a misplaced county courthouse which should have a Civil War statue out front and old men rocking on the veranda, the squat Longworth hides between the Mussolini megalith of the Rayburn Building and the mock-classical style of the older Cannon Building. Viewed from the Capitol, the Longworth appears smaller but no more remote than its prestigious neighbors. The isolation of the building becomes apparent only when the new congressmen try to find it via the tunnels. Wandering through the underground maze, climbing over steampipes, descending narrow staircases, and looking for the Members Only elevator, the young congressman eventually finds out that not only is there no Longworth stop on the congressional subway, but his is the only congressional office building with no tunnel connecting it to the Capitol. The neophyte has two ways of getting to the legislative chamber. He can put on his coat, rubber boots, and hat, walk outside with milling tourists in the inclement weather, risk death among the city buses and mobile campers to enter the Capitol with a third-grade civics class on its fourteenth go-round in the revolving doors. Or, eschewing the common herd, he can go underground from the Longworth to one of the other congressional office buildings, nodding and scraping to every senior congressman he bumps into, and use *their* tunnel or subway stop to get over to the chamber floor, emerging as any self-respecting congressman should from underneath. Through this ordeal, repeated three or four times a day on each rollcall vote, the freshman is constantly reminded of his position in the congressional scheme: he is on the fringe.

Shavante boys are technically married, but during their stay in the bachelor hut, they do not cohabit with their wives, who remain at home until the mature age of nine or ten when they assume spousal duties. Similarly, most congressmen in the bachelor building are also technically married, but the wife is usually back home in the district serving tea and leaflets, trying desperately to help her husband keep his job in the hope that one day he will move up to the Rayburn Building, thus securing their district enough for her to escape Gopher Prairie and move to Washington with him. Consequently, the atmosphere of the Longworth is much like that of a college dorm or Shavante bachelor hut. There are always one or two economy-minded congressmen who defy rules by living in their offices rather than renting an apartment in the city. With a few unkempt congressmen trudging toward the shower room, shaving kit in hand, and the newspaper boy dropping off the morning editions of *The Washington Post* and *New York Times,* the halls of the Longworth are not exactly the corridors of power. Nevertheless, this intimate dorm atmosphere and the mutual experience of mixed euphoria and terror at having at long last arrived in the United States Congress, both bind the inchoate group of freshmen into a class with lasting bonds of amity and enmity common to such collegiate contexts.

Inside the Longworth, the freshman is just one of the boys; but outside, he is nobody. No matter how bright a star he may be in the union halls and Ramada Inns of Pocotaligo, when he gets to the Capitol he is just one of the hundreds of faceless freshmen who come and go in quick succession. It matters not that the Elks Club chose him outstanding man-of-the-year and the chairwoman of the League of Women Voters announced on the "Good Morning, Boise" show that he is destined to be another John Kennedy. For the time being, he is an anonymous entity, hardly a real person, just one of an amorphous class of beings.

Such an effacing role does not come naturally to freshmen legislators, who are often called "a bunch of high-school presidents with a few prom queens thrown in." Accustomed to strutting through shopping malls and bowling alleys with great public attention and awe, it is difficult for them to wander the Capitol tunnels and be recognized only by elevator operators and doormen. But there are forces compelling them to accept that role. In previous years, the freshmen were hammered down and kept in place by men like Wayne Hays, who screamed epithets—"potato head," "mushhead," and "scum"—at them like a drill sergeant dressing down recruits. In the Congress of the 1980s, embarrassment through intimidation and rudeness has given way to embarrassment through humor and jokes. This new form of hazing was evident when Paul Tsongas attended his first meeting of the Senate Energy Committee in January 1979.

At the time, Tsongas had just finished a well-publicized race against Senator Edward Brooke, his name having thus appeared almost daily in the Washington newspapers for weeks. Taking his seat quietly at the far end of the table as befits a freshman, he listened intently as Chairman Henry Jackson welcomed everyone back for the new Congress and greeted the new members, including Senator "Ton'gas." Repeatedly stumbling over the name, Jackson drew ripples of laughter from the audience of lobbyists, staff, and press while Tsongas squirmed in the mandatory silence of freshmen.

The ritual mispronunciation of the new senator's name may not seem very humorous by television comedy standards, but it has a little more impact in Congress where most of those names were launched in million-dollar name-recognition campaigns. The name is the most sacred part of the politician's mana. It is devastating when the name that sparkled from a thousand car bumpers, rained from a hundred billboards, and blasted from every television set, car radio, and portable transistor in the state for five months, is quietly gnarled, gnashed, and gutted in the mouth of the committee chairman. The import of that local *Tribune* headline on the morning after election day never made it to Washington. Had the chairman not seen him on the "Today Show," or the public television panel on nuclear arms and the elderly?

Of course, the chairman becomes overly solicitous, with profuse apologies when another senior on the council leans across the table and in a stage whisper informs him of the correct pronunciation. But by then the damage has been done, the point driven home. No matter who he thinks he is, the newcomer has to start all over from the bottom to prove himself here. This ceremonial means of informing and reminding the newcomer of his place in the pecking order supposedly owes its origin, like so many other legislative practices, to the almost mythical abilities and practices of Senate Majority Leader Lyndon B. Johnson. The man with the fabled memory who could recall the names of a supporter's children across three decades and as quickly recall the names of his detractors' children, would suddenly forget or mispronounce the name of a junior senator who had voted the wrong way. While slapping the young chap on the back and telling him he understood, Johnson would break his name into shreds in a metaphorical statement of what would happen if the disloyalty persisted. Since that time the practice has become a standard part of Hill culture, understood by everyone there, and one of the first and most bitter lessons every freshman learns.

Only one or two of the big names in the freshmen class need be singled out for this ritual. Like most political anecdotes, the story carries quickly and the point is graphically impressed on the others. After all, if it could happen to a well-known freshman from a big state like Massachusetts, it could certainly happen to the guy from Iowa or Vermont. Just to keep the freshmen on their toes, others of their number will be singled out in the first few years for slightly more elaborate forms of humor hazing.

Donald Riegle became one of these victims shortly after his election as the Republican congressman from Flint, Michigan. With his stylish hair covering the tops of his ears, and his 1967 award as the Junior Chamber of Commerce's Outstanding Man of the year, Riegle assaulted the Capitol in what his seniors took to be too cocky a manner. Congressmen were soon chuckling in the elevators and gathering around the television set in the cloakroom to talk about Riegle's ambition to become President. Some of the congressmen referred to him as "the President" behind his back, and a few older congressmen would call him "Mr. President" and treat him with exaggerated deference and politeness when encountering him on the chamber floor or anywhere there was an audience of other congressmen. Riegle became the butt of a series of jokes and anecdotes, all of which were brought to mind any time his honorary nickname was used. After leaving the Republican Party in 1974, Riegle also left the House in 1976 and was elected to the seat of Senator Phil Hart. But the whole series of jokes followed him to the new chamber. Unknown to him, Riegle who had worked so hard criticizing Nixon's refusal to release the Watergate tapes, had himself been recorded on tape by an assistant as they made love in his office. In the public spirit of publishing all political tapes available, the transcript was printed in verbatim in a Michigan newspaper. That article was a goldmine of laughs, innuendos, and snide comments throughout the Congress.

Riegle, admittedly, helped to prepare his own fate, and some might argue that it was deserved; but the harassment began long before those tapes, back when he was a newcomer. And Riegle's treatment stands as a perpetual reminder to young legislators of what may befall them if they step too far off the proper path. Sexual anecdotes, whether true or not, constitute the most appropriate vehicles for such ritual hazings; women as well as men fall victim to this locker-room humor.

One of the early female victims was a representative who was a serious feminist. Soon after arriving in Congress, she broke propriety by audaciously proposing an amendment to a military bill of Edward Hebert, Chief of the Defense Clan. When the amendment expectedly received only a single vote, she supposedly snapped at the aged committee man: "I know the only reason my amendment failed is that I've got a vagina."

To which Hebert retorted: "If you'd been using your vagina instead of your mouth, maybe you'd have gotten a few more votes."

Such stories, both apocryphal and true, are passed through the gossip networks of Congress each year and repeated as gospel. They brand the upstart as an outsider and mark certain forms of behavior as simply beyond the accepted pale. As such, they become instructive fables, repeated to new class after class, teaching them the consequence of wandering out of line, criticizing their seniors, pushing the wrong amendment, or in any way presuming upon the powers of the elders. Through these lessons, the young congressman is impressed with the real meaning of Speaker Sam Rayburn's often-repeated dictum, "To get along, go along." In this way, humor becomes the vehicle for expressing deadly serious facts about power. The elders can then save their talents for the real exercise of power plays where they count— against their peers rather than the insignificant freshmen. The newcomers can be handled with just a touch of humor or a well-placed joke.

Yet despite all the joking used to keep freshmen in their places and silent, one of the manifested norms of the modern Congress is that freshmen should speak out. Repeatedly they, and everyone else, are told: "The rule that 'freshmen, like children, should be seen and not heard' is now dead. Freshmen are to be seen and heard." The obituary of that old rule and the repeated proclamation of the new has itself become one of the new clichés of Congress.

Freshmen can deliver short speeches in the House of Representatives, on the chamber floor, in front of television cameras. What the cameras are not allowed to show is that there is no one else in the chamber watching. No one, that is, except for the other freshmen, lined up waiting for their turn to be broadcast to millions of American homes. The only audience in the chamber is his peers, who are checking over notes on index cards, back-slapping and goosing one another, and combing their hair for their turn before the cameras. Freshmen are encouraged to speak up, but to do so at special times in the day's schedule set aside for such appearances. However, when their seniors are around doing real business, freshmen are still expected to be silent.

If they don't get to the chamber at the special times for these brief appearances, freshmen are encouraged to write up their speech and turn it in "for the record." All of these speeches are then published at the back of the *Congressional Record* in a special section called "Extensions of Remarks," but when the speech is excerpted and mailed to the home district, it appears as though the young congressman is actually voicing local concerns in Washington.

In the same way, freshmen speak to local reporters from their home states with little reservation. But if, by some remote chance, they are interviewed by a television network or one of the Washington newspapers, congressmen know that they must be circumspect in their comments. Anything said to the local press in the district is assumed to be politicking for votes, but anything said to the national or Washington press is assumed to be aimed at fellow congressmen. Freshmen, like children, may talk, but they are still not to be heard.

Freshmen are encouraged to speak to the extent that it is important to accomplish the two tasks expected of them: getting reelected and learning congressional procedure. Until the congressman builds a firm electoral base at home and until he demonstrates that he has been fully socialized into congressional culture, he will not be taken seriously by other legislators, lobbyists, or anyone else in the City of Washington.

At the conclusion of his first term in office, the newcomer wages his reelection campaign. If he is successful, he returns as a member of the now sophomore class. With each election the class dwindles. Some quit from frustration or disgust, a few fall victim to an ethics scandal or a politically damaging revelation about their personal, usually sexual, habits. A few make the bid for another office, such as the Senate or a state governorship, and a great many are simply defeated at the polls. At each election, the class is culled; but the survivors slowly ascend the seniority pyramid as an ever smaller, ever more important cohort.

After the freshman term, the survivors of the class leave the Longworth Building, turning it over to the newcomers. The sophomores move across the street to the more ornate Cannon Building, which connects directly via underground tunnel to the Capitol. Eventually, the seniors will make room for them in the congressional palace of the Rayburn Building. Compared with the dank, dark Longworth, the Rayburn is a marble mausoleum with corridors like four-lane highways. By the time he reaches the Rayburn Building, the rising congressman knows that he has a possible slot at the top of the pyramid. But the long climb up from the Longworth takes much time—anywhere from one to two decades, as the classes above him slowly dwindle and die away.

THE SENIORITY PYRAMID

With each new election, each of the classes shrinks somewhat from that year's losses, while the survivors move up a notch in seniority and power. The resulting hierarchy of congressional classes, beginning with the oldest members at the top and the newest at the bottom, is shaped like a pyramid. In some decades the pyramid bulges with a broad base, indicating a high degree of congressional turnover with a large number of freshmen and sophomores but comparatively few elders. In other decades the pyramid attenuates into a thin, tapering structure, with a long spire at the top representing a hearty generation of elders surviving from elections thirty to forty years previously.

The seniority pyramid of the 97th Congress, which took its place in January 1981, is fairly close to normal in shape. At the top of the pyramid for the House of Representatives rests Jamie L. Whitten, the Dean of the House. As a young man of thirty-one, Whitten entered the 78th Congress representing Mississippi in November 1941, just a few weeks before the Japanese bombed Pearl Harbor. At the bottom of the pyramid are the seventy-four freshmen elected to Congress for the first time in November 1980, nearly four decades after Whitten's freshman class. Even though the span between Whitten and the new freshmen covers twenty congressional elections, the seniority pyramid has only twelve layers to it since eight of the twenty classes elected since 1941 have died out completely. Among the survivors, however, power is distributed primarily among those who were elected in the 1940s. Seven Democrats from that decade control an equal number of committees, including most of the major ones—Appropriations, Rules, Judiciary, Foreign Affairs, Armed Services, Education, and Labor, and the smaller committee on Standards of Official Conduct. The lower positions in the House are distributed over the remaining twenty members elected in the 1950s and the eighty-five congressmen elected in the 1960s.

Of the 256 congressmen first elected in the 1970s, Congressman Ronald Dellums of California was the first one to chair a committee within his first decade in office. His chairmanship, however, was of the lilliputian committee overseeing the District of Columbia. At this rate of change, the bulk of congressmen elected in the 1970s will reach their most powerful position in the 1990s, while the congressmen elected in the decade of the eighties will have to wait until after the beginning of the twenty-first century before their real grasp of congressional power is complete.

The seniority system in Congress operates as a delaying mechanism that postpones the complete effect of an election for anywhere from ten to twenty years. Some of the effect is, of course, immediately seen in the bustle of conservative activity after the election of President Ronald Reagan and his allies in Congress or the liberal activity after the election of President Franklin Roosevelt and his associates. Despite the immediate drama, the long-range effects are more like those of a tidal wave at sea. Even though the initial shaking of earth may be spectacular in itself, the real impact ripples out in an innocuous wave, only showing its true power when it crests near land and crashes down as a tidal wave far from the original movement that started it. As dramatic as was the election of all those Roosevelt Democrats in the

1930s and the concomitant turbulence that arose in creating a round of alphabet soup agencies, the real impact of those elections crashed down on America in the 1960s. Nearly three decades later, the survivors of those 1930s elections finally rose to the top of the congressional pyramid, and then the profusion of New Deal programs began under the name of the New Frontier. This built-in power lag means that the full impact of the elections of 1980 and 1982 will not be felt for another two decades, if the freshmen from these classes survive that long; otherwise they may join the ranks of cohorts like the class of 1950, which quickly died out. For the classes that survive the long rise to the top of the pyramid, the impact of their election changes from a mere ripple to a permanent mark on legislative history. Other classes may have a tremendous impact on the society at large, but they certainly do not leave a legislative impact commensurate with the attention generated in their transitory causes.

This legislative power deferral spawned in the seniority system is reinforced by the party system. Were each freshman class not divided into the two groups of Republicans and Democrats, they might be able to wield a great deal more power. Instead, their power is fractured. This means that it is generally necessary to have two or three successive elections favoring the minority party before it takes complete control of the Congress. Even though the Republicans picked up new seats in the election of 1978, they remained the minority party in both houses. By 1980, they acquired enough seats to take over the Senate organization, but they still held only one of the two chambers. The House remained in control of the Democrats for the 97th Congress. Only when the freshman class is overwhelmingly of one party does it have the numbers to exercise any real power in the congressional pyramid. This happened in the elections of 1932 and 1974, and a miniature version of the same thing happened in the Senate in 1980. Often these elections are heralded as the end of the seniority system in Congress: at last an active class seems to have arrived on the scene to sweep the old curmudgeons away. But a closer look at these classes reveals that they only begin the process, and before it progresses too far the attackers of seniority become its beneficiaries. This is illustrated in the case of both the Roosevelt Landslide and the Watergate Babies.

The legislative activity of the class of '32 was fast and furious. Owing their political allegiance to the new President, Franklin Roosevelt, and throwing out the old Republican leadership, they passed a record number of bills. In Roosevelt's first hundred days he introduced and had Congress pass almost all of the recovery programs associated with his name. The bills were so numerous, and so new, that many of them were only bundles of blank pages voted on and approved by the Congress which knew only the number, name, and vague contents, to be added to the bill as soon as the printer had time. When the Supreme Court balked at some of these new bills on grounds of possible unconstitutionality, Roosevelt made his famous threat to pack the Court with new appointees and the Congress appeared ready to follow him. Even though these bills did not bring the United States out of the Depression, they did inaugurate a new era in congressional politics. For at least a short while in the 1930s, Congress was under the total domination and leadership of a new force. This new force was not the freshman class; the force was Roosevelt, but the young representatives were the tool Roosevelt used to control Congress. By the end of Roosevelt's life he had lost that control over the Congress, but he, more than any other President, managed to overcome the intractability of Congress and for a while, at least, become its leader. As the freshmen who came to Congress on his coattails slowly became accustomed to their position, they also became more independent. After Roosevelt's death the Congress quickly passed a constitutional amendment limiting any future President to only two terms in office.

By comparison with that flurry of activity in the 1930s, the Watergate Babies of 1974 were rather tame. They entered Congress in the elections which occurred only six weeks after the resignation of President Richard Nixon. The Watergate Babies, however, did not have a new Democratic President like Roosevelt to give them direction. The Republicans controlled the White House under Gerald Ford until January of 1977. Nevertheless, the freshmen were determined to have a large and immediate impact as they supposed the voters who elected them had intended. Even though there were seventy-six of them, they were still a minority in the House; their group was not large enough to take over from the senior Democrats already in power. They

joined forces, however, under the handful of senior liberal Democrats, and together forced some changes on the reluctant chamber.

For nearly a decade prior to the arrival of the Watergate
Babies, a liberal minority in the House had been pursuing a set of
procedural reforms. Following the suggestions of congressmen
like Richard Bolling of Missouri, Morris Udall of Arizona, and
the commission chaired by Congresswoman Julia Butler Hansen, a number of significant changes had been made in the
House. Electronic voting reduced the time it took for a rollcall
vote from nearly an hour to only fifteen minutes. This allowed
more votes on more issues and less time for last-minute political
dealings in the hall and doorway prior to voting. An entirely new
budgetary procedure had been introduced by the Congress and a
special Congressional Budget Office was created. The Democratic caucus had been strengthened at least enough to have
monthly meetings as opposed to annual ones. Probably as much
as anything else, the enforced retirement of Wilbur Mills in 1974
following the Fanne Foxe scandal ensured the possibility for real
reform in the next Congress.

This context, plus the presence of a relatively weak Speaker of
the House, Carl Albert, opened up great possibilities of change
for the Watergate Babies who took office in January 1975. Under
the old liberals, they attacked the strongholds of the old conservatives. Mills's departure was used as an occasion to force his
Ways and Means Committee to divide its power among a set of
subcommittees, and its power over committee assignments was
taken away and given to the Democratic Steering and Policy
Committee. The chairman of the Armed Forces Committee,
Edward Hebert of Louisiana, was expelled from his position and
the power of that committee divided among subcommittees. A
similar blow was dealt to Wright Patman and his Banking, Cur-
rency, and Housing Committee and to W. R. Poage's Agriculture Committee. The demise of these three conservative, old
chairmen, plus the fall of Wilbur Mills and Wayne Hays in sex
scandals, meant an end to the conservative power monopoly.
Many observers and insiders at the time interpreted these
changes as the end of seniority, but as the intervening years have
indicated, it was merely the end of a particular breed. Seniority

survived, only now it was controlled by a more liberal set of congressional seniors. Although many people assumed at the time that more chairmen would eventually be displaced, it never happened.

The major impact of the Watergate Babies was not that they dealt the death blow to seniority but in their further decentralization of power in the House. Since the beginning of the century, authority in the House of Representatives had been slowly spread out over more and more of its members. At the beginning of the century, power was centralized in the hands of the Speaker of the House; by the end of the Roosevelt era, it was concentrated in a dozen autonomous committee chairmen. The Watergate Babies carried that diffusion one step further by dividing the authority of the chairmen among several dozen subcommittee heads. There the process came to a quick halt.

By the time the Watergate Babies had orchestrated that final set of changes, a new freshman class was entering Congress. The class of '76 was largely responsive to the same concerns as the class of '74, but they were not quite as liberal. By 1978, the new freshmen were decidedly conservative, and with the election of 1980, the complete takeover by conservatives in the House loomed as a real possibility. The defense of the liberals, with their decreasing numbers, lay in the subcommittees, which they had helped to liberate from the committees. It was now in the interest of the Watergate Babies to shore up the power of the subcommittee chairmen, since they themselves were stepping into that role. The enemy was no longer the old conservatives; it was the new or neo-conservatives, and the liberal bastion was now in subcommittee chairmanships. Thus within only six years, the revolutionary class of '74, which had attacked seniority and the power of chairmen, was picking up the remnants of the old system and reassembling it as their own defense against the new freedom.

It is just this repetitious scenario that preserves the importance of seniority in Congress. Even though it is occasionally updated or modified for slightly different reasons, the importance of seniority persists because it is always a *new* weapon for a rising group of congressmen. Today's young reformers who want to do away with it are the same ones who will benefit by it tomorrow. If the young reformers are a large enough group, as was the case in 1932 and again in 1974, they may begin the reforming process; but before those reforms are complete, it becomes advantageous for them to retreat.

The occasional violations of the principle of seniority do not imply the death of the system, any more than the coronation of Queen Elizabeth I or the arrival of Margaret Thatcher as Prime Minister meant that male dominance of British society had ended. Great Britain remains under the rule of men just as Congress remains under the rule of its seniors. Even as such, however, seniority never attained the status of a fixed law. Throughout its history in Congress, it has been superseded or laid aside as major political considerations required. In markedly conservative times, ways have been found to keep liberal chairmen out, just as in liberal eras conservatives have been barred. Seniority is a major part of the story of congressional organization, but it is by no means the only principle operating. The other organizing features of Congress would, however, be difficult to understand without the awareness of the constant background theme of seniority.

In this regard the organizing role of classes and seniority in Congress parallels that of the Shavante of Brazil. For his first few terms in Congress, the new representatives, like a young Shavante man, struts around the political arenas making an impressive image with his carefully groomed appearance and occasional displays of skilled bravado, but he remains essentially without power. Periods of apprenticeship are the times for trying on adult roles, cultivating the appearance of respectful authority, and continuing the practice of the skills that will be needed later in life. Gradually, the neophyte learns the system and carves out his own niche within it. At this point in his career, the personal talent of the individual comes into play more. The individual congressman or Shavante warrior can be propelled only so far up the power pyramid on the basis of his group affiliation. Then his ability to play the game, to strike out from the group, and to forge his own path takes precedence.

Through almost automatic promotions, a Shavante man becomes an elder, just as any congressman who survives enough elections becomes a congressional elder. Not all elders become chiefs. That elevation depends on the work and strategy of the individual. In both the Congress and the Shavante tribe, age is a necessary criterion for power and a chieftainship, but by no means sufficient. Being a congressional chief means more than being just a congressional elder.

As the freshman works his way out of the anonymous classes at the bottom of the power pyramid, the rising politician finds himself confronting that tangled organization described previously. Confronted by those dozens of committees and caucuses, the myriad party offices, and the constantly changing political themes, where does the would-be chief make his start? How does he build a power base within the Congress, and how does he ever get to the top of the power pyramid?

3

❦

Gathering a Clan

ONGKA, A TRIBAL elder of the Kawelka in highland New
Guinea, knew that he had finally arrived as a Big Man
when he was able to give the biggest *Moka* the region had ever
witnessed. At this huge feast, Ongka made speeches to all of his
assembled relatives, friends, and allies. Dressed in his finest
feathers and decorations, he distributed the roasted pigs and
yam puddings made by his wives, and to cement his position as
a leader and patron, he presented a great many gifts to the assembled tribesmen. To some went live pigs or a bird; a few got
cows and cassowaries. In addition to these traditional gifts,
Ongka gave away a motorbike and a Toyota Landcruiser, making his *Moka* without doubt the finest and most modern ever
known in New Guinea; as such, it was the culmination of a lifetime of hard work by Ongka to become a Big Man.

In parts of tribal New Guinea and Melanesia where there are
no hereditary chiefs, politics are dominated by these successful
old warriors known as Big Men. The arduous path to become a
Big Man is one of hard work and careful strategy, but any
young man who applies himself to it can attain this preeminent
status. The young politician begins life, as do most of his peers,
with a meager patrimony of a small garden plot and a wife to

work it. The yam crop from this garden feeds not only the fledgling family but their pigs as well. If the young couple works hard, they can produce an excess of yams, which can be used to raise more pigs. As they become prosperous, the young warrior acquires another wife, who can help to grow even more yams and more pigs. The repetitive acquisition of wives, pigs, and yams lies at the heart of his political power. Through the distribution of pork to other less successful men, he acquires followers, and through his marriages to new wives and the carefully orchestrated marriages of his own children, he acquires allies.

By the time he becomes a senior warrior, he can thereby head a large group of fellow tribesmen bound to him by these pig alliances. He has become a Big Man. The great *Mokas* crown the process like a combination election and inaugural celebration. Even though the raiding parties that traditionally centered on these Big Men have now been outlawed, the practices have never been completely banished from the hinterlands, where Big Men are still known by the title "Slayers of Pigs and Men."

The political path of becoming a Big Man in the United States Congress resembles the route followed by Ongka and other Big Men in New Guinea. The baked chicken dinners and paper hats of American politics may lack some of the color of roasting pigs and cassowary feather headdresses, and American oratory may pale before the eloquent rhetoric of a New Guinea Big Man, but underneath the process remains the same. The distribution of pork represents the heart of the organization in both cases, even if the Americans have substituted a metaphorical distribution of grants-in-aid and water projects for the living, squealing variety. The more pork he distributes, the more followers he attracts, and the more followers he attracts, the more pork he acquires to distribute.

In New Guinea and on Capitol Hill alike, the system rests on a delicately synchronized spiral of growth, in which followers and goods increase each other. Any boost to one part creates a chain reaction that increases all the other parts. By the same set of interrelations, however, a breakdown at any single point in the process can reverse the whole spiral, rapidly depleting power, production, and followers. A sudden plague that wipes out the pigs, a yam blight, massive budget cuts, or the abolition of a favorite program can destroy a lifetime of careful work and orchestration. Similarly, a rupture in domestic relations and the departure of several wives amid much rumor and gossip or an ethics scandal with public ridicule can deprive a Big Man of his reputation, labor force, and thereby his political clout as well.

Few men in New Guinea survive the ravages of jungle disease and war to become senior members of their tribes, much less Big Men. In the United States Congress, few politicians survive the vicissitudes of voter opinion long enough to become senior congressmen. Of those who do survive, fewer still have the combination of ability and luck to become Congressional Big Men. The key to their success lies in their ability to organize and run a personal political organization within the Congress. Most congressmen get some training for this by putting together an electoral organization in the home district, but in contemporary politics an inept politician who is rich can just buy an election campaign staff, public relations firm, and lots of advertising. Once he gets in the Congress, however, he must learn to pit his own organizational skills against other congressmen for control of the resources available. His ability to do this determines whether or not he will ever become a Big Man.

The origins of every New Guinea Big Man's career arose from his ability to organize his domestic household to produce as many yams and pigs as possible. From this rather undramatic skill develops his opportunity to be a real leader of men in politics, war, and the big hunt. In parallel fashion, every congressional Big Man's career originated from his capacity to organize his personal staff to maximize his political output. This basic skill provides him with the means to be a real political leader within the Congress. The congressman does not begin his legislative career as a leader of other politicians; he begins as the leader of a small staff. Only if he plays the game correctly can he turn this group into one that includes other politicians as well as staff. Consequently, our examination of the Congressional Big Man should begin with his relations with his staff, for in the final analysis that, more than anything else, determines how far up the power pyramid he rises.

A FAMILY AFFAIR

Personal staff is largely a twentieth-century addition to Congress. Even though a few clerks assisted in committee work as early as the 1840s, the first personal staffers assigned to work directly for the legislators were not authorized until the 1880s. Before that, congressmen and senators performed all of their chores, though not entirely on their own, since most of them had wives, sons, and daughters whom they could press into answering constituent inquiries, sending out seed packets to farmers, and distributing almanacs. More affluent members used personal servants or a personal secretary in this capacity. No matter which combination of these a member of Congress used, the assistance was taken directly from his own household. Even a hired secretary would be virtually part of the family household, working out of the member's home, since private offices were not provided until the twentieth century. In this capacity they made frequent trips with the member to the home district or political conventions, and divided the year between the Washington residence and the home estate.

In 1885, the House of Representatives authorized an additional allowance to its members to help them pay these personal clerical costs; the same provision was added for senators in 1893. These innovations did not provide for Congress to hire more staff; rather, they simply provided compensatory money for expenses already incurred. The member could then use this money as he saw fit: hire a new clerk, pay his wife, or do the work himself and keep the cash. This allotment was loudly denounced at the time by a number of senators who claimed that it was nothing more than an underhanded pay raise for members of Congress. It would have been more accurate to describe it as a family allowance rather than a staff allowance since, in one form or another, most of the money went into the congressman's own household.

Not until 1946 did Congress undertake the direct payment of the clerks themselves, and as late as the 1970s they were still paid in cash, computerized checks not arriving until 1972. The direct payment to the staffer by check rather than by cash to the congressmen has been the *only* congressional interference in the member-employee relationship since 1885. The member, not Congress, decides who will work for him and how much they will be paid, in keeping with a resolution explicitly stating that a member could remove any employee at any time "with or without cause." In 1946, Congress defeated an amendment to establish a Director of Personnel who would certify the qualifications of employees. Similar attempts in the 1970s to create boards of appeal for civil rights violations of employees were also defeated.

Throughout the twentieth century Congress has instituted a variety of laws governing the employee-employer relationship in private industry and in the civil service, but in every case it carefully excluded itself. These exclusions prompted Senator Patrick Leahy of Vermont to accuse Congress of acting as though "what is good and fair for the country is not necessarily good and fair for Congress." In deciding what is good for the country, congressmen have exempted themselves and their employees from the provisions of the Fair Labor Standards Act of 1938, the Civil Rights Act of 1964, the Equal Employment Opportunity Act of 1972, and the Social Security Act. The operations of their offices are exempt from the Occupational Safety Act (which created OSHA), and they do not have to answer requests under the Freedom of Information Act and the Privacy Act. Congressmen do not have to pay social security, health benefits, or unemployment insurance on behalf of their staffs.

Exemptions from these labor laws emphasize the unique relationship of a congressman to his staff. The staff grew out of the congressman's private household, and members do not want to interfere in another member's family life. This attitude is reflected in the common designation of Congress as "the last plantation." Technically, a member's employees are no longer a part of his domestic household; but conceptually, members and their staffs are allotted the privacy befitting an extended family.

This changed slightly once the staffers were paid by check: family workers rapidly gave way to hired workers. The extent to which family and staff were synonymous even after World War II is illustrated in the staff of Georgia Congressman Gene Cox.

Representative Cox, nicknamed "Goober" in honor of his district's peanut crop, ran his Washington office under the direction of his wife. In this endeavor the Coxes were assisted by their son, who was also on the payroll. His Georgia office employed the congressman's sister in the same capacity. Cox's brother-in-law also worked in the House of Representatives as Assistant House Bill Clerk. An extended network out of the personal office included a nephew in the Agriculture Department (looking after the interests of peanut farmers), a brother who was a postmaster of one community in Cox's district, and a sister who was postmistress of another community, as well as various cousins spread throughout the federal empire.

The Cox family was not alone in the practice, for nepotism was the rule in Congress, not the exception. This close tie between staff and family helped many congressional wives get elected to succeed their husbands. Margaret Chase Smith is probably the best-known example of the wife-secretary turned congresswoman on the death of her husband. Nepotism, however, extended to males as well, as when young Robert Kennedy took a job as Senate staffer when his brother John was first elected Senator. In similar fashion, Senator Sam Nunn of Georgia also began his political career as a House staffer for his uncle, Congressman Carl Vincent of Georgia; just as Congressman Dingell began his career as a page for his father, Representative John Dingell, Sr.

Persistent press criticism of these practices, particularly from columnists Drew Pearson and Jack Anderson, sharply reduced congressional nepotism. The watershed came in scandals emanating from the staff of Harlem Congressman Adam Clayton Powell, who paid over $20,000 in 1966 to his wife while she lived in the Caribbean. The technical violation was the fact that she did not live in the United States. By that time, however, wives and other family members had largely changed from being full-time office staff to being full-time campaigners. The habit of hiring relatives was falling into disuse for practical rather than ethical reasons.

Gradually over the course of the last century the personal staff evolved out of the domestic household; yet in many ways the organization remains a very personal, domestic one. Even the labels used to describe it by the employees themselves reflect the familial organization. When not disparaging it as "the last plantation," they often speak of it as "one family." When Daniel Minchew and his boss, Senator Herman Talmadge, were under investigation for corruption, Minchew pleaded in court for leniency on the basis of being led astray by a man who was like a "father" to him. Part of the reason these relationships are more familial than bureaucratic is that the relationships exist prior to actual staff employment. A 1977 study by two political scientists found that nearly two thirds of the Senate staffers had known their bosses in some capacity before joining their staffs. If anything, that may be a low estimate.

These close ties in Congress resemble what the British anthropologist F. G. Bailey in describing politics in India calls "personal bureaucracies." Groups of personal retainers coalesce around individual politicians within a bureaucratic setting, the underlying principle of organization being the relationship of patron to client. Each of the 20,000 employees of Congress is the client of one (and only one) of the 535 members of Congress. In turn, some of the members become clients of other members, as we shall see in subsequent chapters. As a principle of organization, the patron-client relationship supplies Congress, despite its large size, with a peculiarly nonbureaucratic form. Because of this, the organization of Congress is socially closer to that of a New Guinea tribe, an Indian village, or an African clan than it is to most Western institutions such as a business, a school, an army, or even other branches of government. The American Congress more closely resembles the ancient legislatures of Rome, Byzantium, and Greece than it does the modern legislatures of Great Britain, Germany, Canada, or France.

In the operation of the Roman Senate, the patron-client relationship reached such importance that the patron and client were exempt from having to testify against each other in court cases. The sacred bond was held to be as personal and intimate as the husband-wife relationship on which it was modeled. According to the Greco-Roman historian Plutarch, the sanctity of the patron-client relationship received its most severe test when Gaius Marius was tried for bribery in his election as praetor in 116 B.C. After prolonged consideration, the court exempted

Gaius Herennius from having to testify against Marius because of their patron-client relationship, thereby reaffirming an ancient tribal tradition that still survives today in the U.S. Congress.

Over two thousand years later the United States Supreme Court issued a similar ruling when an aide to Senator Mike Gravel refused to testify before a grand jury investigating Gravel's reading of the Pentagon Papers. Not only did the Court rule that the aide did not have to testify against his senator-boss, but it added that many of the constitutional privileges of a member of Congress extended to include "his aides, insofar as the conduct of the latter would be protected if performed by himself." The Court went on to declare that for most legislative purposes, a member and his staff assistants are "treated as one." A relationship can hardly be more personal and less bureaucratic than that. Even the Roman Senate stopped short of declaring patron and client to be a single legal entity.

This style of intimate familial organization seems unique in contemporary society to institutions that exist above or beyond the law. It operates in the Supreme Court, which has been traditionally called "the Brethren," both before and after the book of the same name. And it has persisted in the organization of the Mafia which, like congressional staffs, grew out of real family clans. The Congress and the Supreme Court have maintained this archaic organization because they are in a sense above the law (to wit, the congressional exemptions from most laws). The Mafia has been able to preserve the same style of familial organization because it operates beyond the law. Government and the Mafia are the only major institutions in America that can exempt themselves from paying social security, complying with OSHA standards, or meeting the Freedom of Information Act standards. It is hardly a coincidence that both institutions center on the patron-client relationship derived from and still organized as family units.

Just as a Mafia member works for a single Don and not the Mafia as a whole, a congressional aide serves the member and his career needs, not the Congress as a whole, the constituency, or something as vague as the American people. The livelihood and success of the individual staffer will prosper or decline as does the career of the member and the staff as a whole. If the member goes on to higher office, so will his staffers. If the member is thrown out of office by the voters or disgraced by scandal, so is his staff. As in the Mafia, the fate of the individual hangs on that of his family.

After two or three terms in office, when the staff has had time to consolidate its hold on the congressional seat, they work to build new constituencies for their politician. A congressman's staff tries to make the member known outside of his district so that they may all advance to the office of state governor, mayor of a metropolitan area like New York, or possibly to the Senate. Similarly, a senator's staff cultivates a national constituency in hopes of that ultimate political prize: the presidency. Even if they fall short of that goal, the staff will help him seek the vice presidency, a cabinet post, judicial appointment, or an ambassadorial position, for whither he goes they follow.

With the great importance a staff has for a congressman's future career, the selection and cultivation of that staff is as important to him as finding the right political wife. The choice of staff is one of the first decisions he has to make upon entering Congress, and in the long run, it will prove even more vital than his choice of committees in determining how successful he becomes. Part of his campaign staff can be incorporated into his personal staff; but, in addition, he will need some experienced people who already understand how Congress operates. These experienced hands are usually supplied by other politicians who are already in Congress and have large operating staffs of their own. A new member can turn to them for help, seeking out senior congressmen of his own party, his own ideological interest, or his own state delegation.

This exchange of staffers, like the marriage arrangements made for New Guinea children by their parents, forms the first bonds of alliance for the new member. They immediately connect him into a network that will have a decisive imprint on the kind of legislator he turns out to be. A conservative Republican like Jesse Helms of North Carolina started up his staff with an infusion of personnel from the like-minded Strom Thurmond.

The impact of these initial staff acquisitions is illustrated in the subsequent voting records and legislative activities of both these senators.

To finance his staff, the new member receives a start-up fund. This varies from approximately $1 million for the average senator to about a third of that for a congressman. The fund becomes a guaranteed allowance, which the member will receive each year, irrespective of how much he may be able to increase this through his committee work. The initial allowance makes each office something of a small independent business. A million-dollar business may seem fairly large to the average taxpayer who has to support it, but on the scale of government enterprises, it registers as only a millionth of the annual federal budget—or 0.0000015 of the budget, to be more exact. The entire cost of running the Congress was a little over $1 billion for fiscal year 1981, less than one fifth of 1 percent of the total federal budget. Thus, by government standards, a congressional staff is small, but the congressman exercises a flexible control over his private budget. Most of the money allocated to each member of Congress is used to pay the salaries of his retainers. The actual office space, along with furniture and equipment, is provided directly. A separate allowance supplies letterhead stationery; postage is, of course, free through the tradition of congressional franking privileges. Other allowances pay for telephones, computers, travel, newspaper subscriptions, and even postage stamps for mail that cannot be franked.

Once assembled, the staff has a single goal that dominates and is the focus of all their activity: to ensure the reelection of the member. The various assistants approach this task from a multitude of perspectives, but the ultimate goal is the same for all of them. Some of the assistants will busy themselves writing press releases on every subject imaginable. Others will be making use of the franking privileges to blanket the constituency with newsletters recycled from press releases the newspapers rejected. Others again arrange for television and radio interviews. If no reporter shows an interest in interviewing the new member, the staff will use the congressional recording studios to make their own video and audio tapes for distribution. Other staffers will possibly write a weekly column (or two) for hometown newspapers eager to fill up the printed page. Another set of staffers will work on "constituent problems"—a rubric that accounts for anything from chasing social security checks and mailing out agriculture yearbooks to assisting schoolchildren in writing term papers. A more sophisticated ombudsman known as the Grants Officer guides local agencies in applying for federal funds and contracts.

Helping Aunt Emma get her Medicaid payments or arranging for Pineville to receive federal money for an international airport may not be very dramatic as politics, but such work is the stock and trade, the *sine qua non,* of congressional activity. These activities take up so much staff time and effort that the average congressman can afford to hire only a single assistant to work in legislative issues. It does not behoove a new member to hire several legislative experts, if he does not take care of the constituency back home. Legislative work will not win elections; public relations will. Any politician who thinks otherwise rarely lasts long enough in office to make effective use of those legislative assistants.

Once this personal staff is in place, the next step in attaining power is through the committee structure, where there are more staff slots to be acquired. The acquisition begins in earnest when the congressman or senator becomes chairman of his first subcommittee. For members of the minority party, the equivalent is the position of ranking minority member of the subcommittee. This is the first rise out of the anonymous ranks of the lower orders, and with this step the politician begins legislative work.

THE "UNITED FUND CAMPAIGN"

The size of each congressman's personal staff is fairly standardized, while those of senators vary according to the population of the state, with only modest room for manipulation. For the freshmen and sophomores, particularly in the House, there is little opportunity for political expansion beyond this. Most of their political efforts focus on the home district rather than on congressional politics. For senators and representatives who survive the first few terms, playing the insider game of congressional politics begins when they vie for subcommittee jurisdiction and for the accompanying staff. If a member is to expand his following, he must do so in either the committee or the party organization. It is there that both jurisdiction and staff are available.

Until the reforms of the Watergate era, a new senator joining a committee could do nothing but wait until the years passed and he rose to the chairmanship of that committee. Today, however, senators expect and get a small piece of the action from the very beginning. How they handle this responsibility will determine how quickly they rise in the power structure. Initial authority comes in the form of a subcommittee chairmanship. The three essentials for a subcommittee are (1) a staff to run it, (2) space in which to operate, and (3) a piece of jurisdiction to manage. These are acquired through a form of "United Fund Drive." The senior senators on the committee, who all chair their own subcommittees, are expected to donate something in one of these three categories to the freshman member. One senator may have a small room he uses for storage in the annex building; he donates that for an office. Another senator has oversight over the census, but since there won't be another census until 1990, he hands over that jurisdiction. A third senator is responsible for consumer fraud; since consumer issues generate so much crank mail with decreasing press attention, he is willing to donate that piece of jurisdiction and the sole accompanying clerical position. The chairman of the committee has been having trouble with the subchairmen and thinks it might be beneficial to win over the freshman as an ally, so in a generous spirit the chairman throws in another clerical position and responsibility for a sewage program that has lost its funding.

If each of the senior senators donates something to this "United Fund Drive," bit by bit a subcommittee can be assembled. It may have only one staffer and one secretary, a windowless storage room for an office, and jurisdiction over an area for which there are no bills or pending legislation, but nevertheless it is a start. This miniature chimera is decorated with a title— preferably one that reflects a trendy topic or a relevant campaign issue. The title does not necessarily have to reflect the function of the subcommittee since the subcommittee does not necessarily have to have any function.

By means of a "United Fund Drive" for each of the two or three committees on which a new member serves, a freshman senator within a few months of election can be chairman of two or three very impressive-sounding subcommittees. Senator Max Baucus of Montana entered the Senate in 1979. From a "United Fund Drive" in the Senate Finance Committee, he was made chairman of the "Subcommittee on Oversight of the Internal Revenue Service." This was a perfect subcommittee. The title was important-sounding, since every voter knows how important taxes are. It was also highly relevant to the big issue of tax cutting. At the same time it was very specific; unlike vague issues such as consumerism, this subcommittee was concerned directly with one particular government agency—the IRS. The subcommittee was tailored to impress voters. Only a government insider would know that the mention of "oversight" in the title is a code word for powerlessness. In the Congress only "authorizations," which create programs, and "appropriations," which fund them, are a part of the power structure. "Oversight" implies the right to look, but not to touch.

Senator Baucus also served on the Judiciary Committee. From the "United Fund Drive" there, he became chairman of the "Limitations of Contracted and Delegated Authority Subcommittee." The name alone is formidable enough to prevent anyone, inside or outside the government, from bothering to ask what it means. If Baucus was to be chairman, however, he needed someone over whom to preside. The Judiciary Committee then assigned the other freshman, Senator Howell Heflin. In the spirit of fair reciprocity, Baucus joined Heflin's newly created subcommittee on "Jurisprudence and Governmental Relations."

Members of the minority party are entitled to their proportion of all committee and subcommittee seats, so Senator Baucus's subcommittee needed a member of the "opposition." Freshman Republican Thad Cochran was assigned to the subcommittee, and, as the only Republican, was made ranking minority member. Baucus and Heflin could then have an opposition faction to represent the minority view on the limitations of contracted and delegated authority, just in case the issue ever came up for discussion.

This modern procedure assures that no one is left out of the power facade. Gone are the days when it took two decades of sitting on one's hands and waiting for the elders to die before a chairmanship became available. In the 96th Congress, the 60 Democrats divided amongst themselves 105 chairmanships; there were a corresponding 105 ranking minority member positions for the 40 Republicans. Every man a chairman. With the Republican majority in 1981, the proportions changed, so that Republicans became the chairmen and the Democrats took the ranking minority positions. Nevertheless, each senator can be the *head* of two separate subcommittees, or, as was the case with Senator James Abdnor, the freshman may get three subcommittees from the "United Fund Campaign."

PERPETUAL REORGANIZATION

Be it ever so humble, the first subcommittee chairmanship initiates a senator's political career. Like a young New Guinea man beginning his political life with a hand-me-down widow, a poor parcel of a yam field, and a crippled hog, it may not be much, but it is a start. Hard work might turn even that into a family of several young wives, acres of lush fields, and a herd of prize porkers, just as a hardworking senator may eventually build a powerful congressional clan from his meager subcommittee.

Every two years, in January following the November elections, Congress goes through a reorganization. The jurisdictions of departing members are divided up, after which the crumbs are gathered in the "United Fund Drive" and presented to an entering freshman as a subcommittee. Even though the freshman largely has to take only what is given the first time, in subsequent reorganizations he will try to increase his meager share of what the departing Big Men left behind. He will also use that opportunity to fob off insignificant parts of his jurisdiction on the new cohort of freshmen.

When Donald Riegle of Michigan moved from the House of Representatives to the Senate in the 95th Congress, he joined Senator Proxmire's Committee on Banking, Housing, and Urban Affairs. His "United Fund Committee" was given the then hot title of "Consumer Affairs." When consumer issues gave way in the press to more severe economic problems, Riegle used the reorganization for the 96th Congress to expand his title to "Economic Stabilization Subcommittee." The same pressing economic concerns moved Senator Paul Sarbanes from chairman of the "Western Hemisphere Affairs Subcommittee of Foreign Relations" to that committee's "International Economic Policy Subcommittee." The Foreign Affairs panel tries to keep a stable subcommittee nomenclature (in the interest of better international relations), so Sarbanes's old subcommittee title was passed unchanged to committee newcomer Edward Zorinsky of Nebraska.

For the first few reorganizations in a senator's career, the "gains in jurisdiction" are more apparent than substantial. Reorganization is a public relations exercise of senior members trying to make the juniors look and feel good. Gradually, however, the senator is able to acquire a bailiwick of real jurisdiction. The process by which he does this is more one of slow accretion and aggrandizement than of dramatic political coups. For the first few terms the gains come as superficial name trades, exchanging words like "application" for "oversight" and "consumer issues" for "economic affairs." Eventually, the senator acquires small bits of the real authorization and appropriations process. Once this begins, the senator loses interest in the subcommittee name. If he has a piece of real power, people will know it, and he does not need to impress them with a fancy name. At this point in his career any old name will suffice, as he abandons word games for power politics.

When a senator captures another staff position, he immediately fires the employee who occupies the job and fills the position with one of his own clients. Every congressional reorganization involves a major shuffle of staff. When control of the Congress changes parties, as the Senate did after the 1980 election, these staff changes reach monumental proportions. Within hours after the election returns were announced, Senator Strom Thurmond, as the incoming chairman of the Judiciary Committee, the largest employer in the Senate, put all of Ted Kennedy's staff on notice to vacate their jobs. Thurmond was moving in his own people in a quantum jump in power.

Over the next three months corresponding chain reactions reverberated through all the committees and subcommittees of the Senate, as Republicans took over each of the chairmanships.

The process of committee and staff shuffling continues throughout the politician's congressional career. If he is not ever vigilant in protecting or expanding his staff, he will forfeit it to more aggressive senators. This happened in 1981 when Strom Thurmond successfully abolished the antitrust subcommittee which Senator Charles Mathias was taking over as chairman. In abolishing it, Thurmond assumed responsibility for the issues and staff in his capacity as full Judiciary Committee chairman. The same scenario was played out on the Banking and Urban Affairs Committee when Chairman Jake Garn managed to appoint his own staffer to be director over Senator Richard Lugar's subcommittee. Refusing to be chairman in name only, Lugar resigned from the subcommittee. On the House side, Commerce Committee Chairman John Dingell managed to abolish the consumer affairs subcommittee and thereby take away the staff of the second ranking committee member, James H. Scheuer of New York.

Occasionally, this game of musical chairs forces the politician to transfer jurisdiction from one of his committees, where it is in danger, to another better fortified one. This is what Senator William Fulbright did when he surrendered the chairmanship of the Banking Committee for Foreign Relations. On the Banking Committee he had spent years acquiring control over the World Bank and the International Monetary Fund. Rather than abandoning it when he gave up the chairmanship of that committee, he simply transferred that jurisdiction to the Foreign Relations Committee. Subsequent Banking chairmen, like William Proxmire, have been fighting unsuccessfully ever since to get these programs back in their original committee.

That kind of juggling, however, is less necessary in the wake of recent committee reforms. Subcommittee chairmen can be much more independent today. Were Fulbright around now, he could take over Foreign Relations and still keep his banking interests within a subcommittee. When Fulbright made his move, however, relinquishing the Banking Committee chairmanship meant relinquishing all of the power in it. Today, as a subcommittee chairman, he could retain that power within both spheres. The big struggles now are within committees rather than among them. Subcommittee chairmen struggle against each other and against the whole-committee chairman, while committees fight less against each other. In this Congress of rapidly changing jurisdictions, in which some changes are substantive and some are pretense, how is it possible to tell where power is actually located? Is the power in the committee or the subcommittee? Is it in the hands of the chairman, or divided among the subchairmen?

The nominal jurisdictions and the titles belong to the facade of Congress. As part of that facade they are rearranged every other year, when new shingles are made and hung out to represent the shifting tides of public concern and media attention. Behind this ever-changing facade, however, is a simple arrangement that clarifies the location of power. Power is where the staff is.

No matter how grandiose the name and the official jurisdiction, if a subcommittee has only one lonely counsel and a single secretary, it is obviously not equipped to exercise much power. By the same token, no matter how innocuous the name and how vague the title, if it has a dozen lawyers, three Ph.D.'s, a battery of secretaries, and four interns, it is certain that some real power is being exercised. It may not be immediately apparent what they command, but staff is a sure sign of dominion over something.

A junior senator may fuss over his subcommittee name and supposed territory, but the middle-level senators—the rising comers—go straight to the heart of the matter: they fuss over staff. As Stephen Isaacs of *The Washington Post* described it, senators are "scrambling after staff bodies like hunters in pursuit of prey, hungering for the impact that extra staff person, or two, or three, or even dozens can give to them and their political careers."

Rochelle Jones and Peter Woll call staff "the surrogates of power." As they explain it, "Committees . . . are mere symbols of power, not power itself, unless they are accompanied by adequate staff. A good staff is necessary if a Senator wants to wield power through his committees. If he wants to exert influence beyond his committees, a capable staff is essential. Staff and power go together. . . ." Not only is a senator's staff size directly correlated to the amount of public attention he receives in the media, but it is also related to the amount of work he can get done. Having broad jurisdiction and no staff is like a New Guinea tribesman's having a claim to two large yam fields but no wives to tend them. The fields then belong to the jungle, and they will be expropriated by someone who does have wives and children to cultivate them.

The broader implications which this impact of staff has on legislation and policy will be examined in the next section of the book. For now, it is important in the way that it helps to turn an average new member of Congress into a Big Man. The member strives for new staffers with each new reorganization, adding a few here and there. As he gains these new positions, he moves people from his personal staff (who already have close loyal ties to him) to occupy these staff positions. Then new people can be brought onto the personal staff. The staffers who had filled these committee slots are then on their own to find new jobs, unless their old boss is moving into a higher position himself, in which case he may carry them with him. In any event, the clients of the previous boss must move on.

This constant expansion of the personal staff is the means by which a domestic household can eventually become a far-flung clan stretching throughout the Congress. Beginning with the guaranteed allotment and a staff of personal retainers, the senator picks up other staff slots one at a time on various committees—getting a toehold here, a nominal grip there, then turning the toehold into an enclave and the nominal grip into power.

Conceptually, the scheme is a simple one. Like the tribal politicians of New Guinea and the complex of wives, land, and pigs, congressional politicians have to unite the variables of staff, jurisdiction, and pork. This synthesis depends on skill, luck, and hard work. Most important of all, it depends on the strategy devised and pursued by the individual politician. All the politicians know the basic ingredients of power, but each one must conjure a plan appropriate to his own needs, goals, and abilities. What works for Edward Kennedy would be much different from the approach needed by John Stennis or Howard Baker. To appreciate these differences and the implications they bear, we have to examine some of the more common approaches and their practitioners.

4

Extending the Clan

LIKE ALCHEMISTS EVER in search of the recipe for gold, politicians eternally search for the formula of power, as though it could be reduced to a single maxim or checklist of acts. In classical myths and folktales, the hero receives a list of feats from the king, and if he performs them, as he always does, he wins the hand of the princess and the imperial crown, ensuring that he will live happily ever after. Unlike the labors of Hercules, however, the rise from the lower rungs to the upper ranks in any society or organization depends on skills, luck, and intuition, which must evolve with newly emerging situations and does not depend on a mere list of deeds. In the abstract, the principles of the process may be easy to understand, as in the conceptually simple scheme by which a New Guinea hunter becomes a Big Man or an entering congressman becomes an authority eventually. In practice, however, it is a chancy procedure, in which what works for one politician at one time only partially resembles what works for another at a different time.

One New Guinea Big Man concentrates on producing large yams as the key to acquiring more wives, pigs, and followers, while another devotes his energies to arranging good marriage alliances through his children to achieve the same goal. Both strategies may work, or fail, depending on a number of factors beyond the control of the would-be Big Man. Similarly, within the Congress, one politician concentrates his efforts on a single committee staff as a route to power, while another one searches out a wide range of committees to achieve power through diversity. Each strategy produces a slightly different yield, but each aims for the same ultimate goal of procuring and exercising power. Each strategy has its own unique advantages as well as its pitfalls, but under the right circumstances any one of a number of such strategies may be the right one.

Every member of Congress uses a different, individual strategy in pursuing that elusive goal of power, but these various strategies can be grouped together into three primary approaches. In looking at these examples, we should bear in mind that no member of Congress sticks absolutely and irrevocably to any one; nevertheless, certain consistencies in their careers do emerge.

SHAMANS

When the nuclear reactor at Three Mile Island, Pennsylvania, malfunctioned and forced the evacuation of the surrounding countryside under threat of a possible nuclear meltdown, Capitol Hill, like the rest of the nation, became mentally riveted to the drama. Normal work ground to a halt as radios and televisions were set up in the offices for a continuous monitoring of news reports, and everyone phoned everyone else searching for information. Offices were deluged with constituents' and reporters' requests for statements on the accident, on nuclear facilities in the home district, or on the politicians' opinions about nuclear energy in general. As with all national or international crises, there was a tinge of excitement in Congress, for every crisis brings with it the potential to thrust a new senator or little-known congressman into the national limelight or to mangle the reputations of some of the congressional powers who emerge as scapegoats. The prominent question echoing in each mind was who would profit from the crisis—and who stood to lose.

The race to gather glory and dispense shame began immediately. Dozens of committees and subcommittees each claimed some authority or oversight on the matter, and each wanted to hold the first set of public congressional hearings as proof that they were the most interested in the issue, the least responsible for it, and the most likely to correct it. By implication the blame, but not the remedy, lay with one of the other committees that had failed adequately to monitor its part of the federal bureaucracy. The most likely candidates for holding the first hearings in the Senate were Gary Hart, who chaired the Nuclear Regulation Subcommittee of the Environment and Public Works Committee; Henry Jackson, who chaired the Energy and Natural Resources Committee; or Bennett Johnston, who chaired the Energy Subcommittee of Appropriations. The corresponding committees on the House side were also poised to snatch the glory. Hearings could be conducted by Representative Tom Bevill, as chairman of the Energy and Water Development Subcommittee of Appropriations; Toby Moffett, as chairman of the Environment, Energy, and Natural Resources Subcommittee of Government Operations; Morris Udall, as chairman of Interior and Insular Affairs and its Subcommittee on Energy and the Environment; or John Dingell, as chairman of the Energy and Power Subcommittee of Interstate and Foreign Commerce. Even though each of these panels claimed some bit of jurisdiction over the issue and all of them sought the credit without the shame, none of them was the first to display their orchestrated rage on national television. That honor went to Edward Kennedy, chairman of the Subcommittee on Health and Scientific Research of the Labor and Human Resources Committee. On grounds that the accident posed a major health hazard, Kennedy's staff organized hearings for the weekend following the crisis, a full week before any other staff could marshal a complete review of the incident.

This was neither the first nor last time that the Kennedy staff scored a publicity coup by initiating a full legislative spectacle of inquiry by the senator. The Kennedy organization stood ready to spring into action at a moment's notice, launching a public performance on any issue that popped into national headlines, or to whisk their chief off to any part of the country commanding news interest. Not by coincidence, Kennedy had built the largest Congressional Clan on the Hill up to that time.

Kennedy's clan-building strategy was simple and persistent: to get as many staffers as he could in as many places in the congressional hierarchy as feasible.

On first entering the Senate in 1962, Kennedy sought seats on the Judiciary Committee and the Commerce Committee. Majority Leader Mike Mansfield arranged for him to get the Judiciary seat, but he had to take the less popular Labor and Public Welfare Committee rather than the Commerce position. Within the Judiciary Committee, Kennedy forged a staff around the issues of monopoly and antitrust legislation. Within the renamed Labor and Human Resources Committee, he focused on health and scientific research. In 1979, when Judiciary Chairman James Eastland retired, Kennedy was the ranking Democrat and became the committee chairman, giving him command over the largest committee staff in the Senate.

In addition to these major enclaves in justice and health, Kennedy acquired toeholds in several other legislative areas. He chaired the Energy Subcommittee of the Joint Economic Committee, giving him a platform from which to approach the problems of gasoline prices, oil imports, and nuclear power. As a member of the Select Commission on Immigration and Refugee Policy, he addressed the needs and problems of the large Hispanic population in the United States. His position on the congressionally operated Office of Technological Assessment provided him with a rich source of information and assistance on a variety of issues from space travel and mass transportation to world population.

In 1981, when the Republicans took organizational control of the Senate, Kennedy, like all the other Democrats, lost his chairmanships and half of his 120 staffers. He then switched the base of his operation from the Judiciary to the Labor Committee, choosing to become its ranking minority member.

Kennedy's strategy was to cast a wide net, covering a broad range of issues and thereby being able to speak impressively and officially, even if not authoritatively, on any one of them. He could reap the first round of television and newspaper coverage on an issue, as he did with the Three Mile Island accident, and leave other staffs the tasks of sorting out the technical information and details in the ensuing months. The press, however, generally downplays these second, third, and fourth rounds of congressional hearings after the immediacy of the crisis has passed. Kennedy's ability to react so swiftly and decisively rests on his large and diversified staff, for no matter what the issue, someone in that circle is expert enough to assemble a panel of appropriate witnesses and authorities, write a quick speech or press release, and raise some provocative questions.

The benefits of such a clan are obvious. They keep the senator in the public spotlight as a congressional activist, and as such, this strategy is perfectly suited for a would-be President. The staff operates as something of a cabinet-in-waiting, keeping the chief active in all aspects of the national arena. What this strategy does not do, however, is give the senator much power within the Congress. It produces a lot of light, but not much heat. This lack of inside power is evident in the career of Kennedy, who, despite his renown and large staff, never managed to get a major bill through Congress—a point that was frequently and effectively argued by Jimmy Carter when Kennedy challenged him for the Democratic presidential nomination in 1980.

This abundance of light shines forth in his handling of all kinds of legislative issues. The Kennedy staff arranges a constant procession of hearings in Washington and throughout the nation, dragging up victims of every kind of disease imaginable. With crying old folks, bereaved widows, impoverished orphans, migrant workers, and amputees, the shows always make good press images suitable for sixty-second clips on the national news. His highly trained cadre of lawyers and health experts has written dozens of major health bills, including the first proposal for a national health care program. None of these pieces of legislation got through Congress, despite their publicity. Even in the area of Judiciary where Kennedy has chaired the committee, he was unsuccessful in passing his many bills calling for major changes in the federal penal code or improvement in the court system. Kennedy had a large popular following, but lacked inside congressional power.

In the political jargon of Washington, politicians like Kennedy are frequently referred to as showhorses, who command a great deal of public attention, as opposed to workhorses, who plod along unnoticed in the background. Convinced that their political destinies are really in the White House rather than on Capitol Hill, the majority of politicians in Congress at some time or other pursue this path to national prominence. It was a strategy followed by Richard Nixon in his early investigations of Alger Hiss, and later it worked as well for young John Kennedy. For them, Congress was a platform from which to speak to the nation and gather a wide political following. In this regard they resemble shamans, who exist in almost every society under a variety of forms and names. Also called medicine men and witch doctors, shamans are jacks-of-all-trades, willing to tackle any problem beyond the powers of the ordinary people. They heal the sick, appease the fates, end droughts, arrange love matches, ensure a good hunt, and dispense magic to protect warriors on the field. They practice their crafts to produce a good harvest or to fight black magic, to end an epidemic or increase a woman's fertility.

Shamans always carry a bag of amulets, potions, magic stones, and assorted ritual objects. Their primary tool, however, is the faith which they can generate, the conviction in their performance, and the charisma of their role. Shamans are expert in conjuring belief from the most skeptical in an audience, giving them at least a minimum of security in the face of the world's uncertainties. Unlike the chiefs and war leaders in a tribe, the shaman's power derives not from the authority of his position or from the practical results which he produces, as much as from the confidence he displays and the emotions he can extract from his followers. They publicize, play upon, and eventually help to allay the worst fears of the common people. They make real the threat of unseen demons, which they then exorcise. In the political world of Washington, shamans do not invoke the dread of evil spirits as much as the dreaded forces of world communism, the Mafia, monopoly cabals, the moral majority, or immoral minority. They play on the common man's fear of being squashed by overwhelming forces or of falling victim to some dread disease that will leave him disabled and his family impoverished. Like shamans everywhere, they mix together the real dangers and tragedies of the world with a host of unseen and

unreal ones to provoke a fear of things from which only the shaman has the power or the willingness to protect the potential
victims.

Political shamans rarely make good behind-the-scenes manipulators; their power flows from their ability to generate popular support and belief more than from their ability to deliver
results. Many of them, however, fail to attract the public attention and approval which their shows are designed to capture.
For every Joseph McCarthy, Estes Kefauver, Richard Nixon, or
Edward Kennedy who succeeds in tapping some emotional, national following from the congressional pulpit, there are dozens
of Howard Metzenbaums, Gary Harts, and Larry Presslers who
pursue the same path with only minimal public recognition or
enthusiasm.

Larry Pressler entered the Senate in 1978 after serving two
terms in the House; at the age of thirty-six, he was one of the
youngest men in the chamber and one of the least experienced.
His prior career included a stint as a Rhodes Scholar at Oxford,
which he left after only a year to volunteer for military service in
Vietnam. With his officer's credentials and war veteran record,
Pressler went on to Harvard Law School. After graduating, he
failed in two efforts to join the South Dakota Bar, but was later
admitted to practice in the District of Columbia. Aside from the
failure to pass the bar exam in his home state, Pressler's accom-
plishments read like a checklist of what an aspiring politician
should have behind him. However, his failure to do anything
beyond public relations with those abilities made him a constant source of jokes in the House, as well as the Senate. Upon
entering the Senate, he joined four different committees and got
seats on several spots in the party organization too, indicating
the desire to become a real activist. Once on these panels, he
seemingly spent more time appearing at Washington parties accompanied by photogenic or newsworthy companions than he
spent in committee work.

No sooner was Pressler in the Senate than he decided to announce his candidacy for the Republican nomination for President in 1980. Like Kennedy, he was out on the campaign trail,
making public speeches and soliciting money while other politicians were back in Washington legislating. Pressler was cut from

the field of candidates early in the primary process, but he popped up in the news a few months later as a self-proclaimed hero of the Abscam scandal. As one of the senators who visited with the fake sheiks in an FBI house in the Washington suburbs, Pressler refused a proffered bribe. He then made repeated public appearances, basking in the glory of being the only clean politician in the Abscam mess. That theme died a quick death, however, when word was leaked that the FBI had video recordings of the incident in which, even though Pressler did not take the bribe, he did not appear as quite the hero his version of the encounter maintained. Mocked as something of a charlatan, he dropped out of political sight, staying well beyond the limelight for the duration of the 1980 campaigns and the Abscam trials.

While Edward Kennedy epitomizes the successful shaman who enjoys genuine public acclaim and can inspire great confidence and support, as well as hate, Pressler appears as a near parody of the role, inspiring neither strong support nor dislike. In deliberate cultivation of the press and of public attention, he generated more mirth and mockery than anything else. Nevertheless, both Kennedy and Pressler adopted strategies that emphasized casting a wide political net, being involved with a diversity of issues, and trying to stay constantly before the public eye. Because of this public attention, such politicians often appear to the public as the real powers of Congress. They symbolize the whole political process; yet the real powers of Congress are men much different from either Kennedy or Pressler and usually much less known. These are the Congressional Warlords, who build a fortress around a well-delineated territory and then defend it with the might of a samurai.

WARLORDS

While Congressional shamans run around grabbing staffers and offices wherever they find them on Capitol Hill, the Warlords pursue the opposite strategy. They carefully choose one piece of organizational terrain, slowly dominate it, strengthen it, and gradually extend it outward, increasing the scope of that special area. By taking control of all the different spots in the organization that relate to one issue, capturing all of the staff positions associated with it, and then uniting them into one operation, the Warlords concentrate on intensive, rather than extensive, politics.

When Senator Mark Hatfield became chairman of the Senate Appropriations Committee in 1981, he stepped into a position with the potential for dominating energy issues in the Senate. The energy issue was spread throughout the organizational matrix, with each committee owning a small piece of the action, but Hatfield controlled two of the major spots. Before becoming Appropriations chairman he had been ranking Republican on the Energy and Water Development Subcommittee of Appropriations and ranking Republican on the Energy and Natural Resources Committee. In the two-tiered committee system of Congress, one set of committees authorizes legislation, but the money for any program they establish must be approved by one of the various appropriations subcommittees. Hatfield's clan straddled both of these tiers, concentrating on a single major issue, but pursuing that issue throughout the committee system.

The best practitioners of this strategy in recent decades have been Senators Russell Long of Louisiana and John Hampton Stennis of Mississippi. Stennis ranks with the most gracious, gentle, and polite men ever to have walked the corridors of the United States Senate. With his lank, rangy frame, gray hair, and slow dignified gait, he personifies the "courtly gentleman," a phrase that seemed to be a part of his name. Opening doors for young women and men alike, holding elevators for aides, speaking to everyone he passed, and knowing hundreds of the Hill workers by their first names, Stennis exudes the *noblesse oblige* of the Old South in ways that contrast with the other Southern stereotype of the redneck populist. His reserved, quiet style knows nothing of the glad-handing, good-old-boy or the media-hype of the twentieth century. John Stennis can afford to be nice to everyone; he has played the game of congressional politics and has won.

Unlike the diverse committees and broad assignments of Kennedy, Stennis sits on only two committees: Appropriations and Armed Services. In the 97th Congress, he is the senior Democrat on both, and prior to the Republican takeover, he chaired the Armed Services Committee and the Subcommittee of Appropriations dealing with military funds. He was the latest in a dynasty of southerners bearing the title "Mr. Military." By chairing both key positions, he exercised a monopoly on defense matters in the Senate. If Senator Stennis wanted a new aircraft carrier or another contract for his Mississippi shipbuilding yards, one part of his clan would authorize the program while the other appropriated the necessary money. This gave Stennis an ultimate form of congressional power over a government agency costing roughly $150 billion per annum—more than the total national budgets of most nations in the world and more than the gross national product of many. With this kind of power, it is not surprising that Stennis once said of the committee system, "I almost worship it," for he had managed to play the system to his needs. Unlike Kennedy, who, even if he could get a major health bill through his authorizing committee, lacks the control over funding for it, Stennis controlled the gamut of military legislation.

As chairman of the Finance Committee, Russell Long did not have to worry about appropriations. His clan had final say over tax revenues and how much money came into the federal government, needing to confer only with Representative Al Ullman who, with Long, headed up the Joint Committee on Taxation. Through a slow and arduous process, Long managed to capture all of the congressional slots associated with taxation. He was the expert on the issues, and his staff controlled all of the major decision points in the legislative process. Even though he lost a large number of those staff assistants when the Republicans took control and Senator Robert Dole became Finance chairman in 1981, Long remains a major power; but he no longer has a pure monopoly.

Warlords like Stennis, Long, and Hatfield are the real powers of the Congress. Although each controls only a part of the whole organization, they have strategically selected every spot to maximize a particular brand of power. Theirs is a patient game of slowly adding staff in one certain area year after year, ignoring those opportunities that may momentarily entice, but lose their public appeal after a year or so. Theirs is also the game of the career legislator willing to spend the remainder of his life in Congress and to eschew the glitter and fame of the White

House. Even though Warlords may be the least-known congressional powers to outsiders, they ultimately have the clans that stretch furthest from Congress and into the bowels of government, exercising an influence that far outweighs the more media-oriented politicians.

GODFATHERS

The third major strategy for building a Congressional Clan largely ignores the committee organization of Congress and pays only secondary attention to the news media. Acting more as back-room politicians, these tacticians concentrate on the political party structure, seeking elected posts within Congress as party whips and party leaders, putting together ad hoc coalitions and deals, and playing a fast game. Like Warlords, they, too, have made a career commitment to Congress, but unlike them, they are usually too impatient to accrue power slowly in a single area. Instead, they act as brokers, keeping the various Warlords in balance and maintaining the minimum amount of cooperation and cohesion necessary for Congress to function as a body. They are the Godfathers of politics.

The prototype of the Congressional Godfather was Lyndon Johnson, assisted by his constant lieutenant, Bobby Baker. Together, they knew all the needs of their flock, and they met them. Treating other senators as any politician treats a constituent, Johnson subjugated the Senate Warlords more than any Big Man in recent history. He also managed to keep them happier than subsequent leaders have been able to do. With lesser success than Johnson, several Congressional Big Men of the 1980s continue to pursue this style of political manipulation.

No one in the present Congress better embodies the deftness of this approach than Thomas P. O'Neill, Jr., the Irish bear who clawed and backslapped his way to becoming Speaker of the House in 1977. His actual assumption of this, the third highest constitutional office in the nation, was a shoo-in with more backslapping than clawing, for the real fighting had taken place in the preceding decade. In 1977, O'Neill's careful crafting and preparation came to its logical fruition as he mounted the podium as Speaker.

This very Irish son of Boston first entered politics in 1936, when he ran for the Massachusetts House of Representatives, a post he won and held for sixteen years. By 1947, he was Minority Leader of the Massachusetts House, and when the Democrats gained a majority, he became the first Democratic Speaker in the history of Massachusetts, traditionally a Republican state. For many politicians, such an attainment would be hard to trade for the lowly status of a freshman congressman in Washington; but when Jack Kennedy decided to give up his eighth district seat in the House and run for the Senate in 1952, O'Neill left the state legislature to launch his congressional career.

Once in Washington, O'Neill ignored opportunities on various committees to go straight for a seat on the Rules Committee. That committee has a great deal of diversified power within the House, but it did not provide much public exposure for a young man wanting to go on to higher office in the Senate or in a presidential cabinet. Nevertheless, it was there that the experienced O'Neill knew he could best learn the procedures, personalities, and idiosyncrasies of the House of Representatives and its 435 members. And he learned well.

Even though O'Neill's strategy did not place him in position to build a large personal following of staff and younger congressmen during the first few years, it gave him the opportunity to capture eventually the largest bloc of staff slots. His first major step in that direction came in 1971. He and his Northern allies supported Louisiana's Hale Boggs for the position of Majority Leader when Carl Albert left that post to become Speaker. In return for that support, Boggs appointed O'Neill as Majority Whip, the third ranking slot in the party hierarchy. Under the normal sequence of posts, Boggs would have become Speaker after Albert died or retired and O'Neill would have moved to Majority Leader. As it happened, however, Boggs died in an airplane crash in Alaska during the election of 1972, and O'Neill advanced to replace him virtually unopposed.

As Majority Leader, O'Neill controlled a large number of staff positions and appointive offices. After six years of meticulous use of those positions, he stepped in to replace Speaker Carl Albert, who retired at the end of the 94th Congress. The much more dynamic O'Neill was by then the only appropriate replacement with the background experience and the demonstrated ability to mesh the disparate elements of the House Democrats. Assuming the job in 1977, O'Neill applied himself as arduously to the task of rebuilding the Speaker's powers, which had been eroded under McCormack and Albert, as he had to the task of getting the office.

O'Neill's ability to accomplish this most politically precarious of all the strategies in Congress derived from his previous long apprenticeship in the Massachusetts legislature and his unswerving purpose. His decision to bypass earlier opportunities and concentrate on this long shot was risky, but the rewards were correspondingly great. In the end, O'Neill's approach yielded more access to power, control over staff, and potential patronage than the more conservative maneuverings of the Warlords.

To a lesser extent, Senate Majority Leader Howard Baker pursued the Godfather game, but mixed with more media cultivation in keeping with his attempts to run for President. An even more typical Godfather in the Senate is Democratic Leader Robert Byrd, who not only tends to the legislative and constituent needs of his fellow senators but massages their egos as well. He sends them birthday cards and delivers flowery speeches in their honor on other special occasions. He attends family events, weddings and funerals, as regularly for his fellow senators as he does for his constituents back in West Virginia. As the timekeeper on the Senate floor, Byrd rearranged voting times and debates to meet the busy demands of senators' personal schedules and out-of-town engagements.

This devotion to detail enabled Byrd to win two major skirmishes with the clans of Hubert Humphrey and Edward Kennedy. Even though both Humphrey and Kennedy were much better known national politicians, neither had the quiet tact to be a Congressional Godfather, nor the time-honed skills of back-room negotiators. Their fellow Democrats voted for Byrd over Kennedy in a 1971 contest for the office of Majority Whip, and they supported him again in 1976 when he vied with Humphrey for the office of Majority Leader upon Humphrey's return to the Senate. Although most of the Democrats in the Senate were ideologically much closer to Humphrey or Kennedy than to Byrd, they had more trust in Byrd's quiet role as a group facilitator than in the more flamboyant and self-centered politics of both Kennedy and Humphrey.

Playing the political Godfather is one of the most appealing roles in Congress because it offers an opportunity to participate in every major decision, while allowing one always to rise above the feuding Warlords to a higher level of statesmanship. It is the fast-track ascent up the congressional power pyramid without the tedious wait and inveterate strife encountered by the Warlords. Nevertheless, the Godfather role is the most difficult to play well, often defeating truly ambitious politicians like Kennedy or Humphrey because of the finely tuned knowledge they must possess about the political and personal habits and fears of all the other members of Congress. A congressional party leader without this knowledge or the requisite tact to mesh disparate interests becomes a mere party spokesman, like former House Speaker Carl Albert or former Senate Majority Leader Mike Mansfield, who presided but left the real running of Congress to the Warlords and their clans.

Much of congressional history seems to repeat itself in the ebb and flow of power between these two different kinds of Big Men, the Warlords and the Godfathers. Power becomes centralized around Godfather figures like Nicholas Longworth, Joe Cannon, Richard Russell, Lyndon Johnson, or Sam Rayburn, only to be dissipated in the next generation by lesser known Warlords. Somewhat to the side of these congressional struggles, the shamans entertain and cajole the public in a separate political game of presidential politics. The politician who is not clearly aware of which game he is playing or when he moves from one arena to another stands to get lost in the shuffle. Trying at one moment to be a Warlord, then switching to the public arena to run for President, only to go back to Congress to play the Godfather role, can cripple more careers than it benefits. Occasionally, a Lyndon Johnson can take advantage of a peculiar situation to act the chameleon, but for most it leads to obscurity.

THE PATH WRONGLY TAKEN

Each of the three clan-building maneuvers works best when the politician adopts one of them early in his career and sticks to it. Kennedy, Stennis, and O'Neill pursued distinctively different plans, but each adhered to his choice carefully through the decades. Eventually all became a type of Congressional Big Man. In a national milieu of volatile ideological stances, voters, and tactics, there is still a need for a certain underlying constancy in tactics if the politician is to succeed. An official like Robert Byrd may change from being a Ku Klux Klan supporter to being an advocate of civil rights, or he may shift from defending the war in Vietnam to opposing it. What he cannot afford to do is change his own personal political organization or switch from one clan type to another.

Such consistency is difficult in the vicissitudes of the political arena, where a chance for rapid advancement may pop up, or a sudden wave of interest in a particular issue propel a politician before the attention of new groups of people. Occasionally, a decisive move can be made at such a juncture; but more often than not the politician fares better by slowly expanding his original organization. The damage an erratic strategy renders is illustrated in the career of Senator Frank Church of Idaho.

First elected to the Senate in 1956 at the age of thirty-two, Church cut a cultivated, though extremely youthful, figure at a time when the Senate was still very much under the domination of the Southern *ancien régime*. Church arrived on the Senate steps with a set of whiz-kid credentials: Phi Beta Kappa and law degree from Stanford; extensive experience as a young officer in military intelligence in Asia; private practice as an Idaho attorney. Enhanced by his marriage to Bethine Clark, the daughter of Idaho Governor (and later Federal Judge) Chase A. Clark, he combined the best of political professionalism and scrubbed youth with old-fashioned Senatorial oratory and connections with good-old-boy politicians. Along with fellow freshmen Jacob Javits of New York and William Proxmire of Wisconsin, Church joined a growing cadre of young active senators that already included John Kennedy of Massachusetts and Henry "Scoop" Jackson of Washington.

With his broad background of military intelligence in China, India, and Burma, Church wanted to make his mark in foreign affairs, a wish eventually accommodated by Majority Leader Lyndon Johnson, who secured him a seat on the Foreign Relations panel. That committee was and remains one of the most prestigious assignments in the Congress, but it is an impractical luxury because of its lack of access to congressional pork. Work in international relations is a form of political conspicuous consumption that produces little for the politician's followers back home, but ranks high in status in diplomatic circles. It gives a senator plenty of national exposure; however, as William Fulbright of Arkansas discovered, it is easy to lose contact with and support from the constituents when a senator occupies himself too much with such glamorous topics. Idaho's two major concerns, agriculture and water policy, are at best only tangential to the business of international treaties and diplomacy.

To meet some of those constituent concerns, Church also sought a seat on the Interior Committee, which had jurisdiction over Idaho's water interests and those of national lands and natural resources. By going on these two very different committees, Church bifurcated his potential clan between his personal interests in foreign affairs and his need to serve his state. From the start, this precluded Church's ever getting sole control over one area or ever becoming a Warlord. In order to build a monopoly clan such as Stennis's in the military, Church would have to seek an appropriations assignment that corresponded to one of his two authorizations committees. But just as he could not be a Warlord, he did not have a diversified enough operation to be a Congressional Shaman involved in all areas of politics, as Edward Kennedy did with assignments in justice, health, refugees, economics, and science. Aside from Church's position in Foreign Affairs and in the Interior panel, his only variation was to serve on the powerless Committee on Aging.

Despite these handicaps, Church wanted to go for the big prize, the presidency. His work investigating both the intelligence community and the management of the government's interior policies did bring him some public attention. On the basis of this and the notoriety from his opposition to the Vietnam War, he made his presidential bid in 1976. But his previous work had been too narrow in scope; his only substantial support came from the Pacific Northwest—the area that had most benefited from his work in Interior and Energy. That small constituency, even when added to scattered enthusiasm among college students and the elderly, failed to match the wider appeal of Jimmy Carter, who easily eliminated Church in the primary elections.

Like so many senators who use the Senate as a national platform from which to run for President, Church found himself back in the Senate without a major stronghold or a viable Congressional Clan. Although high in seniority on both the Foreign Relations and the Interior committees, Church had not acquired a large staff on either. His stronghold centered in the Aging Committee, which he chaired; yet that position operated as a congressional showpiece that could investigate issues, but lacked power to pass either legislation or appropriations.

Church's situation changed considerably in 1979 after the retirement of Foreign Relations Chairman John Sparkman of Alabama. Church was next in seniority and therefore next in line for the chairmanship, but his elevation proved to be more in name than in power. Sparkman himself had exerted little leadership and under him much of the chairman's power slipped away from the centralized organization it had been under William Fulbright. In particular, the subcommittee chairmen had won greater power and independence by wresting away from the committee chairman the power to hire their own staffs. Having their own aides in charge of the issue areas, they exercised reasonable autonomy from an elderly and often uninterested Sparkman.

Before Church could even begin consolidating his inheritance over the weakened office left him by Sparkman, a more severe blow was dealt to his control over staff. The Republicans on the committee, especially the conservative ones around Jesse Helms, demanded their own staff which, under the rules, was their due. Even though the Republicans had been willing to share staff under the conservative Sparkman, they refused to continue with the more liberal Church. With the increased importance of staff in the congressional world, it is unlikely that the Republicans would have continued without staff no matter who was chairman; as it was, Church's ascension to the chair only intensified their effort to grab more staff away from the Democrats.

Although a committee chairmanship may be inherited on the basis of longevity, the concomitant clan does not just spring into being. Rather, it must be slowly built, nourished, and extended through the years. Even for those staff positions that Church did inherit, he lacked a loyal following of retainers to move into the slots. Upon assuming the chair of the Foreign Relations Committee, he had to surrender his chairmanship of the Aging Committee, but he abandoned his staff there to fend for itself. In keeping with congressional tradition, most of the old staff was immediately thrown out by the new chairman, Lawton Chiles. For the new positions in Foreign Relations, Church wanted fresh blood, especially foreign affairs specialists from the Ivy League schools.

It may appear that what Church did was proper, but politically it was not very wise. Even though he hired an academically qualified staff, these people held little personal loyalty to him. After all, they were successful before coming to Congress and could return to their outside professions. They owed him their jobs on the congressional staff, not their careers.

In addition to bringing new experts to fill the staff slots, Church simultaneously tried to take back control of staff positions from the subcommittee chairmen, an erosion of several years that could not be reversed overnight. To retrieve that power he would have had to start years before, by slowly picking up the staff positions of each departing subcommittee head. He could not just remove by fiat the staff from presiding chairmen.

In the end, Church occupied a highly prestigious and visible office in the Senate as chairman of Foreign Relations. He had a reasonably large staff, even though it was smaller than those of his predecessors, but he still lacked a powerful Congressional Clan. Instead, he had a long list of employees, rather than the more important integrated following based on personal ties to his leadership. He wore the trappings of a Big Man, but he lacked the power. Church failed to develop and carry through with a single strategy. His efforts stayed divided between his personal interest in international politics and the political needs of Idaho. He vacillated between amassing power within the Senate and carrying out his presidential ambitions. Finally, the voters deprived him of his seat in the Senate in 1980, after nearly a quarter century in office.

Church's predicament is common to many members of Congress, especially among the would-be Presidents. They find themselves in nominally important positions within the Senate, but years of neglecting senatorial for presidential politics leave them weak within Congress. Some of them, like Barry Goldwater or George McGovern, just vegetate for years in Congress after their failed presidential campaigns. Others like Church and Edmund Muskie return their attentions to the Senate, but face severe battles against younger men who were gathering senatorial staffs while they were out on the national campaign trail.

The senators who kept their attention firmly focused on the Congress and eventually became the Big Men still have one more arena for clan expansion. After they have secured the right number and combination of staff positions and have captured their targeted part of the congressional machinery, they can begin to move some of their loyal staffers into congressional seats of their own. So begins the first stage of subclans.

GETTING THE STAFF INTO OFFICE

Throughout the clan-building operations, the staffers advance in tandem with their boss. As the clan expands, they move from personal to committee staff; if he becomes chairman, one of them becomes staff director. Until recently that was as high as an assistant could advance within the congressional bureaucracy. Recent changes, however, have opened up whole new vistas for them, favoring their election to congressional seats.

This new type of politics is another Kennedy specialty. In 1964, Kennedy's former assistant John Culver ran for Congress from his home state of Iowa. After returning to Washington as a member of Congress rather than as an aide, Culver hired Dick Clark to be his assistant. In 1972, Clark ran for the Senate and was also elected. Two years later, Culver decided to leave the House and also go over to the Senate. When the 95th Congress convened in 1975, Kennedy, Culver, and Clark were all serving together as senators. Even though Clark lost his reelection campaign in 1978, the alliance among the three politicians continued to function. Kennedy and Culver assisted Clark in acquiring a newly created ambassadorship for refugee problems, made possible in part by Kennedy's work on the Select Commission on Immigration and Refugee Policy and his contacts as former chairman of a subcommittee in that field. Despite all the work in getting the job, Clark resigned within months of his confirmation in order to join Kennedy's 1980 presidential campaign staff. In that year's election, however, not only did Kennedy fail to get his party's nomination, but Culver himself was defeated for reelection. Thus, in 1981, Kennedy lost his chairmanships in the Senate, his clan was reduced to its core, and none of his former aides was serving with him as a member of Congress. His subclan withered in the political winds.

The same election that deprived Kennedy of his chairmanship over the Committee on the Judiciary and his former aides brought Republican Strom Thurmond to new prominence. As the ranking Republican on the Judiciary Committee, he became the new chairman in 1981. For the first time that year, one of his previous aides was also elected to Congress. Thirty-three-year-old John Napier won South Carolina's sixth congressional district, replacing John Jenrette, who had been convicted of receiving bribes. It is too early to know whether or not Thurmond, who was already seventy-eight when he became chairman, will ever be able to help Napier into the Senate. Nevertheless, the same political process seems to be operating, whether the protagonists are liberal or conservative.

A similar game of musical seats was played by Hubert Humphrey, Walter Mondale, and several of their junior protégés. Mondale served as campaign manager in Humphrey's election to the Senate in 1950. When Humphrey left the Senate to become Vice President in 1964, Mondale moved into the vacancy. While serving in the Senate, Mondale hired as his assistants Toby Moffet and Richard Nolan. In 1974, both of them were elected to the House—Moffet to a Connecticut seat, and Nolan to a Minnesota seat. The multi-generational complex of assistants and former assistants grew more complicated when

Humphrey returned to the Senate as Deputy President pro tempore, while Mondale proceeded to become Vice President and thus the presiding officer of the Senate in 1977. Humphrey's death in 1978 brought Muriel Humphrey to his seat and thereby kept the alliance alive for a few more months.

Such networks of members and their assistants, of patrons and clients, have become as entangled as the genealogy of polygamous families in New Guinea, adding another layer of obfuscation to an already confused arrangement. The full impact of this new tradition seems yet to be felt. Being derived from recent changes in the political milieu, it has only just begun to influence a wide range of congressional activities.

As of 1981, sixty-eight members of Congress were former congressional assistants; a number of other congressmen had served as campaign assistants to congressmen prior to their own elections. For now the importance of this new route to political office lies simply in its being the ultimate extension of the traditional clans that spring up within Congress. This development makes it all the more imperative for any analysis of Congress to examine the politicians and their assistants as units, rather than to look at only one part of the total picture. Viewed in this way, the process becomes something of a cycle: A new member begins with a personal staff, which slowly expands to include subcommittee staffs, committee staffs, and possibly party staffs. When these Congressional Clans seem to have reached their maximum extension within the Congress, the process begins anew with the staff members running for office and thus generating subclans.

This expansion and division of clans within Congress involves only that small part of the clan that remains in Congress. But these clans, no matter how extensive and powerful they become within Congress, also need to extend themselves outside Congress to supplement and reinforce that power. The Congressional Clan is a power base, but only a base. Soon after a representative or senator passes from being a middle-level member to a Big Man, he begins the external expansion of his clan operation.

PART II

❧❦❧

POLITICS
IN WONDERLAND

Congressional Clans live in constant peril. Decades of careful work building just the right clan organization often collapse literally overnight by the sudden break of an ethics scandal, a lost election, a revolt in the lower classes, or a change in the ruling party. The 1980 election drove that point home when not only were a handful of congressmen brought down by the Abscam scandal, but some of the real Big Men of Congress were defeated in the November elections. Such institutional figures as Senator Warren Magnuson, Representative Al Ullman, and Representative Bob Eckhardt were unexpectedly defeated, their clans routed, and followers forced from their jobs. Even the Democratic senators who survived that election suffered catastrophic damage in losing half of their staff assistants and all of their chairmanships when the Republicans took control of the chamber. Big Men including Edward Kennedy, Russell Long, John Stennis, and Ernest Hollings all remained in office, but with severely weakened positions within Congress.

Despite the precarious lifestyle inherent in politics, the

clans can survive such misfortunes; a well-organized clan persists even after the death of its chief. Almost as soon as it gains the first foothold within Congress, the clan begins to expand outside the congressional walls to build enclaves in other parts of the government. Tucked away in various parts of Washington, these subclans enhance the daily operational power of the parent clan on the Hill, but at the same time they offer a long-term insurance against sudden death and destruction to the parent clan in times of political plague. The careful cultivation of the extended part of the Congressional Clan is as important to its survival as the strategy for its development within Congress.

The extensions of these clans, their long-term continuity, and the importance which this has for contemporary American government form the theme of the next three chapters. Crosscutting the formal organization of government departments, political parties, and lobbies, these extended clans form the network base around which government operates. To appreciate fully this more extensive and complex form of organization, we move beyond the comparisons of Congress with the small-scale tribal societies of New Guinea and the Amazon basin. More appropriate analogies arise in comparison with the larger and technologically more diverse peoples of eastern Africa, such as the Watutsi, Hutu, and Twa. Examination of particular features in their complex political organization illuminates some of the problems we have in comprehending the full role played by extended Congressional Clans in modern government.

5

⊷≶≷⊷

Conquering
the Bureaucracy

WHEN PRESIDENT CARTER finished negotiating his treaty to relinquish the American control of the Panama Canal, Congress was beside itself with grief, threats, admonitions, soul searching, and chest thumping. Amidst a spray of oratory and a flurry of press releases, Congress twisted and turned in a public spectacle of its agonizing decision whether or not to ratify the treaty. Citizens listening to the live broadcast of the debates heard repeated panegyrics on American technological sophistication and financing for having built the Canal. The frenzied rhetoric gave the impression that this sacred monument was not only vital to our defense but was truly a one-of-a-kind creation. What few people outside Congress knew at the time, however, was that as Congress groaned through this pageant, it was also quietly proceeding with business as usual, constructing yet another canal even longer and more expensive than the Panama Canal.

Despite the *Sturm und Drang* surrounding the Panama decision, this new canal was even more impressive; it was virtually a new Mississippi River, located less than two hundred miles from the old one. While every congressman could extemporize for two hours on the beloved Panama Canal, few of them could even remember the name of the new one—the Tennessee-Tombigbee Waterway, being built at an estimated cost of $3 billion.

Normal pork-barrel politics would assume that the waterway was being built in the home state of the chairman of the Public Works Committee, or perhaps the home of the Majority Whip or Speaker of the House. It was, however, none of these. That old courtly gentleman, Senator John Stennis of Mississippi, Chief of the Military Clan, was building it and thereby creating lifetimes of jobs for workers and contractors in his home state. How was such a feat possible? How did one Congressional Clan begin work on a $3 billion canal that most Americans never heard of? And why was it being orchestrated by the Army Corps of Engineers when the defenses of the nation seemed so short of cash?

The answer to these questions lurks in the very bowels of government, at the peculiar nexus between Congress and the federal bureaucracy. Ultimately, it is in the anonymous corridors of the bureaucracy more than in the marble halls of Congress that the real power of Congressional Clans manifests itself. The connections between the bureaucracy and the national legislature embody the most important relations in government; yet, as pointed out by Lord Bryce in his nineteenth-century description of America, this connection "is the thing which the nation least notices and has the scantiest means of watching."

Before we examine the details of that connection, we may benefit by looking at an analogous phenomenon halfway around the world in the land of the Watutsi. Despite the discontinuity in appearance between the three-piece-suit politicians in Washington and the tall, feathered Watutsi warriors, a lesson can be found in examining their political life—a lesson that is all too easily missed when we succumb to a myopic examination of our own institutions.

The Watutsi burst into Western consciousness early in the twentieth century as a tribe of tall and graceful warriors. Like the Samurai of Japan, the Apache and Aztecs of America, even the knights of medieval Europe, the majestically proud Watutsi combine ferocity in war with a complex code of masculine beauty and grace. Their ostentatious pride becomes self-sacrificing in battle to the point of apparent recklessness. This cult of the *machismo,* wherever encountered in the world, always fascinates westerners, creating a mixture of admiration and fear. Because of the primitive masculinity and refined elegance of tribes such as the Watutsi, Zulu, and Masai, they are often the only African names readily recognized by many Americans and Europeans.

Western awareness of these groups came late, however, as they were some of the last peoples to be pacified or conquered by the imperial powers. For centuries the Watutsi lived among the numerous lakes of east-central Africa, in "the heart of the dark continent," beyond the pale of European explorer and Arab slaver. Not until the very end of the nineteenth century—after the explorations of John Speke, Richard Burton, David Livingston, and Henry Stanley—was this final enclave of Africa opened to the West. The Watutsi did not yield to the outside until the imposition of Belgian control in 1917.

Following colonization, most of the Watutsi inhabited the modern state of Rwanda, but they are a type of people common to Kenya, Tanzania, Burundi, and Uganda, as well. Collectively, they are often referred to by the anthropologists as "ethiopid" or "nilotic," to distinguish their tall, rangy appearance from that of other African groups. In addition to sharing a slender physique and finely chiseled features, they have a common sociocultural complex centering on cattle. Cattle supply the primary nutritional needs of these people through milk, blood, cheese, and some meat; but almost as importantly, they supply the focal index of the prestige and power system. The herds and concomitant grazing lands under a Watutsi's control indicate his success as a warrior.

Control over cattle, however, is more likely an indication of the Watutsi's success as a good politician than his actual physical prowess on the battlefield. For despite their bellicose bravado and reputation for ferocity, their culture also demands a high degree of political astuteness, oratorical skill, and hard work, if a warrior is to advance to a chiefly status. These mundane skills, more than their ability to handle a spear, underlie successful careers in the quest for cattle and glory.

These business and political talents dominate the maneuvering in the Watutsi hierarchy of Hill Chiefs, Cattle Chiefs, Land Chiefs, Army Chiefs, and ritual offices. Like the Prussian general Karl von Clausewitz, a Watutsi chief knows that warfare is only an extension of politics by another means, but, as such, is a means of last resort, to be employed if all other political means have failed. A good chief rarely needs it. Instead, he manipulates the system of offices and the pursuit of higher positions much as a member of Congress pursues subcommittee and full committee chairmanships. Each rise in the ranks opens a new area of exploitable resources in the quest for the highest office. A Watutsi Army Chief, for example, gets to appoint several retainers to lesser offices. All of these retainers in turn support the Army Chief in his bid for a higher chieftainship, in the hope that each of the retainers will then move up another notch and increase his own following. With each office, jurisdiction over larger cattle herds is expanded, making the chief more attractive as a patron to new retainers.

This hierarchy of offices and cattle rights surpasses in size and complexity the New Guinean yam-pig-wife complex. The matrix of offices approximates more closely that of the Congress, but the major parallel between Watutsi and Congress comes in their relation to another set of people—the Hutu.

Although over six times more numerous than the Watutsi, the Hutu are much less known to the outside. The Hutu belong to a shorter and more squat group of Bantu farmers, and like peasants and agriculturalists everywhere, their lives lack the color and ostentation of nomadic warriors. For centuries before the Watutsi migrated to their part of the world, the Hutu cultivated their crops of beans, sorghum, bananas, and cassava. After the arrival of the Watutsi, the Hutu followed essentially the same economics, but now they did so under the domination of the Watutsi. In addition to farming, the Hutu had to take care of the Watutsi cattle and build their homes. This freed the Watutsi for the full-time occupation of politics and the acquisition of cattle.

In the classic tie of client to patron, each Hutu is bound to a particular Watutsi warrior, who protects him from other Watutsi. The patron supplies the cattle which the Hutu manage; the more cattle a Watutsi acquires, the more Hutu he acquires.

Despite the inequality of the system and the constant tension between Hutu and Watutsi, it stayed remarkably stable for many generations prior to European arrival.

From this tension-filled symbiosis between Hutu and Watutsi comes a striking parallel between the American Congress and its own bureaucracy. As a group, the Watutsi struggle to affirm their dominion over the Hutu; but within the group, the individual Watutsi struggle against one another for power over groups of Hutu. In analogous fashion, the Congress as a group constantly struggles to maintain its control over the bureaucrats, while at the same time the individual members of Congress strive against each other for the exercise of that control. To understand the bonds and the tensions between Congress and the bureaucracy, the duality of the struggle must be clearly kept in mind. At all times, it is both a battle between the Congress and the bureaucracy as groups and a political battle within Congress itself.

THE ROOTS OF THE CONFLICT

The struggles between bureaucrats and congressmen stretch back in time about as far as the struggles between the Hutu and the Watutsi. The difficulties encountered by the Continental Congress of the 1780s in dealing with the nascent federal government during the American Revolution provoked the founding fathers to frequent complaints similar to those still voiced in the 1980s. Lacking an executive branch of government prior to the U.S. Constitution, the original Congresses had to oversee the full gamut of federal activities, from the conduct of the war against Britain to the collection of revenues. Facilitating this task were those old legislative perennials—the committees. The committees wrote the bills, hired people to implement the policies, and tried to oversee the work. So onerous was this task that the Constitutional Convention turned most of it over to the executive charged to act as overseer to the federal bureaucracy and intermediary between it and the Congress.

The creation of this presidency was a momentary whim that subsequent Congresses have regretted ever since. Never before or since has Congress willingly relinquished so much power all at once, and for two hundred years it has worked tirelessly to reassert that authority over the administration of the government. Less than two decades after the Constitution went into effect, just what power Congress had forfeited became evident in an encounter between John Randolph and one of the bureaucrats. As chairman of the House Ways and Means Committee in charge of government revenues, he sought some information on the expenditures for fiscal year 1807:

> I called some time since at the navy office to ask an explanation of certain items of the estimate for this year. The Secretary called upon his chief clerk, who knew very little more of the business than his master. I propounded a question to the head of the department; he turned to the clerk like a boy who cannot say his lesson, and with imploring countenance beseeches aid; the clerk with much assurance gabbled out some commonplace jargon, which I could not take for sterling; an explanation was required, and both were dumb. The pantomime was repeated at every item, until, disgusted and ashamed for the degraded situation of the principal, I took leave without pursuing the subject, seeing that my object could not be attained. There was not one single question relating to the department that the Secretary could answer.

Congressman Randolph's encounter with the bureaucracy was interpreted as an episode of ignorance, but the line between ignorance and obstinacy blurs when dealing with the bureaucracy. The same spirit that confronted Randolph in 1807 appeared in one of the first memos issued by Patricia Harris upon assuming the office of Secretary of the Department of Health, Education, and Welfare.

> Until further notice, there are to be no meetings, calls or staff contact with members of Congress or staff . . . regarding proposed or pending legislation, 1980 authorizations, or policy development without prior discussion with me through the assistant secretary for legislation.

Laboring in such bureaucratic trammels, Congressman Randolph would have been as encumbered trying to pry the details of the 1980 budget from Secretary Harris's office as he was in his

1807 effort. Since Randolph's era, the struggle between legislator and bureaucrat has assumed the demeanor of a ritual battle, each side loaded with a panoply of rhetorical weapons. The congressman asks about an expenditure; the bureaucrat responds in the concrete obliqueness of his argot. The congressman raises the possibility of fiscal castration; the bureaucrat ripostes with minatory comments on the hypothetical damage done to the congressman's constituents if all federal aid to his district were curtailed. Facing each other in this stand-off, both then agree that the problem needs further study prior to any hasty decision or action.

The formal powers of Congress and the bureaucracy seem evenly matched. In the much-touted power of the purse, Congress displays a formidable weapon for use against the bureaucracy, but using it wreaks greater havoc than it eliminates. Like throwing a sledgehammer to hit a fly, the implement is simply too big and clumsy to be practical. The bureaucrats, even while lacking the more awesome powers of Congress, have honed their smaller weapons to a delicate accuracy capable of making a precise strike against the political base of their congressional adversaries—hitting the politicians in their most vulnerable spots, their home districts.

During the long history of this stalemate, each generation of politicians vowed to rectify the intransigence of the bureaucrats and restore the supremacy of the legislative branch of government. Along the way, diverse strategies arose. Congress tried to run the government directly through its committees in the decades after the Civil War, but eventually fighting within the Congress aborted that campaign. Congress tried to force the President to act as its intermediary and agent in compelling the bureaucracy to follow legislative intent, but it proved too difficult to lure the President out of the bureaucratic camp. Congress then tried repeated versions of civil service reform to drive a wedge between the President and his power over the bureaucracy, but the move only served to make the bureaucrats more autonomous from both the President and the Congress.

After more than a century of such wrestling of opposing wills, Woodrow Wilson dolefully decided that "the means which Congress has of controlling the departments and exercising oversight at which it aims are limited and defective." Wilson, like so many contemporary political observers, was echoing a consistent complaint about democracy. Two thousand years ago, Demosthenes complained about the disjunction between the making of a democratic decision and its implementation when he said that in Athens "a motion voted and carried is still as far from execution as before." The difficulty in executing the will of the legislators seems as endemic to modern Washington as to ancient Athens.

This picture of bureaucratic sabotage even in the face of congressional rage has become commonplace enough to pass into our political mythology. Yet at the same time it contrasts sharply with another prominent image in contemporary folklore—that all-powerful congressman or senator who can have a fleet of military transports zooming emergency supplies and reconstruction loans to his district at the first warning of a tornado. Such heroic tales appear regularly in the newspapers with flesh-and-blood protagonists like former Congressman Daniel Flood, whose cape would flutter in the winds as he personally directed a corps of army helicopters to his Philadelphia district. Some congressmen bask in the renown that accrues to them for cutting through the red tape of the Health and Human Services Department to produce a missing social security check within an hour, building as many hospitals and military bases in their district as space allows, or saturating political supporters with government contracts and grants.

How do these two paradoxical figures—the omnipotent congressman and the immovable bureaucrat—coexist in the same government mythology? They persist because a few congressmen, using their clans outside as well as inside Congress, have found a way to circumvent the bureaucracy. The average member of Congress, especially in the first few terms in office, exercises about as much power over the bureaucracy as a welfare mother, except that the congressman is treated a bit more courteously. Unlike the welfare mother, however, the congressman can eventually acquire the means to scale the official walls of the governmental labyrinth. He may not be capable of defeating the bureaucrats in a head-on clash, but he can subvert them or undermine them by infiltrating them with his clan.

INFILTRATING THE BUREAUCRACY

The conquest of the bureaucracy starts, as do so many other congressional activities, in the seemingly innocuous attempt by the political clan to provide services for constituents. As ombudsmen for the district, the congressman's personal staff constantly deals with the various government offices around Washington—over the telephone, at committee hearings or investigations, and through the diverse meetings that fill a bureaucratic day. Over a quarter of all personal staffers on the Hill have contact with someone in the federal bureaucracy at least *once an hour,* according to a recent study by Harrison Fox, Jr. and Susan Hammond.

These contacts range over the whole gamut of government activities, but each congressional district will have specific agencies within the government requiring persistent attention. A congressman from the Miami gold coast or southern California—both Meccas for retirees and tourists—can expect frequent complaints with social security payments and pressures from the travel industry. Congressmen from the Midwest are flooded with requests from farmers needing help on agricultural programs. Suburban districts generate complaints about home mortgages and moving companies. These specialized complaints force frequent interactions between the congressional office and the particular branch of the government dealing with those issues. Constant contact promotes professional friendships between the congressional staffer and the bureaucrats, and in time a job opportunity opens up in the bureaucracy.

With the official support of his patron—the congressman—and with inside information from a bureaucratic ally, the staffer frequently is able to get the vacant job. After five or six years, a typical congressman should have a handful of his former staff spread throughout the bureaucracy at strategic mid-level positions. His former staffers rule on pension eligibility, help write the regulations for agriculture subsidy programs, set limits on small business loans, and execute those thousands of anonymous decisions that directly impinge on the daily life of constituents. Now the social security checks flow a little easier to the congressman's district, rules and regulations are interpreted more favorably for his constituents, and at least some parts of the federal bureaucracy respond more readily to his office and to his constituents' problems.

As ever-vigilant sentinels, these office alumni scatter throughout Washington and the home district looking after the concerns of the congressional patron. What they cannot do themselves, they can warn the congressman about ahead of time. They provide him with an inside voice in the halls of the government administration and a reconnaissance net of early warning.

Joining the bureaucracy is certainly much easier than fighting it. Around these networks of office alumni the well-known tradition of leaking information operates, despite memos from Secretary Harris or anyone else. Even before Harris's memo forbidding contacts with the Hill had been circulated to her own staff throughout the Health and Human Services Department, it had been passed to Republican Congressman Tom Tauke of Iowa. In denouncing the memo on the floor of Congress, Tauke informed many of Harris's own employees about the message before they received it through official bureaucratic channels. In so doing, he signalled to the new Secretary in a publicly humiliating way that she could do very little that would not be known immediately throughout the Congress.

Congressman Tauke did not need to be a Big Man in order to have a well-placed network of allies in the bureaucracy, since any congressman who stays in office more than two terms has such an organization in operation. Once in place, the network relieves him from having to devote excessive amounts of his time to constituent problems. His personal staff, operating in conjunction with the staff alumni, functions as the problem-solving unit for his district, requiring only occasional token acts by him. The congressman is thereby freed for the more important task of playing politics. In this way the successful congressional politician, much as the Watutsi warrior, can spend his time concentrating on politics, while underlings do the work caring for constituents or for cattle.

Although the network of office alumni *cum* mid-level bureaucrats sustains good constituent services and thereby helps meet that vital goal of a satisfied electorate, being a Big Man requires additional influence. As the Congressional Big Man captures the strategic part of the internal organization of Congress and brings it within the domain of his clan, he needs more and more of his former assistants to move out of Congress and into bureaucratic positions. His network of middle management clients lacks the authority to implement his policies on a scale larger than just catering to the basic needs of constituents. The congressman needs to place his own loyal assistants in the top managerial positions of the bureaucracy, for no matter how carefully the clan writes the laws and how ferociously they defend their turf within Congress, an unfriendly bureaucrat can subvert the whole effort. Clan control of all of the relevant spots in the committee hierarchy does not ensure control over the government agencies. As Woodrow Wilson noted, "The committees may command, but they cannot superintend the execution of their commands."

To change that *de jure* authority into real and immediate power, congressmen vie with each other in placing their own aides in charge of bureaucratic programs. It is not enough to write the regulations; the congressman needs his own clansmen to administer them, for as Aristotle wrote in *The Politics,* "It is never easy to frame general regulations covering every particular," and it is the particulars that most need to be covered. One loyal follower in command of a government office surpasses in worth volumes of duly prescribed congressional laws and concomitant regulations and intents.

Taking over a part of the government is the most delicate and difficult task the congressman ever faces. The bureaucracy, by nature, is a conservative organization which, left to its own devices, would never change. When faced with the threat of shifts, turns, or reforms from an outside source, even when the outside source is the Congress, the bureaucratic instinct is to resist. But this rubs against the grain of every politician who wants to leave his mark on public life through one or another pet program. Getting that pet program established by the Congress is only half the battle. To nourish, protect, and guide that living memorial to the would-be Solon, a legislator must send one of his close and most-trusted assistants to manage it. Only a member of the congressman's personal clan can ensure the continuation of the program.

These congressional clansmen stream down Capitol Hill in a perpetual torrent, filling the cavernous halls along Pennsylvania Avenue and spilling into Foggy Bottom. They become commissioners of the Interstate Commerce Commission, directors of the National Endowment for the Arts, assistant secretaries for the Department of Commerce, and officials of every part of the government from the Corporation for Public Broadcasting to the Federal Energy Regulatory Commission. Behind every oak door and around every simulated-wood conference table in the City of Washington is a former Hill staffer, brandishing the colors of his Hill clan and congressional sponsor.

The effectiveness of these former staffers is illustrated in the clash between the House of Representatives and the National Endowment for the Arts in 1980. A study by the House accused the Endowment of being rife with cronyism and of failing "to develop and promote a national policy for the arts" since its creation in 1965. Even though most members of Congress assumed such promotion to be the mission of the Endowment, the head of the Endowment, Livingston Biddle, Jr., argued that this was not so. And he displayed a good claim to knowing exactly what the original intention was: "I believe I can speak with no small authority on the matter since it was I who helped draft the authorizing legislations, who served as the agency's first deputy chairman, as congressional liaison for the Endowment, and as a staff member of the Senate authorizing subcommittee." Such words carry profound weight in the tradition-minded Congress, where it is a cardinal sin to tamper with *precedent,* abuse previous *congressional intent,* or violate the sacred *institutional memory.* Anyway, who would argue with the man who wrote the law?

A decade and a half after the Endowment was established, Livingston Biddle, Jr., was still protecting and guarding his patron's creation. No Congressional Chief could ask for more loyal service. He can rest assured that no matter what congressmen succeed him in office, his own clansmen will still be around to ward off philistine attacks on his works. Building a legislative record is not enough, unless the congressman also builds these personal safeguards to make sure his patrimony survives to spread its good works and, he hopes, its money as the congressman originally saw fit.

Once ensconced in bureaucratic jobs, these former congressional assistants possess virtual life tenure via the civil service laws. Unlike the staffers still working inside the Congress, who can be fired by a new Congressional Big Man, bureaucrats persist immune from this arbitrary authority. The upper echelons of the bureaucracy stand as protected in their positions as the national monuments on the Washington Mall. To circumvent this last set of congressionally installed public servants, a rising Big Man can seek to reorganize the agency. If he intends his newly created programs to succeed as anything more than window dressing, he must reorganize the existing structure. The reorganization leaves past programs largely intact with their old heads, but superimposes on them a new layer of bureaucrats, who will be drawn, of course, from his own clan.

In this process of so-called reform, program chiefs are added to oversee program administrators. Newly created coordinators are wedged between existing supervisors, only to be superseded by an executive director, who in time gives way to a new chief executive officer. Any of these offices may then be affixed to other titles such as deputy, assistant, associate, or acting, to form such combinations as acting deputy chief executive officer or assistant deputy program coordinator. This process results in the noun-heavy grammar of government bureaucracy, which is so difficult for outsiders to fathom. Each new idiom and each new hierarchical stratum is limited only by the rhetorical perimeters of the imagination necessary to think up successive and intervening layers of administration. Each newly devised layer anchors in as a permanent part of the structure, so that subsequent congressional leaders must create yet another layer to supplant the existing one. The federal bureaucracy comes to resemble an archeological site where the preserved remains of past Congresses are permanently sealed for eternity in time-specific strata. Understanding this organization is an act of excavating more than it is an act of studying the dynamics of a living organism. In one stratum are the programs created by the Congress of '54; a few layers up come the creations of '62; and so on, to the final living layer installed by the most recent and still reigning Congressional Chiefs.

Bureaucratic reorganization is one of the primary activities of these Congressional Big Men. As they send in a new cohort of staffers-turned-administrators, these new bureaucratic leaders immediately begin to reorganize the offices and programs of the agency, creating new lines of authority, flow charts, and personnel classifications. Before these can be instituted, however, a new leadership is being dumped on the agency with another plan of organization. In this way the bi-annual reorganization of Congress in each odd-number year is accompanied by a succession of reverberating changes in the bureaucracy. The bureaucracy, like the Congress, is perpetually reorganizing.

The perpetual flow of Hill staffers into executive positions in the bureaucracy preserves the various agencies of the government as virtual subclans of the major Congressional Clans. The bureaucracy is then divisible into a handful of congressional fiefs, each responsible to a different member of Congress and his attendant clan. Traditionally, this division of the government into marked spheres of congressional influence facilitated the easy distribution of pork projects. A senator or representative carves out his jurisdiction in Congress, moves his staffers into management positions within that jurisdiction, and then waits for the benefits to flow into the home district. The system operates as a more sophisticated version of the constituent case-solving network. In addition to finding checks and arranging farmer loans, the more developed network supplies municipal grants, major loans to businesses, and big contracts to local manufacturers. Under this system, if a congressman needs something that is not immediately available from his part of the bureaucracy, he can arrange a trade with another member. A veterans hospital may be traded for a post office, a small dam for a small military base, a federal highway for a new harbor.

These old traditions of pork-barrel legislation—military bases, highways, and water projects—have yielded in the last few decades a new breed of pig. With the great expansion of federal services in the 1960s and 1970s, constituent needs have expanded from a few major projects to dozens of smaller ones. Each part of the constituency wants its own tailor-made project, not just some general enterprise like a dam or harbor meant to improve the overall economy of the district. The small towns want sewer systems, the elderly want Meals-on-Wheels, and the ghettoes want CETA funds. Businessmen have become addicted to low-interest loans, and manufacturers want larger parts of the now diversified government purchases. Local governments depend on revenue-sharing programs, and the schools need grants from the Department of Education. The needs of even the smallest district read like a shopping list compiled from the pages of *The Federal Register*. And most of these projects boil down to money. The people do not want a new federal office building or military base; they want financial fortifications in the form of grants, contracts, or loans.

This need for numerous middle-sized infusions of cash forces traditional Congressional Clans to diversify. Being "Mr. Health" or "Mr. Military" on Capitol Hill is necessary, but no longer sufficient. Being "Mr. Health" may be great for bringing hospitals into the district, but it does little to secure revenue-sharing grants or finance day care centers. Neither does "Mr. Military" net many business loans or new sewers. In order to satisfy this new list of constituent services, Congressional Clans need to graft new projects onto their old clan jurisdictions.

A farm district's congressman may have a clan well connected to handle agricultural needs, but how does he get sewers for the small towns in his district? He must add a sewer-financing program to his jurisdiction within the Agriculture Department. At the same time, the urban representative with a HUD-oriented clan also has a few farmers in the fringe of his district; so, he adds a farming program to HUD. By 1980, sewers were being built or financed through the Department of Commerce, the Department of Agriculture, the Environmental Protection Agency, and the Department of Housing and Urban Affairs. Not counting sewers supported by our government in foreign nations via AID and agencies clustered around the Department of State and money to the World Bank, domestic sewer programs were being planned by agencies as far removed from that topic as the national historic preservation program.

By virtue of diversification, each of these distinct branches of the federal government offers nearly the full range of services and programs. Not only do all have sewer programs, most of them offer some form of rural economic development, as well as their individual housing policies. Education grants come from the Department of Agriculture as well as from the Justice Department, the Department of Health and Human Services, the National Science Foundation, the National Endowment for the Arts and the Humanities, the Department of Defense, and, of course, from the Department of Education. No matter which piece of the government a Congressional Big Man controls, he wants it to be capable of delivering every form of federal largesse his constituents may desire. This mimeograph mentality results in a proliferation of government programs and constant duplication, with each Congressional Clan compelled to be all things to all people. A frequent assumption is that such duplication is an inherent part of bureaucracy, rising automatically from the schemes of government workers. Congress, however, is the real culprit behind the phenomenal duplication. As the political scientist Morris P. Fiorina has noted, "Contrary to what is popularly believed, the bureaucrats are not the problem. Congressmen are. *The Congress is The Key to the Washington Establishment.* The Congress created the establishment, sustains it, and most likely will continue to sustain and even expand it."

Even though Congress as a whole and congressmen as a group may exercise very little day-to-day power over the operation of the bureaucracy, individual congressmen do exercise that power through their private bureaucracies, their clans. Each Big Man runs his own separate part of the government as a sovereign, independent chief, but because Big Men do not interfere with the clan operations of other Big Men, and because the junior Congress members lack the power to interfere, the Congress as a whole has little means at its disposal to oversee the government. Viewed in this light, it becomes easier to understand how a Big Man like John Stennis could build the Tennessee-Tombigbee Waterway, opposed by only minor harping and criticizing from the sidelines.

BUILDING A SECOND MISSISSIPPI RIVER

The Mississippi is without question one of the great rivers of the world. Its importance in the history and economic develop- ment of the United States convinced Congress it would be a great idea to build another one. Building a new waterway parallel to the old Mississippi, but about 150 miles farther east, was first proposed in 1874. Dropping down across the moun- tains of Tennessee and through the state of Mississippi, the Tennessee-Tombigbee Waterway would do for the economy and prosperity of eastern Tennessee and Mississippi what the original river had done for the western parts of those states.

Despite some of the strange schemes enacted by Congress in the latter part of the nineteenth century, plans for the new river lay dormant. As part of the postwar vision of a new America, the 1946 Congress approved its construction, but with some wisdom refused the funds to finance it. Not until 1971 did Con- gress authorize cold cash to pay for the new river, a project that was estimated to cost $323 million. In less than ten years this had increased ninefold, to $3 billion, slightly ahead of the infla- tion rate.

The digging of a "$3,000,000,000 ditch," as *The Washington Post* called it, would seem to be a major policy decision and fi- nancial expenditure of the federal government—a decision large enough to provoke major public interest and lengthy con- gressional consideration and examination. In fact, however, since the first shovelful of dirt was financed, the entire matter has been handled as a fairly routine in-House, or more precisely, in-clan, operation by the chairman of the Armed Services Com- mittee, Senator John H. Stennis, and his allies.

Stennis's political experience stretches back to 1928, when he was elected to the Mississippi House of Representatives. Follow- ing service in a variety of state offices over the next two decades, he entered the United States Senate in 1947. In the traditional manner he worked his way onto the two committees around which he would build his clan—Appropriations and Armed Services. After serving rather quietly, but skillfully, he achieved brief public attention in 1976, when President Nixon, who had been the first President to approve of the canal, chose Stennis to audit the Watergate tapes in lieu of a fully public disclosure of them. Assuming that the public would be satisfied with the opinion of a senior Democrat proved to be but one of the major underestimations of the Nixon White House during its declining months. Although the episode exposed Stennis to some public ridicule, it essentially left his reputation for honesty intact. He then went on to win an overwhelming reelection that year, undaunted by the skirmish with the Watergate affair.

With the patience and detailed attention of a master carpenter, Stennis blocked, cut, and hammered the Senate Armed Services Committee to fit his own blueprint. Two decades after coming to Congress, he assumed chairmanship of that committee as the Vietnam War reached its zenith of unpopularity. Stennis presided, somewhat reluctantly, over the military withdrawal from Southeast Asia, while trying to resist the anti-military mood of the newer members of Congress. As the military dropped from public attention and money from the war was freed for other purposes, Stennis jumped at the opportunity to use those funds for his home state. After prolonged years of waiting, Stennis at last had the opportunity to build that old dream of a new Mississippi River in 1971 when he diverted some of those funds to his project.

As chairman of both the Armed Services Committee and the Appropriations Subcommittee that funded the project, Stennis exercised complete control. The money was approved annually by one of his subclans, while the other routinely directed "congressional oversight" of the work in progress. With Stennis's authority over the budget of the Army Corps of Engineers, his committee's responsibility to approve the promotions of all its officers, and his legislative powers over them, Stennis helped them reassess their original opposition to the project. Even though in the pre-Stennis era the Corps estimated a benefit of only 28 cents for each dollar of cost, under Stennis's leadership the projected benefits rapidly escalated. A new study found additional sources of benefit, such as the annual shipment of 2.4 million tons of coal from the Tennessee town of Graysville; the report neglected some of the details of exactly how that coal would ever get to Graysville in the first place since the area did not have the mines capable of producing it. The new study also found it necessary to increase slightly the width of the canal originally authorized by Congress, from 170 feet to 300 feet.

While the country was preoccupied with the political drama of Watergate, little attention was paid to Stennis and his Military Clan. Even under the administration of President Carter, sworn enemy of wasteful water projects, the Tennessee-Tombigbee Waterway was never added to the list of hit projects. Anyone who criticized it faced the unpleasant prospect that a new study from Stennis's committee might find the military base or navy yard in his home state an unnecessary expense. In the absence of any real opposition, Stennis and the Corps were able to rearrange the geography of North America as God probably would have done if He had had the money.

Early in 1980, however, as the price of the waterway approached the $3 billion mark, difficulties surfaced. The country was in the mood for cutting expenditures (as it often seems to be in presidential election years), and there was growing dissatisfaction with military unpreparedness. The military foray to rescue the diplomatic hostages in Tehran went up in flames in the Iranian desert. The press overflowed with reports of military disorganization, malfunctioning computer systems, and illiterate enlisted men. The resultant pressure on the military to make better use of its money cast criticism on the Tennessee-Tombigbee Waterway as an unnecessary government expenditure.

In the same year the Government Accounting Office, which serves as fiscal watchdog over government spending, lambasted the project as economically unfeasible and wasteful. In response to that report, Senator Mike Gravel threatened to hold an official investigation of the matter. At the time, Gravel faced a tough campaign for the Democratic renomination to his seat and desperately needed campaign issues reflecting a money-conscious activism. His short-lived and ill-advised challenge to Stennis proved the wrong issue. After an extended private meeting between the two, Gravel announced rather bluntly: "I decided a hearing was not necessary." Senator Stennis immediately denied reports that he had threatened to use his position on the Appropriations Committee to suspend funding of important federal projects in Alaska. Gravel not only lost the bout with Stennis but his party's nomination and thereby his seat, as well.

A similar scenario unfolded in the House involving Stennis's ally, Representative Jamie L. Whitten, who also happened to be from Mississippi and chairman of the House Appropriations Committee. The complainant against the Tennessee-Tombigbee was Joel Pritchard, the Republican congressman from Seattle, Washington. As luck would have it, however, Mount St. Helens exploded in Pritchard's home state and the citizens of Washington suddenly fell in desperate need of federal assistance. Whitten, none too obliquely, raised the possibility of extended study of the eruption before appropriating money for its relief. As chairman of the Appropriations Committee, he could withhold funds indefinitely from Pritchard's constituents smothering under the volcanic ash. Like Gravel, Pritchard lost not only his contest against the Tennessee-Tombigbee Waterway but his seat in Congress as well. In the end Whitten held up his half of the project as capably as Stennis had done, and work on the canal was authorized to continue on through 1982.

Even after a century of planning and a decade of digging, the ultimate fate of the Tennessee-Tombigbee ditch is uncertain. With growing opposition to fiscal extravagance and with Republican control of the Senate, the project may be scrapped. Like George Washington's only half-completed dream of a canal from the City of Washington to the Ohio River, the Tennessee-Tombigbee Waterway may remain an unfulfilled folly. Whether it reaches completion or not, it will go down in history as just one more footnote confirming the bureaucratic bungling, misjudgment, and waste generated by Washington, D.C. The Tennessee-Tombigbee boondoggle, however, was not conceived, encouraged, or supported by the bureaucracy; its paternity originated on Capitol Hill in the politics of the Congressional Clan system.

The magnitude of such an undertaking as the Tennessee-Tombigbee project indicates just how extensive and independent Congressional Clans can become and how they can make whole sections of the federal government into virtual subclans. In this process, the Big Men who achieve power over the mili-

tary have not only the ability to move their own staffers into ci-
vilian positions in the Pentagon, but they have an added dimension of control in that they must approve each officer's
promotion within the military ranks. For the most part this
grant of commissions and approval of promotions is routine, but
its occasional exercise and its persistent potential are enough to
give the congressional staff a stranglehold authority over every
career officer in the armed services. This extreme authority over
a part of the government exists only in the Military Clan; but,
to a lesser degree, a similar form of power is exercised by all the
clans over their respective pieces of the government. Only the
magnitude of the Tennessee-Tombigbee project separates it
from other examples of bureaucratic agencies forced into works
that are essentially beyond their mandate or capabilities.

What arises from these combinations and permutations of
clans and subclans is a series of miniature governments within
the overall federal framework. The congressional staff becomes
the vortex and training ground from which a much larger entity, encompassing hundreds of high-level bureaucrats, spreads
through American government. A Congressional Chief such as
John Stennis, Tip O'Neill, Mark Hatfield, or Russell Long presides over an organization within Congress—and also over its
affiliated agencies in the Washington bureaucracy. The connecting bonds are not so much derived from the formal powers,
procedures, and precedents of Congress as they are from the
clan network itself, held together by the present congressional
staffers and the former staffers who have left the Hill to administer the bureaucracy. In this way the Congressional Clans are
more than just the primary power units of Congress; they form
the main components of contemporary American government.

Despite this development, and despite the repeated debacles
of recent presidential administrations stretching back through
Carter, Ford, and Nixon, there persists the notion that the President acts as the primary power over the federal government.
Congress, with its 535 different members, only vaguely shares
the blame for bureaucratic growth, a culpability that is often
deflected by repeated congressional denunciations of the bureaucracy and of big government.

Since the first years of Franklin Roosevelt's administration, most new federal programs have been sponsored by the White House. Roosevelt initiated a long series of agencies, first to combat the Depression, and then to assist in the war against Germany and Japan. Two decades later, Lyndon Johnson proposed another set of new government agencies under his War on Poverty. Even Nixon, the avowed enemy of big government, fathered that complex of programs and grants known as revenue sharing, and Jimmy Carter pushed for creation of the Department of Energy and the Department of Education. Since 1932 and Roosevelt's emergency policies for dealing with the Depression, the expansion of the federal government is measured in the various rhythms of each presidential administration. With the possible exception of Roosevelt, however, it is not at all clear how much these Presidents led the way for these programs and how much they were responding to Congress and its own internal dynamics.

The 1980 creation of the Department of Education, for example, did not spring fully grown from the head of Jimmy Carter. For nearly two decades Senator Abraham Ribicoff championed that cause, and in the course of his persistent efforts he picked up considerable support within Congress and from outside groups, including the National Education Association. Although the idea was endorsed by Carter as a 1976 campaign pledge to the politically active teachers' union, the plan was mapped out and already well under way before Carter ever left Georgia. The fruition of that plan had more to do with Ribicoff's coming of age within the Senate and leading a large clan of his own than it did with Carter's halfhearted efforts on its behalf.

Similar circumstances surrounded many of Lyndon Johnson's creations. Critics of governmental growth, particularly conservative commentators, repeatedly blame him for the bureaucratic hypertrophy of the 1960s. Although the federal expansion of that era surpassed even that of the Roosevelt administration, it is often forgotten that of all the Presidents in American history, none equalled this son of the Senate in legislative skills. He wrote the book on "knowing what Congressmen want and giving it to them." Johnson's fabled virtuosity of "playing Congress like an organ" expressed itself in his instinct for filling these wants. He used the same acumen to cultivate his own national constituency among the American people, and in the process made these diverse programs into a living, legislative memorial to himself.

Johnson makes a colorful and flamboyant target for both critics and proponents of the expanded governmental role in the 1960s. That decade, however, was also the time when congressional staffs really came into their own as the extended clans which now occupy such a prominent position in Washington politics. The benchmark for congressional staff expansion was the 1946 Legislative Reorganization Act, and in the decade following its enactment, the halls of Congress became swollen with aides and assistants. By 1960, these whiz kids were eager to remake the government according to the new economic, social, and philosophical principles of modern, scientific policies. They yearned to move off the Hill to administer their own bailiwicks, fearful that the new programs they labored to enact might be sabotaged by the older, more entrenched bureaucrats left from the Eisenhower years. Everything from the Peace Corps and Vista to the Arts Endowment needed their personal leadership.

And these new programs proliferated and were inevitably capped by new layers of directors, executives, and coordinators, some of the government departments split into whole new departments. With the addition of the departments of Housing and Urban Development, Transportation, Energy, and finally Education, the total number of cabinet secretaries reached thirteen by 1980. The logical next step in the process was the creation of super-departments, a proposal frequently bandied about Washington over the last decade and considered by both Presidents Carter and Reagan. The Presidents, such as Lyndon Johnson, may have been leading the way in these developments; but the major impetus for them seems to lie in the horde of eager congressional aides bursting with enthusiasm to ride herd on the programs they have authored. It was a watershed time in American politics when Johnson, the great congressional insider, ascended to the presidency just as Congress's own baby boom of staffers prepared to swoop down the Hill and storm the bureaucratic redoubts. The combination of events left an enduring mark on American government, and the new creations defied Richard Nixon's political machinations to dismantle them and impound their funds just as furiously as Jimmy Carter's attempts to reorganize them. Regardless of whether the President favored or opposed the growth, it continued apace under the Congressional Big Men with the same regularity that new generations of congressional workers were inducted into the government and provided with their own domains to administer.

Presidents have been as incapable of stopping the steady growth fostered by Congress as have private citizens. Even when they recognized and denounced the danger, their efforts to end its hydra growth have exacerbated the problems. The result is a gigantic chimera of unrivaled historical proportions, which dwarfs even the infamous bureaucracy of ancient Byzantium.

In its final decades, the Byzantine Empire became so bloated in bureaucracy as to lose the ability to protect itself from either internal or external threats. Michael Psellus, one of the latter presidents of the Byzantine (Roman) Senate, was painfully aware of the problem, but as helpless to stop it as modern American Presidents seem to be. Writing in the year 1057, Psellus penned the following description of the government that had been under his administration:

> We can liken it to a monstrous body, a body with a multitude of heads, an ugly bull-neck, hands so many that they were beyond counting, and just as many feet; its entrails were festering and diseased, in some parts swollen, in others wasting away, here afflicted with dropsy, there diminishing with consumption.

While the tone and metaphors may be different, the sentiment of Psellus a thousand years ago closely resembles that of President Reagan's speeches and press releases in the twentieth century. It seems a credit to American ingenuity that what it took the ancient Byzantine empire ten centuries to accomplish, the United States has effected in two hundred years.

Whereas the congressionally created bureaucracy resembles that of Byzantium in many of its manifestations, the internal dynamic of political patron-client relations more closely parallels that between the Watutsi and the Hutu. Just as the individual Hutu knew that his and his family's personal prosperity depended on that of his patron Watutsi, modern bureaucrats know that their individual careers hinge on the ability and support of their congressional patrons. Watutsi warriors acquire chieftainships and distribute cattle to the management of their client Hutu, whereas Congressional Big Men acquire office in Congress and use it to distribute larger pieces of the bureaucracy to the management of their former assistants and clients. The ritualized cry of the Hutu, "Give me milk; make me rich; be my father," reasserts their dependence on the Watutsi. It differs only slightly from the ritualized appropriations hearings in which bureaucrats ask their clan father for more funding, more power, and more protection.

6

❦§❧

Domesticating
the Lobbies

THE TRUK ISLANDS in the South Pacific claim one of the world's largest collections of ghosts. Unlike the wispy, translucent creatures of Europe and America, the ghosts of Truk retain a real, physical body easily encountered by any unwary islander out at night. Since these ghosts fear the light, they do not appear in the daytime, and at night the best precaution against them is to carry a torch or lantern with which to frighten them away. Bathed in this protective shield of light, the wanderer can easily hear the ghosts and occasionally feel one as it flutters by, trying to escape the inimical rays.

The Trukese and their ghosts live on several islands inside the Truk atoll, which is a large coral reef containing the world's largest lagoon. It is to this tropical lagoon that the American anthropologist Marc Swartz went to study the society of Truk with its strange ghosts. Swartz found the people of Truk to be as intelligent, shrewd, and endowed with common sense and empirical reasoning as any other people in the world; nevertheless, they could not be dissuaded from their belief in the existence of ghosts. The empirical evidence abounded in the strange noises circulating at night, in the ominous shadows and figures moving through the jungle, and in inexplicable little events for which no animate culprit could be found. For the Trukese, ghosts were facts of life, not so much supernatural as merely a handy explanation for everything that was preternatural.

Of course, the Trukese were not able to show Swartz a "living" example of a ghost, for whenever they went out at night searching for one, it would disappear as soon as he turned the flashlight on it. To the Trukese this confirmed, in a scientific manner, that indeed ghosts do fear the light. For them, both the evidence (such as noises in the night) and the lack of evidence (such as seeing nothing in the light) stood as sound proof for their belief in the existence of ghosts. As Swartz explained it, the beliefs about ghosts form part of the basic understandings the Trukese hold about the world, which as such "are closed to experience." Accordingly, "anything that happens confirms them, and nothing can occur to prove them wrong."

It is easy to smile at this seemingly naive type of uneducated reasoning, but before we laugh, we should take a look at some of our American commonsense perceptions of the world. When considering the Congress, for example, almost all observers agree that lobbies are the real evil influence in politics. They corrupt, suborn, distort, and abuse our democratic liberties. Frequently, we have evidence of this in the numerous scandals unfolding from Capitol Hill. Often, however, we have no evidence. But the lack of evidence just proves how successful lobbyists are at avoiding the light of public scrutiny. Thus the evidence for the pernicious nature of lobbyists abounds: we hear them go bump in the political night, catch only glimpses of them fleeing from scandal, and presume that their invisibility is proof of cleverness. These ideas about lobbyists constitute a closed set of understandings equally impervious to evidence or lack of evidence.

Neither we nor the Trukese are alone in using such closed systems of thought. Every culture creates some category of being into which they dump the unexplained. The sudden death of a healthy pig, failure to bag a bird on the hunt, or a poor harvest may be explained as the work of gremlins, spirits, ghosts, or just bad karma. In lieu of these animistic explanations, the residual concept can be moved out of the supernatural realm and into some human category. A lost war or an economic depression may be explained as the work of capitalists, communists, Zionists, racists, Baptists, or any other disfavored minority. The difference between the two explanatory systems is that when people rather than spirits are blamed, the accused can also be made into actual scapegoats. After all, there really are people who are communists or capitalists or Baptists, and they can actually be hauled into court, lynched, persecuted, or just pilloried as objects of obloquy. Unlike the Trukese, who can never see the objects of their fears, Americans can always drag forth some real, living person to represent the evil of society and to bear punishment for it.

Within our democratic system of government, the lobbyists play this role of scapegoat for everything that cannot be explained otherwise. At times their activities are pernicious, at times innocuous. Regardless, every evil aspect of the political system falls upon them. From the Teapot Dome scandal to Bobby Baker, from the Credit Mobilier case to Koreagate, lobbyists are at the root of the malady. No stone is unturned by any muckraker without revealing a cabal of rich lobbyists practicing their "unethical" trade.

Despite this reputation, lobbyists flourish in the 1980s even more than before. The ranks of Washington lobbies have pushed past 15,000, and they have been augmented by the recently developed political action committees, of which there are approximately 2,000. By 1979, for the first time more people in Washington worked in service-oriented jobs, including lobbyists, public relations experts, and specialized lawyers, than worked for the federal government itself. Their total budgets run to the billions of dollars and their political campaign contributions to the tens of millions. The facts, and especially the figures, of lobbying always impress; the stories and anecdotes titillate with scandal. Lobbying is to Washington what sex is to Hollywood. The sensation surrounding lobbying makes it difficult to see clearly and impractical to analyze objectively. In dealing with such an institution, any observer risks being blinded and confused by too much sensational information pouring out at once, too many figures, and too many preconceived notions.

To avoid these pitfalls and to understand the real importance of lobbying in the congressional scheme, we need, at least temporarily, to set aside moral judgments, preconceived ideas, and some of the more flamboyant parts of the picture. Instead, we need to take a cold look at these lobbying practices, what they are and where they came from, separating solid evidence from conjecture and myth from behavior. Trying to avoid the rhetoric of both apologists and critics, perhaps we can also avoid Swartz's paradox of closed beliefs.

THE BASTARD CHILD OF CONGRESS

One of the common clichés of American politics explains that "If lobbies didn't exist, Congress would have to invent them." Like so many pearls of Potomac wisdom, it overlooks one crucial fact: Congress did invent lobbies. In the broader sense, lobbying began when the first caveman asked a favor of his local chief. But as an institution, lobbying originated in the United States Congress. The word itself first popped up in the records of the 10th Congress in 1808, and derived from the habitat of special-interest representatives waiting in the ornate lobby off the chamber floor. There they would collar entering politicians just before a vote. By an analogous procedure, the word in England came to mean the political journalists trying to collar politicians as they left the floor after a vote.

In the earliest days of the Republic, before the present Capitol was built with its ornate lobbies, the lobbyists were often called by the looser term of "factions," which also had to do double duty at that time for the concept of political parties. The definition proposed by James Madison, writing in the *New York Packet* of Friday, November 23, 1787, is still one of the best on record. He described lobbyists as "a number of citizens whether amounting to a majority or a minority of the people, who are united and actuated by some common impulse or passion, or of interest, adverse to the rights of other citizens, or to the permanent and aggregate interests of the community." Madison went on to give examples of such factions as debtors, creditors, landed interests, and merchants—in brief, the full gamut of the citizenry. Despite the potential for abuse, Madison knew that it was impossible to control the creation of such interests, for "Liberty is to faction what air is to fire," and to subdue these factions would be to stifle the free air of liberty. Instead of controlling the causes of such factionalism, only its results can be controlled. Not until several decades after Madison's writings did parties and lobbyists bifurcate into separate entities. Part of this early confusion of parties and lobbies stemmed from the fact that often it was the members of Congress themselves who were the lobbyists. Only much later in the nineteenth century did lobbyists emerge as separate individuals, performing a distinct function within the political process.

This combination of politician as representative of his district and lobbyist for special causes is evidenced in an early letter of Daniel Webster's. While serving as the senator from Massachusetts, Webster also acted as representative of the United States Bank. In 1833, when the Bank was threatened with destruction by Andrew Jackson and his forces, Webster wrote to the Bank president, Nicholas Biddle: "If it be wished that my relation to the Bank would be continued, it may be well to send me my usual retainers." The retainer came through, and Webster continued to lead the fight to preserve the Bank. The Bank was not Webster's only customer. For a while he received an annual fee of $100,000 from a consortium of Boston merchants to ensure his opposition to the trade tariffs of President Polk. Webster lobbied for so many private interests that in a single day he brought thirty different people onto the Senate floor while he presented their legislative needs to the Congress. So successful was he in combining lobbying with legislation that John Quincy Adams eventually remarked that all of Webster's political systems "are interwoven with the exploration of a gold-mine for himself."

The combination of elected public representative and paid private advocate in the same politician has declined, but has not been eliminated in the intervening century and a half. Even the latterday champion of political probity, Senator Sam Ervin, represented clients before the Supreme Court while simultaneously serving as a senator and a member of the Judiciary Committee.

By and large, however, the lobbyists and the legislator have split into separate roles; but institutionally these roles are still

two sides of the same coin. Lobbying never has been and probably never will be an outside force impinging on Congress. It is a
political factor born, nourished, and reared in the congressional
bosom.

To appreciate just how integral to the system lobbying is, we
need to look at the various kinds of relationships existing between legislators and lobbyists. The lobbyist is not the same to
an entering freshman as he is to an experienced Big Man. To
understand this crucial difference, we must examine the lobbyist-legislator tie first as it pertains to the entering congressman and then as the relationship changes through the
years.

THE HELPING HAND

There is probably no one in the City of Washington so out of
his element as the new congressman. In a city filled with a hundred ambassadors, the President and his cabinet, the nine Justices of the Supreme Court, a battalion of generals and admirals, anchormen of the nightly news, directors of the World
Bank and the Organization of American States, as well as the
powerful Chiefs of Congress, the freshman from Peoria cuts a
lonely figure. It may be difficult for constituents to appreciate,
but their local congressman is usually a nobody in the Capitol.
Even Alexis de Tocqueville was struck by the fact that in the
House of Representatives, the "members are almost all obscure
individuals whose names bring no associations to mind."

Washington is not impressed by learning that the new congressman was captain of the football team at Lincoln High the
year they won the state championship, that he was selected Jaycee Young Man of the Year, or that his wife was Miss Peach
Festival back in 1977. Aside from the Doorkeeper and the elevator boy assigned to his corridor, no one on the Hill seems able
to remember his name, much less his past glories. Local reputations never travel well, at least not to Washington.

His isolation is matched only by his political distrust of anyone who offers a helping hand. The orientation classes provided
through Harvard University for entering congressmen seem
suspiciously academic and do not teach him where the bath-

rooms are or even how to answer a constituent's appeal for information on when to plant petunias. The Big Men of the Congress appear to him only in reception lines and on the podium addressing the newcomers. Insecurities maximize his paranoia. Does the senior senator want to make him a protégé? Does the political science professor just want a job? Do the party leaders only want his votes? Does the consultant want a contract or the constituent a favor?

The only person about whom there are no doubts or questions is, paradoxically, the lobbyist. His position is clear, aboveboard, and understandable. He wants the freshman's support on a few specific issues and presents his case in a straightforward manner with no oblique political rhetoric. Even if they are political foes, the congressman and the lobbyist know precisely where each other stands. John Kennedy described this relationship in an article he wrote for the *New York Times Magazine* in 1956: "Concededly, each is biased; but such a procedure is not unlike the advocacy of lawyers in court which has proven so successful in resolving judicial controversies. . . ."

To their allies in this advocacy process, lobbyists provide the one service available nowhere else in the system: political knowledge. Mountains of substantive materials (reports, background briefs, legislative opinions) are available from many sources, including the committees, the government agencies, and the legislative research service. But the kinds of questions most important to a newcomer are usually best answered by lobbyists. What is the chairman really like? Who allies with which coalition on the Appropriations Committee? Which one of the many claimants really has final say on energy matters? Who hates whom, and why? What role do the blacks play in this issue? Does being a Catholic matter to that congressman? Thousands of such questions are important during a freshman's initiation into Congress. Some of them can be answered by a colleague down the hall, by an experienced staff aide from the committee, or by a senior member of the state delegation; but who knows what biases lurk behind their answers? One knows immediately where a lobbyist stands and exactly what his biases are. In this inverted sense, the lobbyist's answers are more reliable and usable than those from any other source.

Lobbyists function as the primary agents of socialization in the congressional system. As one Washington attorney-lobbyist said, they teach the newcomer "how to be an effective member of the House, and how to advance." Once established in this paternal role, lobbyists play a permanent part in the congressman's career as information broker. They explain the details of bills, supply computer analyses of how an issue affects different parts of the constituency, and which groups oppose or support the issue with how much enthusiasm. As John Kennedy described them, "Lobbyists are in many cases expert technicians and capable of explaining complex and difficult subjects in a clear, understandable fashion." Among the specific tasks lobbyists perform, Kennedy listed preparing briefs and legislative analyses, as well as writing legislation. They keep detailed score cards on past voting records of other members, as well as important political information on the other members' supporters. And these facts and figures are laced with appropriate bits of inside gossip, which may be of even greater importance than the technical information.

To the new member forced to devote most of his staff workers to constituent problems, lobbyists supply scarce legislative assistance. Long before the new member commands his own clan and information sources, lobbyists fill the void. Former New York Congressman Allard Lowenstein, one of the most liberal and anti-lobby representatives to serve in Congress, explained the influence of lobbyists as follows:

> How much can anyone do with limited staff, and all the mail and what not to cope with? If you aren't independently wealthy, you can't have a staff that is capable of putting things together much beyond what you can come up with from the sources available to everyone—the executive departments, the lobbies, the staffs of congressional committees, the Library of Congress. That's one reason why the lobbies are so influential.

No matter what position a member takes on any issue, some lobby will rally to his aid. Whether he votes anti-abortion, pro-oil, anti-tobacco, or pro-consumer, every issue has a lobby. With so many lobbies, the congressman can pick and choose his assis-

tance from a smorgasbord of ideas. As former Senator Frank
Moss of Utah said: "I would use the lobbyists' information and
research on my own. Or I'd see what a counter lobbyist had to
say." When the choice is between doing one's own research or
turning to lobbyists, time alone compels the member to take the
proffered aid. Even if the legislator wants to introduce an anti-
lobby bill, an anti-lobby lobby stands ready to assist, just as the
pro-lobby stands ready to take the opposite position.

The use of lobbyists even if they are members of the opposition appears in an episode surrounding Edward Kennedy's
commencement address at Howard University in the spring of
1979. At the time, Kennedy was percolating plans to challenge
President Carter for the Democratic presidential nomination in
1980. One of the prominent debates of that primary campaign
revolved around energy, in particular windfall profits for oil
companies and their oil depletion allowances. Kennedy insisted
that Carter's proposed windfall profits tax was much too low
and that it was only a token tax imposed for the upcoming elections. Others, most notably the oil industry and Senator Russell
Long, charged that the tax was inexcusably high, and worked to
lower it.

Kennedy chose that issue as his first major volley against the
Carter camp, and in gathering ammunition for attack, he sum-
moned Mobil Oil lobbyist Bob Bates for help. According to
Bates, he met with Kennedy and his aides several times "to help
prepare the Senator's commencement address," despite the
anti-oil position which Kennedy propounded.

Six months later when the Kennedy presidential campaign
launched into full battle with Carter, Herb Schmertz, the controversial Mobil Vice President for Public Affairs, went on leave
from Mobil Oil to work full time on Kennedy's campaign. On
the same staff was James Flug, another former senatorial aide to
Kennedy and former director of Energy Action, an anti-oil
group that had particularly castigated Mobil Oil. Explaining
that "it is a signal that the Senator is able to bring under his
umbrella a whole variety of people who have confidence in his
leadership," Flug put aside his bitter rivalry with Schmertz in
order to work together.

Despite all of that assistance from the oil companies, Kennedy had been, and remained through his campaign, an anti-oil politician, holding stances that substantially threatened the goals of the oil companies and their profits. The very week that Schmertz joined the Kennedy campaign, the Judiciary Committee, which Kennedy chaired, considered a bill to prevent companies such as Mobil from acquiring smaller companies, an issue which the oil companies all fought. Because Kennedy, like every other politician, works with lobbyists on all sides and has former aides in both camps, the losers in any issue always blame some set of lobbyists. The oil interests blame Kennedy's association with Flug and other anti-oil interests; but had Kennedy at any point softened his opposition to the oil companies, fingers could have quickly pointed to people like Schmertz, Bates, and other oil lobbyists as the reasons. In these relationships, it is difficult to decide where congressional staff ends and the lobby-as-staff begins. By the time a bill reaches conclusion, even the participants hardly know which parts were written by whom. This obfuscation of authorship is readily exploited by everyone in claiming credit or assigning blame.

This role of lobby as surrogate staff is the only one that the lower ranks of Congress ever know. The anonymous members of the freshman and sophomore classes rely on lobbies for assistance and in turn feel the pressure from lobbies for support. The process is weighted unevenly, with young congressmen always on the receiving end of either assistance or pressure. For the Big Men of Congress like Senator Kennedy, however, this inequality of relationship changes through time, as they slowly acquire power over the lobbyists. If the congressman survives those initial years to enter the ranks of the elders and to lead his own clan, he will develop an entirely different form of alliance with the lobbyists.

To appreciate this new legislator-lobbyist connection, we need to take a closer look at that quintessential political activity of logrolling or exchanging favors. All too often this practice is seen by political observers as the real core of politics, and particularly of lobbying. If a journalist can detail who exchanged what favor for which vote, he has uncovered the ultimate roots of the explanation why an issue passed or failed. Logrolling, however, is the last thing that any legislator wants to do, for to ask another politician for a favor is to incur a debt. Congressional Big Men strive to stay out of debt as much as possible; only when absolutely necessary will one of them ask another for a favor. The British anthropologist F. G. Bailey, who analyzed political behavior in Europe and Asia, found that throughout the world such asking for favors reduces the status and effectiveness of the asker. Seeking a service from another politician is asking in essence for a gift, a word that in German means poison—an irony well appreciated by any young politician who has to ask a senior for a political favor. In *The Gift*, Marcel Mauss, the French anthropologist, notes that by receiving a gift or favor from another, one always incurs a debt that must be repaid eventually—and not necessarily at a time convenient to the debtor. A good politician, in any society, always endeavors to maximize the debts owed to him but to minimize his debts to others.

The major means by which Congressional Big Men avoid asking other legislators for favors is to get the lobbyists to do it for them. The lobbyist tries to convince the younger legislator to vote the way of the Big Man on grounds that it is in the younger politician's interest to do so. If this fails, then the lobbyist can ask the younger politician for the favor and, thereby, the lobbyist inherits the political debt. Here lobbyists function as the legmen doing the real political work, while the Big Men rise above the rough and tumble of lowly politics. Because the Big Men usually have a virtual life-or-death power over the interests represented by at least some lobbyists, they can use them as political surrogates while attending to the business of being statesmen. This makes for peculiar twists in lobbying when lobbyists have to spend a great deal of time working on issues that are of little concern to their employer, but are of interest to the Congressional Big Man who has power over their employers' interests. Such a twist arose in an encounter between labor lobbyist Marvin Caplan and the office of Democratic Representative William Hughes of New Jersey. As a member of the House Judiciary Committee, Hughes was to vote on a Fair Housing Bill for which Caplan was lobbying. Together with an attorney from the National Committee Against Discrimination and fellow lobbyist Evelyn Dubrow of the International Ladies Garment Workers Union, Caplan met with Hughes's staff:

> We tell our story to two aides—and they in turn lobby us. Will labor support Hughes in an attempt to get social security for Holocaust victims who, for self-preservation, told the Nazis, and, later, U.S. Immigration officials that they were younger than they really are? We think labor might.

Even though they were employed by two important labor unions to lobby for labor issues, Caplan and Dubrow fought for a housing issue which at most could be only marginal to their primary mission. Yet in the process they were led to another task even further from that mission: they were asked to help secure aid for Holocaust victims, an issue of importance to Hughes's constituents. In this way lobbyists become the general factotums for all kinds of political work, not just one single interest.

As a relative newcomer to Congress at the time of this episode, Representative Hughes was still in the position of asking for or trading favors with lobbyists. Not yet a Big Man who could automatically command a battery of lobbyists to work his will, he had to haggle with them. Big Men like Russell Long do not need to ask lobbyists to go out of their way to support pet issues; lobbyists of all stripes automatically fall in line behind him even when his issue has little to concern them. Such an instance seems to have been behind a problem experienced by Senator Ernest Hollings in dealing with the textile lobby.

Representing South Carolina, a major textile producer and cotton grower, Senator Hollings frequently voted in agreement with the textile lobby. Back in 1975, however, Senator Hollings announced that the textile lobbies were pressuring him to stop his vociferous public denunciation of oil depletion allowances. While it was true that the textile industries, like most manufacturers, consumed petroleum products, the matter of depletion allowances was not one that directly concerned them. But the champion of these oil allowances was Russell Long, who, as chairman of the Finance Committee, exercised jurisdiction over imports, an issue that was of great concern to the textile industries in their fight to preserve oil depletion allowances. They were doing his politicking for him.

In this respect, lobbyists are by no means just outsiders trying to influence the system of legislative processes. Rather, they are the internal conduits by which the process operates—the communications links among members of Congress. Lobbyists act as the foot soldiers fighting the political battles of the Congressional Big Men; without them, the practice of politics would grind to a halt.

TAKING OVER THE LOBBIES

In much the same way that Congressional Big Men take over parts of the bureaucracy by moving their own followers into prominent positions in government, they also extend their control over lobbies by placing their staffers in prominent lobbying jobs. Each move has similar benefits for both the legislator and the lobby; the clan chief who has his staff alumni scattered throughout the lobbies controls a network that can pull in rich and diverse resources.

When Senator Kennedy turned for assistance to Mobil Oil lobbyist Bob Bates in writing the Howard commencement address, he was not turning to just any lobbyist. Bates was Kennedy's own former legislative assistant of eight years. Even though Bates was now employed by Mobil Oil, he had a much older and more substantive tie to Senator Kennedy, who had helped him launch his own political career. How much better it is for a senator if he can retain the speech-writing or legislative skills of a former aide while some corporation underwrites the salary and ancillary costs. Having such former assistants on their staffs is important to both the lobbies and their congressional patrons.

The lobby benefits by having access to the inner sanctum of the clan. These ties provide an early warning of impending changes in policy and the assurance that the lobbyist's position will be conveyed to the clan leader, even though the leader may reject it. By being more the clients of Big Men than the masters over them, the lobbyists can expect protection from their patrons, despite the fact that the Big Men occasionally make decisions and policies which the clients do not like. Being subject to the whims of a clan chief may have some disagreeable aspects for the lobbyists, but it is generally better than having no patron at all and is thus similar to the situation of the unaligned Hutu who is subject to the whims of all the chiefs.

From this results a seamless web connecting Congressional Big Men and the lobbies. Nowhere is this closeness better illustrated than in the career of Daniel Minchew, the Georgia-born and Oxford-educated protégé of Senator Herman Talmadge. Beginning as an elevator boy in the Senate, Minchew worked his way through the Capitol Hill police to become Talmadge's administrative assistant in 1971. In the fall of 1974, Talmadge helped him secure a position as International Trade Commissioner, a high-paying bureaucratic plum. After his work at the ITC, Minchew quickly managed to double his salary to $100,-000 by taking another job representing the trade interests of the Japanese. Even while he was working as a lobbyist for Japanese manufacturers, his wife continued her employment as a lawyer on the staff of President Carter's White House trade representative Robert Strauss. The Minchews were one of Washington's up-and-coming couples who, according to a Department of Justice investigation, amassed nearly $2 million in assets during their tenure in Washington.

Minchew was constantly on the move from congressional staff to the bureaucracy to lobbying—a classic example of Washington's revolving door. All the while, however, he continued under the patronage of Senator Herman Talmadge. It was this intimate association which gave Minchew access to these other jobs, and in the end it was just this intimacy which brought down both of their careers. In a long series of investigations, court trials, and Senate hearings in 1978 and 1979, Minchew was convicted of pilfering money from campaign contributions and various uncertain sources while serving as Talmadge's aide. Through the use of illegal bank accounts and large stashes of cash, Minchew and Talmadge had managed to sustain their patrician lifestyles. Minchew was ultimately sent to prison for his part in these schemes; Talmadge was subsequently denounced by the Senate and thrown out of office by his Georgia constituents in 1980.

On the surface, Minchew might appear to be just another example of the blind ambition common to so many who come to Washington. The story seems like a repeat of that good old boy, Bobby Baker, the South Carolinian who worked his way up from page to millionaire Secretary of the Senate, dealing in a series of illegal schemes on the side. But unlike Baker, who rose under the patronage of Lyndon Johnson, Minchew and his patron Talmadge both benefited from their criminal activity. No matter who Minchew worked for—American textile interests, Japanese manufacturers, or the government—his ties persisted with Talmadge, whom he described as "a father" to him. In the end, Minchew broke the sacred trust of "protect thy patron." As Art Harris summed it up for *The Washington Post*, "Daniel Minchew . . . has committed the cardinal sin," and in so doing destroyed himself and his patron.

The criminal nature of the relationship between Minchew and Talmadge is probably not unique, but neither is it typical of congressional client-patron bonds. Without ever violating the letter of the law, all Congressional Big Men have former assistants like Minchew who leave the fold of the Hill clan to work as lobbyists, but never terminate their intimate ties to the clan. Like their bureaucratic counterparts, these individuals operate small subclans, which form a part of the extended Congressional Clan. Such enclaves are found in the offices of weapons manufacturers as well as power utilities, in the Direct Selling Association just as in the Federation of American Hospitals, in Nader's Raiders as much as in the Moral Majority.

In addition to ex-staffers working for lobbyists, one finds the family of congressional members doing the same thing. In recent decades these clan extensions have become less frequent and more prone to journalists' attacks as conflicts of interest, but they do persist. Tom Boggs, for example, is one of the most efficient lobbyists in Washington, representing sugar interests, dog food manufacturers, and a host of other concerns. His mother is Congresswoman Lindy Boggs, an active legislator; his father was the former House Majority Leader Hale Boggs. Tom Boggs's wife is in turn the business partner of Senator Proxmire's wife in a private convention planning service catering to groups meeting in Washington.

Occasionally these extensive and complicated relationships cause political embarrassment for a politician, as happened to ex-Senator Jacob Javits. Mrs. Javits worked for the Iranian government of the Shah, doing public relations work in the United States while her husband served in the Senate. The heavy criticism of this work from Javits's Jewish constituents finally forced Mrs. Javits to resign her job, but many similar situations never receive public attention. If the congressman is less known than Javits, the practice can often be justified as just another modern marriage in which husband and wife each pursues an independent career.

These extended branches of kin and former aides bind together the congressional community and lobbies in a tight, intimate network of associates. As inside members of the same establishment, they share cultural and social allegiances to one another that far outweigh other ties. As the Washington journalist Charles Peters points out: "A lobbyist knows that the folks at Mobil or Exxon may forget him one day, but his network won't." In the same way that congressmen often loosen the ties to their constituents back in the district, lobbyists loosen their ties to their corporate sponsors in the hinterland, becoming instead intimates of the Congressional Clan system.

Even if a Congressional Big Man is unable to infiltrate or take over any lobbying groups in Washington, he can always start his own lobbies. In recent years, this new technique has arisen to compliment traditional tactics used to turn various lobbies into subclans. The major requirement for such a strategy is that the politician have access to a large sum of money.

BIRTHING NEW BASTARDS

The creation of new lobbies has been a particular expertise of Senator Jesse A. Helms of North Carolina and his clan. As an outspoken and imaginative strategist of conservative issues, Helms rose to national leadership in the anti-busing, anti-abortion, anti-sex education, and anti-Equal Rights Amendment movements. His persistently negative stances earned him the epithet "Senator No" until the reelection campaign of 1978, when he raised enough money to earn the new nickname of "the Six-Million-Dollar Senator." Through pioneering efforts of national mail-order solicitations for his campaign, Helms raised the largest election war chest ever in congressional history.

Using his evangelical talent to raise money in five- and ten-dollar donations, Helms established a series of his own lobbies headed by his staff assistants, following the successful example of the Heritage Foundation, which was created by congressional aides in 1973. Under the guidance of aides Howard Segermark, John Carbaugh, and James Lucier, the Institute on Money and Inflation was born. Another aide, Carl Anderson, was sent to head up the American Family Institute. The same aides managed Helms's Centre for a Free Society, and together with Dr. Victor Feiday, a former aide to Senator Strom Thurmond, they also ran the Institute of American Relations. Like most lobbying organizations in the City of Washington, they are not technically registered as lobbies, but operate under the rubrics of institutes, think tanks, and public affairs groups. Nevertheless, their primary mission is to finance work that is essentially lobbying.

Just how extensive these lobbying efforts are became clear in September of 1979 when two of the group's officers, Carbaugh and Lucier, travelled to the London peace talks between Ian Smith's Rhodesian government and the Zimbabwe guerrillas. According to press reports, they encouraged Smith's government to continue resisting black government until Senator Helms could rescind the economic boycott of Rhodesia-Zimbabwe. On the same issue, Helms himself had travelled to London earlier to meet with British Prime Minister Margaret Thatcher, all expenses paid through his Institute of American Relations. Similar expeditions were sent to Central America at the time of the fall of Nicaragua's General Somoza and the subsequent takeover of the country by the Sandinista guerrillas.

By running his own organizations, Helms's clan operated with a degree of freedom not available within the rules and regulations of the Senate regarding official travel and expenses. According to research by Richard Whittle, the combined groups under Helms's leadership provided nearly $1 million for use by its officers in these lobbying endeavors between 1976 and 1980. Access to such funds propels staff activity to a whole new dimension when they are able to act as an independent diplomatic corps beyond control of either the Congress or the President. It also further blurs the rather feeble distinction between congressional staff and congressional lobbies.

In his extensive creation of lobbies as subclans of his congressional organization, Senator Helms perfected a ploy first developed by Harlem Congressman Adam Clayton Powell. During his twenty-five years in the House of Representatives, Powell's outspoken and unusual style kept him in repeated court cases and ethics investigations. For part of his tenure he presided over a group he called the Tenants' Protective Association, through which flowed a large amount of money and personnel from his Capitol Hill office. Together with his personal staff, his staff as chairman of the Education and Labor Committee, and his lobby staff, Powell's extended clan stretched from Capitol Hill to Harlem and to Bimini in the Caribbean, where he headquartered his operation. Former aides, including Powell's wife, served at various times on both his government payroll and the payroll of his lobbying group. Through a series of congressional investigations in the 1960s, Powell's misuse of funds and irregularities in his hiring practice finally destroyed his entire clan. After losing his committee chairmanship and being temporarily deprived of his congressional seat, his Harlem constituents rejected him in the 1970 election in favor of Charles Rangel, and Powell died two years later without making a comeback.

Even though Jesse Helms has avoided the technical violations of congressional rules that destroyed Powell's career, the mesh of staff and lobby was much the same in both cases. The flow of money and of personnel directed by such Big Men unites lobbies and parts of congressional staff into a single political clan under the domination of one Big Man.

In examining the relationships between lobbies and politicians, it is usually assumed that a flow of money somehow indicates a flow of power. As a general principle, that idea seems to hold true, but exactly how the money and power correlate is actually quite uncertain. Does the exchange of money mean that the giver is exercising undue influence over the receiver, or does it indicate that the receiver has an undue power over the giver? All too often the automatic assumption is made that the giver, which is usually the lobby, gains power over the receiving politician. It comes close to being a virtual, though legal, form of bribery; but the distinction between bribery and blackmail is arbitrary. Particularly in the practice of campaign contributions, money donations may more often be a form of expected political tribute to a Big Man than any attempt to bribe him. The flow of money between lobbies and politicians can just as easily be seen as an index of the power a Congressional Big Man wields over the lobbies as it is an example of how much influence they have over the politician.

This unclear distinction received ambiguous expression in the 1980 election campaign of New York Congressman James Hanley. As chairman of the House Post Office and Civil Service Committee, Hanley had before his panel a bill to decide whether or not low postage rates would continue for magazines and mail-order companies. While the bill was pending, he distributed invitations to various publishers and lobbyists for his first campaign fundraiser and received from them $40,000 in immediate contributions. In his perverse style, Hanley then decided not to run for reelection. Unlike either Helms or Powell, Hanley did not have complete control over these organizations; they were not parts of his clan. Nevertheless, he exercised enough authority over them that he could cripple them with a single decision. Knowing that he had that power and was not adverse to exercising it, only the most foolhardy of companies and lobbies would refuse to contribute to his campaign. In each election year, a host of such episodes is repeated as politicians raise money from the people directly affected by their legislative work, and newspapers chronicle these as further attempts by lobbyists to exert improper influence over legislation. They could, however, be just as easily interpreted as the improper use of influence over legislation by Big Men seeking to extract money from the lobbies. All too often politicians approach the lobbies like Persian satraps collecting tribute from their subjects. It is probably this attitude as much as anything else that keeps the lobbying practice alive, despite so much public condemnation of it.

In addition to extracting money from lobbies, Congressional

Big Men are also able to influence how much money goes to junior members of Congress. Big Men direct the flow of lobbying funds toward or away from specific junior politicians, thereby enhancing the power of the Big Man over younger congressmen. The power which this money gives a congressman over colleagues has been successfully exercised by Hollywood Representative Henry Waxman.

Just prior to the 1978 election, Waxman made campaign contributions to ten of his House colleagues from funds which he raised through a consortium of labor, consumer, and environmental groups, together with some of his wealthy constituents. While not an illegal practice, it was certainly unusual for one congressman to donate directly to the campaign of another, but the fruits of Waxman's effort materialized in the 1979 opening of the 96th Congress. Even though Waxman lacked the seniority, he announced his intention to run for chairman of the Health Subcommittee of the House Commerce Committee. All ten of the recipients of his money served on that committee, and all ten of them voted for him. The Waxman case was unusual only in that such power is usually directed by senior Big Men rather than by a junior congressman. Waxman's ability to raise money and to use it so effectively made up for several terms of seniority, proving that in some cases money does speak louder than seniority, even in Congress.

All of these examples, from Adam Clayton Powell to Edward Kennedy and Jesse Helms to Henry Waxman, distort the usual perception of who lobbyists are and how they operate. They illustrate how politicians themselves are able to take over lobbying groups and their diverse resources for use in their own political schemes. Lobbyists are not so much outsiders trying to influence what goes on within the legislative process of Congress as they are integral parts of the inside operation. They act as pawns under the ultimate control of some Congressional Big Man more often than they work independently. And as pawns they end up doing the dirty work of politics, permitting their congressional patron to rise above it all. While the congressman plays the clean statesman role in public, lobbyists do his bidding behind the scenes, making the deals for him, trading horses, and performing the truly political chores.

Throughout the world we find societies in which some marginal, seemingly outside group of people is retained to perform services which the members of that society find distasteful. In India, the Untouchable castes tan hides and remove dead carcasses so that the clean castes need not break religious taboos by touching dead animals. By their very name, the Untouchables are excluded from the normal boundaries of proper Indian society; yet in reality they play an integral part in it. In similar fashion the Jews of Europe were always defined as aliens, not really a part of German, French, or British society; yet they performed indispensable roles as moneylenders and merchants, filling vital positions prohibited to Christians by the biblical injunctions against usury. In turn, Orthodox Jews often needed Gentiles in their communities to light fires on the Sabbath and perform the tasks they themselves were proscribed from doing by their culture.

Among the Watutsi and the Hutu live a third group of people called the Twa, who are jungle pygmies and not a part of either the Hutu or the Watutsi, but who perform services vital to both. Traditionally, the Twa supplied honey to the other two peoples, who were reluctant to enter the jungle areas where the honey was found. The Twa also made pots and performed artisan services for the Watutsi, who consider such tasks beneath their dignity. Over the centuries, some of the Twa settled around the courts of important Watutsi chiefs to serve as jesters and entertain the warriors and their followers. Being neither Watutsi nor Hutu, the Twa often acted as intermediaries between the two groups and as reconnaissance teams for the Watutsi chiefs, spying on rival chiefs and on the client Hutu. The Twa were a part of neither group, but nonetheless performed very important roles for them.

Being at once outsiders and insiders, such marginal groups often play the scapegoat for shortcomings of the social system. For almost two millennia the Jews would periodically bear the blame for outbreaks of plague, famine, economic depression, or war. When banking families like the Rothschilds played a prominent role in financing the exploits of European monarchs and businessmen, it was often easier to blame them for causing the war, losing the war, or creating the economic calamities than it was for the countries to blame themselves. Just as Jews were periodically slaughtered in pogroms and nearly annihilated in the Holocaust, the Twa were killed and maimed by the Hutu after the nation received its independence from Belgium.

In far less dramatic and less bloody fashion, the lobbyists of Washington are treated as outside spoilers who pollute the political arena, which would otherwise be more honorable and less corrupt. In this role, they are more likely to bear the scorn of the public and much more likely to be prosecuted than the politicians who are supposedly their victims. As we have seen in this chapter, however, lobbies are central parts of the internal process of Congress. Rather than outside forces acting on the Congress, they are the very creations of Congress, designed as channels of politics. In this capacity, lobbyists perform those vital functions that are technically and legally beyond the limits of what the politicians themselves can do. The lobbyists are more the tools of Congressional Clans than the manipulators of Congress. They are the means by which Congressional Chiefs control the junior politicians and sometimes each other. The exercise of power is frequently a painful act, and the truly powerful often exercise it from behind a facade of intermediaries who deflect the heat and hatred arising from it. Kings and czars can be powerful and still loved by the common people as long as their power is mediated through a circle of counsellors and lower functionaries, who then bear the contempt of the people. This principle of politics operates as effectively in contemporary America as it did in Imperial Rome, czarist Russia, or Tokugawa Japan. Today's circle of retainers is made up of congressional staff, bureaucrats, and lobbyists, who absorb the public derision and criticism while the public continues to elect and reelect their political masters.

7

❦

Recycling Congress

WHEN A PRIMITIVE tribe changes into a nation, or several of them unite to form a single state, the most powerful clans become aristocratic dynasties. The royal houses of Europe, China, and Egypt were only one step removed from the chiefly clans of the Watutsi, Zulu, or Iroquois. The history of European nations in large part becomes the genealogy of aristocratic clans like the Hapsburgs, Bourbons, Stuarts, Romanoffs, and Medicis. With almost boring continuity, one generation of kings, emperors, and princes gives way to another with largely the same set of names. The Hohenzollerns blend with the Hohenstaufens and Henry III succeeds Henry II, making it quite difficult for the modern student to keep one century of history separate from another. Was Louis XVIII the son or the grandson of Louis XV? Did Tutankhamen take over the throne from Amenhotep IV or III? Which King James sponsored translations of the Bible into English, and which Charles had his head chopped off?

All of those names seem to blend together in that monotonous pageant we call world history. It feels so remote from our own time and system of government in America, where leaders earn their offices of power through election and not through birth.

Our contemporary political system seems more dynamic and more alive than those of the past, which are interesting only when exceptionally bloody or particularly romantic. Otherwise history takes on the archaic tone of the Bible in which Arphaxad begat Salah, and Salah begat Eber, and Eber begat Peleg, and Peleg begat Reu, and so on in a litany of successions. Future historians and anthropologists, however, may have just as much difficulty remembering the names and understanding our own times as we have recalling those of Europe or in the Bible. Already the American politicians fuse together. Was President William Harrison the grandfather or the grandson of President Benjamin Harrison? Adlai Stevenson I was elected Vice President in 1892, Adlai II failed to defeat Eisenhower in 1952 and 1956, and Adlai III became senator in 1970. Wasn't it Theodore Roosevelt who said, "Speak softly but carry a big stick," and his cousin Franklin who said, "All we have to fear is fear itself"? Howard Taft was President, but his son Robert Taft I and grandson Robert Taft II were only senators. Was it Huey Long who was assassinated for defending the poor and his son Russell Long who grew rich as a senator championing the oil companies, or was it Earl Long?

Every few years America holds one of those supposedly watershed elections in which the slate is wiped clean, the old leaders tossed out once and for all, and a new era inaugurated. Yet, two or three years later, it is hard to tell the difference; once the rhetoric settles, Congress and government seem to be continuing much as before. The key to this static dimension of politics can be found in examining who gets to Congress and who is likely to rise to become its chiefs. These people are literally the sons, and sometimes the daughters, of the old Congress, with a handful of wives, cousins, brothers-in-law, and staff assistants thrown in. The incestuous lines of relationship in congressional genealogy are as complex and convoluted as those of a pasha and his harem or the in-laws of King Henry VIII. Despite their complexity, however, their importance demands attention if we are to comprehend politics in the modern Congress, for in the final analysis these connections often determine who gets the chance to play the game and which of the players stands the best chance of winning.

THE CONGRESSIONAL FAMILY

Prominent American families have always sent their children to serve in Congress. A list of congressmen from any decade in our history invariably reads like a roster from the blue book. An exceptional number of seats belong to the Byrds of Virginia, the Adams, Cabots, and Lodges of Massachusetts, the Fish family of New York, the Tafts of Ohio, and the Roosevelts of New York. Although newly arrived on the scene, the Kennedy family is entering its fourth decade in Congress and seems destined for a lengthy membership in the ranks of political perennials. Families such as these become important and sometimes colorful parts of American folk culture, as significant to the tabloid press as to the political journals. They are almost always depicted as unique in the number of politicians they produce. The proliferation of politicians from one family is rarely seen as part of an overall pattern in American life; yet just such a pattern is there, making these families the political norm rather than the exception.

This same pattern is visible in a variety of lesser-known names, as well as in the families of the famous. They include names like Dingell of Michigan, Byron of Maryland, Gore of Tennessee, and Burdick of North Dakota. These everyday-sounding names neither reek of old lineage nor resonate with authoritative consonants and crisp vowels. Although not recognized by the general public outside of their home states, each of them represents a family that has been in Congress for up to five generations.

Frequently, kinship ties are dismissed as being of importance in only a few backwater districts that have not caught up with the times, or else they are seen as symptomatic of an aristocratic, almost un-American strain of thinking, peculiar to New England or the Old South. Congressional kinship, however, knows no geographical boundaries. Just as a Kennedy can win election to Congress from New York as easily as from Massachusetts, so a Goldwater can win in both Arizona and California. Before being elected Vice President, George Bush served as congressman from Houston, Texas, carrying on a family tradition as son of the senator from Connecticut. Kinship dominates the power relationships of the Western states like California, Washington, and even Alaska as readily as in Massachusetts or South Carolina; the only difference is that in the East the tradition is older, but not necessarily more important.

A quick overview of the congressional kin in 1981 reveals fifteen sons of former members, three widows, two sets of brothers serving concurrently, two others who are brothers of former members, as well as assorted cousins, brothers-in-law, and nephews. More important than just the numbers, however, is the success these congressional kin have in playing the clan politics of Congress. Beginning their careers with obvious advantages, they parlay these into positions as the really big Big Men of Congress.

The way in which sons build on their political patrimony is well evidenced in the career of Senate Republican Leader Howard Baker of Tennessee. Baker is the son of six-term Congressman Howard H. Baker, Sr., of Tennessee. His stepmother, Irene Baker, served as congresswoman from the family stronghold of the second district when the senior Baker died and she was elected to the remainder of his term in 1964. Supplementing this heritage, young Howard Baker married Joy Dirksen, daughter of Senate Republican Leader Everett McKinley Dirksen of Illinois. Baker tried to assume his father-in-law's position as leader when Dirksen died in 1969, a wish not fulfilled until 1977 when Baker became Senate Minority Leader. Four years later, in 1981, he surpassed his father, stepmother, and father-in-law by becoming Majority Leader—the first Republican to do so in a quarter of a century. Meanwhile, over in the House, Baker's brother-in-law William Wampler represents Virginia's "Fighting Ninth" district as another Republican congressman.

On the Democratic side of the political aisle, a parallel to Baker is obvious in Senator Russell Long of Louisiana. Whereas Baker's parents served in the House, Long is the only senator who is the son of two senators. Both his father, the legendary Huey "Kingfish" Long, and his mother, Rose McConnell Long, held his seat before him. Young Russell Long could not inherit his rightful patrimony until he reached age thirty, the minimum age specified in the Constitution for senators; he was elected at twenty-nine and began serving as soon as he turned thirty in 1948. In 1965 he became chairman of the powerful Finance Committee, but lost the title in 1981 when Republicans took control of the Senate committees. In the same year, however, his cousin, Representative Gillis Long, was elected by his fellow congressmen to a House leadership post, keeping the family prominently displayed in Congress. Before Gillis Long, the district was represented by his cousin Speedy Long and by two of old Kingfish's brothers, George Long and Earl Long, making Louisiana in general and the eighth district in particular a virtual family preserve.

Every election seems to bring at least one more congressional son to the Senate. In the 1980 election, young Christopher Dodd was elected to the Senate from Connecticut, exactly ten years after his father, Thomas Dodd, was thrown out of office by the same voters. The senior Dodd had been censured by the Senate, the ultimate disgrace of opprobrium from the senatorial peers, for unethical conduct. In the election before Dodd's arrival, Wyoming elected Alan Simpson, son of former Wyoming Senator Milward Simpson. Other senatorial sons include Democratic Senator Quentin Burdick of North Dakota, who replaced his father, Republican Usher Burdick, and Independent Harry Flood Byrd, Jr., who replaced his father, Democratic Senator Harry Flood Byrd, Sr. Rhode Island Senator Claiborne Pell is the son of former New York Congressman Herbert Pell.

On the House side, the list of congressional heirs and kin is both longer than that of the Senate and generally less known. It includes obscure names such as William Pattman, Andrew Jacobs, and William E. Goodling, as well as slightly better-known ones such as Barry Goldwater, Jr., Albert Gore, Jr., and Hamilton Fish. Of all these congressional pedigrees, that of Fish is the oldest. A succession of politicians, all with the name Hamilton Fish, has represented New York's Hudson district since 1842. The list includes Secretary of State Hamilton Fish from 1869 to 1877; another Hamilton Fish left Congress to serve as Assistant United States Treasurer from 1903 to 1908. The next-to-the-last Hamilton Fish served in Congress from 1919 to 1945, when he was defeated by Katherine St. George, a cousin of the family's archenemy Franklin Roosevelt. After that defeat, the family did not regain its seat until the present Hamilton Fish was elected to it in 1968, although in the meantime various cousins and relatives by marriage held other seats in other states.

The family of Thomas Ashley occupied a similar position in Ohio politics to that of the Fish family in New York, until Representative Thomas Ashley was defeated in 1980 after twenty-six years in the House. The first Ashley came to Congress as an anti-slavery Republican from Toledo during the Civil War and played a prominent role in the postbellum reconstruction of the South. Afterwards the family switched to the Democratic Party, but continued its activist role in whichever issues arose. The most recent Thomas Ashley chaired a special House committee charged with designing a new energy policy—a project about as successful as the reconstruction of the South by his grandfather.

The twentieth-century role of women in political office has added a new wrinkle to congressional politics. In addition to having sons, nephews, and grandsons among the members, Congress was joined by wives, daughters, and other female relatives of the congressional horde. Between 1789 and 1981, 10,930 people served in Congress. Of these, 108, a little less than 1 percent, were female. The majority of those elected in recent years achieved election on their own merits, but over the last fifty years many of them were elected to what is known as the widow's bench. There are only three widows in office in the 97th Congress: Cardiss Collins of Illinois, Beverly Byron of Maryland, and Lindy Boggs, wife of former House Majority Leader Hale Boggs of Louisiana. Marilyn Lloyd Bouquard is a borderline case, having been elected as a fill-in candidate, replacing her husband who was killed during the 1974 campaign in an airplane accident. She took his place on the ballot and was elected to the next Congress, even though he himself had never served in Congress.

The blend of widows and sons in congressional politics is aptly evident in the Byron family of Maryland's sixth district. In the 1930s, when the young sportsman William Byron was just beginning his political career, he was greatly assisted by marrying Katherine Edgar, granddaughter of Maryland Senator Louis McComas. This political merger helped the unknown Byron get elected to the sixth district seat in 1938. Despite his athletic prowess, William succumbed to a fatal heart attack only three years later, whereupon his young widow Katherine moved into his seat in 1941. Almost four decades later the story repeated itself with her son Goodloe Byron, who was by then also in Congress. In 1978, while jogging in a preparation for a marathon competition, Goodloe died of a heart attack, after holding the sixth district seat for only eight years. His young widow, Beverly Byron, then stepped forward and took his place on the ballot. Winning the 1978 race, she went on to be re-elected in 1980 as the fifth in their family to represent Maryland.

The genealogy of the Byrons is short in comparison with that of the Fish or Ashley family, but even so, such accounts quickly take on the monotony of the "biblical begats," as one generation of congressmen propagates another with seemingly indistinguishable traits and names. What is of greater importance than the kinship per se is the way in which these Congressional Clans become permanently associated with specific areas of political territory. All of the Byrons were involved in environmental issues, even though they never grew beyond a small district clan. Similarly, the Fish family maintained a persistent involvement with international finances—an involvement that stretched well beyond government to include a long line of stockbroker and banker brothers in a miniature version of the Rockefeller clan.

In the contemporary Congress, this continuity of domain and issues appears in the careers of the Kennedy family in the Senate and the Udall family in the House. All three of the Kennedy brothers used their seats in the Senate as presidential campaign platforms, but while in the Senate they were also heavily involved in the issue of crime and criminal investigations. Robert Kennedy got his start in Senate politics as aide to Senator Joseph McCarthy, whom he assisted in his anti-communist investigations. After those hearings faded from public interest, he worked for Senator Estes Kefauver in his anti-crime and racketeering investigations. When John Kennedy became President in 1961, Robert became Attorney General. Meanwhile younger brother Edward Kennedy, upon winning election to John's Senate seat in 1962, immediately sought a position on the Judiciary Committee, bypassing several more senior senators to get it. In 1979, Edward became chairman of the committee after holding a succession of subcommittee chairmanships, but in 1981 he was replaced when the Republicans took over the Senate and South Carolina's Strom Thurmond became chairman. Whether the issue was communism and racketeering in the 1950s, civil rights in the 1960s, government surveillance in the 1970s, or criminal code reform in the 1980s, one of the Kennedys always played an active role in judiciary issues.

The Udalls of Arizona represent a parallel situation for the issue of natural resources and environment, or what is traditionally referred to as "the Interior" in Washington. After working closely with those issues in the House of Representatives, Congressman Stewart Udall became Secretary of the Interior in 1961 under President John Kennedy. When Stewart resigned his House seat, brother Morris Udall was promptly elected to it and then joined the Interior and Insular Affairs Committee. In 1977, after running unsuccessfully for President in 1976, Morris Udall became chairman of the Interior Committee, a position he retained in the next two Congresses.

The much more aristocratic forebears of Senator Claiborne Pell have maintained a similarly persistent involvement in foreign policy, but for a far longer time than either the Kennedys or the Udalls. Claiborne's father, Herbert Pell, was a crony of Franklin Roosevelt and under him served in both the Congress and the ambassadorial corps. This diplomatic interest of the Pells stretches back to pre-Revolutionary times when John Pell (1610–1685) served as Cromwell's ambassador to Switzerland, later taking refuge in the American colonies after the Stuart Restoration to the throne in 1660. Like many aristocratic families, they have dabbled in academic pursuits while engaging in diplomacy. Just as the present Claiborne Pell is the former chairman of the Subcommittee on Arts and Humanities, the original Pell's academic pursuit was also a sideline. John Pell introduced the division sign ($\div$) to the English-speaking world. Other congressional ancestors of Claiborne Pell include Senator William Claiborne (1775–1817) and Senator George Dallas, who served as minister to Russia and Great Britain as well as Vice President of the United States from 1845 to 1849. The present Pell in Congress is the ranking Democrat on the Senate

Foreign Relations Committee in the 97th Congress, continuing the diplomatic traditions of the family.

Sometimes in addition to or in lieu of a particular legislative bailiwick, a family will claim an ideological niche. To some extent this was apparent in the liberalism of the Udalls and Kennedys or the conservatism of the Tafts and Goldwaters. But it is by no means confined to the presidential candidates coming out of the Congress. The use of ideology as a focus of clan territory is illustrated in the Crane and Burton families of the House.

When Phillip Burton was elected to Congress from San Francisco in 1964, he passed his seat in the California Assembly to his younger brother, John. Once in the House, Phillip became a leader in the "radical" anti-war elements of the Democratic Party. This stance appealed to his California constituency, and partially on the basis of that popularity, he was able to help brother John win the congressional seat in neighboring Marin County in 1974. This was just in time for John to assist Phillip's pursuit of a leadership position over the cohort of progressive Watergate Babies. Working as a team, they boosted Phillip to office in the party hierarchy over the Democratic Study Group, and among other feats, were instrumental in bringing down the Military Clan and its chairman, Edward Hebert. They failed by a single vote in the campaign to have Phillip elected House Majority Leader, losing to Texas Representative Jim Wright. Despite this failure, the duo has stayed in the forefront of liberal causes in Congress into the 1980s.

A mirror image of the liberal Burtons soon appeared in the conservative Cranes of Illinois. Philip Crane was first elected in 1969, and as a young charismatic speaker became a favorite of House Republicans. His success in mail-order fundraising was impressive enough for him to help his two brothers, David and Daniel, use the same techniques in their bids for Congress. David was rejected by Indiana voters in 1976 and 1978, but Daniel was elected from Illinois's twenty-second district in 1978, shutting out another political clan in which the administrative assistant and brother-in-law of the retiring congressman also competed for the seat. Once in the House, Daniel threw in his support as a junior partner with his brother's conservative causes; but, unlike the Burtons who sought party office within the House, the Cranes launched Philip's presidential campaign as "the Kennedy of the right." The campaign fizzled, yet both were reelected to the House in 1980 and continued their ideological skirmishes with the Burton brothers.

With the increasing number of women in politics and the rise of divorce in American society in the 1970s, congressional kinship has become even more complex than these examples. A recent example involves Colorado Senator Gary Hart and former Kansas Congresswoman Martha Keys. Keys got her start in Kansas politics through Gary Hart, who was married to her sister. As chairman of George McGovern's presidential campaign in 1972, Hart made Keys chairman of the Kansas campaign, even though her only prior experience in politics was that she was married to political science professor John Keys. Two years later, both Martha Keys and brother-in-law Hart waged their own campaigns for Congress and assumed their respective seats in January 1975. Politics, however, proved a drain on both of their marriages. Keys divorced John in favor of Indiana Representative Andrew Jacobs, Jr., who was himself the scion of a political family, having inherited his congressional seat from his father, Andrew Jacobs, Sr. After Martha Keys and Jacobs were married in 1978, Kansas voters declined to return her to the Congress, fearing that she would be more of a congresswoman for her husband's state of Indiana than for her own Kansas. Meanwhile, ex-husband John Keys decided to keep the family active and launched his own campaign for Martha's seat in 1980. John Keys, like his former wife, was defeated, but Andy Jacobs, the second husband, managed to be reelected, as did the former brother-in-law, Gary Hart. Keys, meanwhile, managed to get back in politics through an appointment in the bureaucracy by President Carter.

When not resembling biblical lineages, congressional kinship quickly takes on the quality of contemporary soap operas, with incessant domestic dramas of marriage, divorce, remarriage, fighting over inheritance, and forgotten characters suddenly reemerging from the past. Neither the soap operas nor congressional politics seems far removed from the political and marriage squabbles of the royal houses of Europe, in which alliances were made and broken through marriages and inheritances.

The complex script of congressional relations, however, has yet another dimension in the recent rise of congressional assistants who graduate from the staff to hold elective office in Congress. These staffers often fill in genealogical holes when there is no wife or child to assume a departing congressman's office; and in increasing cases, the staffers actually rival some of the real kin for the spoils of inheritance. To understand the full impact of this new development, we must examine how these institutional bonds between politicians and their protégés are blazing a new path to elected office.

INSTITUTIONAL KIN: CONGRESSIONAL CLONES

The frequency with which family members step into the position of a fallen politician is not based solely on the sentimentality of the voters. Often the assumption of office by the wife or son is much more practical than it seems. Prior to the anti-nepotism rules imposed by Congress in 1967, family members were frequently on the congressional payroll and consequently well acquainted with running the office. They knew how Congress operated, had campaign experience, and knew their constituents. Congressman John Dingell, Jr., was not only the son of a congressman, but through his father's patronage had worked in the House prior to his election. Similarly, Senator Sam Nunn worked for his granduncle, Carl Vinson, on the House Armed Services Committee before his own election to the Senate in 1972.

This type of transition was best exemplified by Maine Senator Margaret Chase Smith, who began politics as secretary to her husband, Congressman Clyde Smith. When he died in 1940 after having won forty-eight elections to political office in Maine, his logical successor was Margaret. After being elected to the House, she went on to parlay that position into a Senate seat in 1948. As she herself admitted, "I'm a real product of nepotism. I wouldn't be in Congress if I hadn't been a member of my husband's staff." But it was her extensive experience on the staff, rather than her marriage, that qualified her for the job as his replacement.

This same mixture of staff and kin is evidenced in the career of Katherine Langley, Republican congresswoman from Kentucky. Katherine Gudger Langley was the daughter of Congressman James Madison Gudger, Jr., of North Carolina's mountain area around Asheville. When she married Congressman John Langley from the Kentucky side of the Appalachians, she came to Washington as his secretary, a position she held for fourteen years. In 1924, John was sentenced to federal prison for moonshining, a not atypical sideline in the prohibition era. Katherine came forward, took his place on the ballot, and won his seat as a caretaker until he could be parolled. She then hired her own daughter as secretary, in the continuation of what appeared to be a family dynasty. The dynasty was interrupted in 1930, however, when John was released from prison and wanted his congressional seat back. By then Katherine had grown to enjoy the office, had acquired seniority, and had proven successful in three election campaigns. In the internecine squabble, the whole family was defeated, and the seat went to a Democrat.

It has become increasingly difficult in recent decades to combine kin and staff. Some members of Congress do have relatives on someone else's payroll, but it is considered unethical for them to keep family members directly on their own payroll. Consequently, it would be more difficult for someone like Katherine Gudger Langley or Margaret Chase Smith simply to step in and take over; widows are more likely to be defeated today. In the 1980 election, Dorothy Runnels, widow of Congressman Harold Runnels, was defeated in her campaign for his New Mexico seat. A similar fate overtook Maryon Allen of Alabama in 1978; even though she had been appointed to the seat of her husband on his death, she failed to win election to it. Allen directly attributed her defeat to trouble with the staff, who treated her as an outsider, unqualified for the office.

This new development has led to a proliferation of staff in Congress in the latter part of the 1970s and early 1980s. By 1981, sixty-nine former congressional aides were serving in elected congressional seats; these included sixty-one congressmen and eight senators.

Some of these cases of staff being elected to Congress have already been mentioned in conjunction with the building of subclans within Congress. They included the Kennedy-Culver-Clark triad and the Thurmond-Napier relationship. The majority of staffers, however, are elected after their bosses leave office or with only a short overlap between their own and their bosses' terms. Like wives, sons, and nephews, they are the inheritors of the political patrimony of their former bosses.

Congressman Keith Sebelius decided to retire in 1980 after twelve years representing Kansas's first district, one of the largest geographical districts in the union. Sebelius had built up an operation focused on the agricultural concerns of his rural constituents, and he rose to become the ranking minority member of the House Agriculture Committee, with a similar position on a subcommittee of the Interior Committee. Upon announcing his retirement, he supported for his replacement Pat Roberts, who had served as his aide for all of his six congressional terms. Roberts, who came originally from Dodge City, Kansas, had no trouble overcoming opponent Phil Martin, who had served five years in the Kansas legislature. Martin's local experience was no match for the Washington experience and connections of Roberts and Sebelius.

Such congressional races tend to lack drama and often get ignored in the wash of political campaign coverage, where the more interesting stories involve orphans who fought their way up to become millionaire heads of fiberglass companies and then launched into politics, or a grandmother who jogs across the state searching for votes. Yet it is races like that of Pat Roberts which give continuity to Congress. Even in an election such as 1980, which in some ways moved a major political upset and brought seventy-four new congressmen to the House, the radical change is mitigated when it is realized that 15 percent of these newcomers were recycled staffers from the old Congress. Although there were some dramatic defeats, such as the downfall of Senator Frank Church, chairman of the Senate Foreign Relations Committee, there were also some undramatic newcomers, such as Church's former aide Tom Lantos. Lantos was elected to the house from California in the same election that saw Church go down in defeat.

Staff and kin become interchangeable parts in the congressional scenario. This mixture is illustrated in the history of Florida's eleventh district on the gold coast north of Miami. The district was first created in 1944 and was won by Paul Rogers, Sr., running on the Democratic ticket. When he died ten years later, the district passed to his son Paul Rogers, Jr., who presided over it for the next quarter of a century until 1978. Even though he had built up an impressive congressional operation and presided as "Mr. Health" in the House, Rogers decided to leave Congress in order to earn a little more money in his later years. To replace him, he supported his long-time administrative assistant, Dan Mica. Together with the bureaucratic programs established by Rogers and the lobbying coalition which he formed prior to his retirement, continuity of his political clan was assured. Since Rogers retired voluntarily, he was able to lend his continued presence and leadership to assist the clan through its transition and to help Mica get elected in 1978 and reelected in 1980. In this way the eleventh district has never passed out of control of their dynasty, despite the fact that the area around it and Florida in general have grown increasingly more Republican.

A similar transfer of power to a former staff assistant occurred when Edmund Muskie became Secretary of State in 1980. Muskie had led a very active but somewhat erratic life in congressional politics. In his first decade in the Senate, he concentrated on building an organization around the old pork-barrel Committee of Public Works. His emphasis switched from congressional to national politics when he made the 1968 bid for Vice President and in 1972 ran for the Democratic nomination for President. Only after losing both of those did Muskie again seriously reenter congressional politics. This began another phase of organization for his clan. Rather than returning to the old area of Public Works, which now looked rather mundane after the highlights of a national campaign, Muskie worked for and got a whole new committee. Through this Budget Committee, he built an entirely new congressional operation. In the process, he battled every major and minor clan in Congress. Against the minors, he scored a number of victories by limiting their spending authorizations. He repeatedly took on Stennis's military operations, and capitalizing on the anti-military mood of the 1970s, defeated the old warrior on a number of funding issues. His really big rivals in money matters were Russell Long (of Finance) and Warren Magnuson (of Appropriations). In most major battles with them, Muskie was a surprisingly good match; nevertheless, he lost, particularly on Long's taxmaking policies, against which he fought a perpetual but doomed war.

Despite the losses against the two biggest clans in the Senate, Muskie's record was substantial, creating, in essence, a clan from scratch. Within the last decade of his twenty-two-year term, he was able to do battle against the biggest and oldest clans in the Senate. His unexpected departure to become Secretary of State in 1980 caused almost immediate division of much of his territory. The bulk of the Budget Committee staff fell to South Carolina Senator Ernest Hollings, whose diplomatic Southern style contrasted markedly with the temperamental outbursts of Muskie. Muskie's clan was cut back to a personal staff, which went to his former administrative assistant, George J. Mitchell, appointed to fill the unexpired term until the election of 1982. Just to get Mitchell the appointment to the Senate, Muskie forces had to fight off former Maine Senator William Hathaway, who had been defeated in the 1978 election by Bill Cohen and who wanted to use Muskie's promotion as an entry back into Congress. Senator Mitchell was not the first of Muskie's staff to get a congressional office. Michael D. Barnes, who had worked as Muskie's special assistant, was elected to the House in 1978 and again in 1980 to represent Maryland's eighth district in the Washington suburbs.

Both the Rogers and Muskie cases show how generations of congressmen can spring from one source. The same cycle began in the Goldwater family when Barry Goldwater, Jr.'s, assistant, David Dreier, ran for Congress in 1980, adding a third member to that family's dynasty. In that election the senior Goldwater was reelected to the Senate, the younger Goldwater was reelected to the House, and Dreier made his debut. This same progression is evident in the career of John Dingell, Jr., who became chairman of the House Interstate and Foreign Commerce Committee in 1981. Dingell had worked as a House page when his father was congressman, and then gone on to replace his father in 1955. In 1964, his assistant John Conyers gained election to the House from the Detroit district neighboring on Dingell's, and by 1981 both of them were serving together in prominent positions in the House hierarchy.

The most common form of replacement today occurs when a congressman runs for the Senate and one of his assistants then runs for the House seat. Six such staffers held office in 1981, having replaced their former bosses in the Senate. When Dan Quayle defeated long-time Senator Birch Bayh of Indiana in 1980, Quayle's seat in the House was taken over by his assistant, Daniel Coats. The same thing happened in the election of 1978 when Bill Cohen left the House to become senator, handing over his seat to Olympia Snowe, just as Thad Cochran moved to the Senate and left his seat to Ron Hinson.

Of course such transfers of power are not automatic, and frequently the staffer is defeated at the polls, just as wives and sons are sometimes defeated. When Dawson Mathis, Democratic congressman from Georgia's second district, gave up his House seat to run against Senator Herman Talmadge, Mathis's assistant Julian Holland filed in the campaign for the open position. Both Holland and Mathis lost in the primaries, with the House seat going to another Democrat, Charles Hatcher, and the Senate seat to Republican Matt Mattingly.

A single defeat, however, does not necessarily mean a clean sweep from Congress; the defeated staffer may try again. It took Congressman Pat Williams two tries before he won the seat of his former boss John Melcher. Other defeated candidates may simply return to their work on congressional staffs and await another opportunity. Donald Watson served as administrative assistant to Illinois Democratic Congressman George Shipley until Shipley's retirement in 1978. Watson, who was the congressman's brother-in-law as well as aide, failed to win the election, but he then signed on as assistant to the Republican who did win it, Representative Daniel Crane. In the same election, Chuck Pike lost his bid to replace his former boss, but he then became the assistant to Representative Robert Whittaker who defeated him in the primary election.

The way in which staff assistants and family members can substitute for one another in clan politics is nowhere better illustrated than in the struggles of the Military Clan. As one of the most coveted sources of power and prestige within Congress, control over defense issues always evokes keen competition. Both houses of Congress vie with each other for control of the Pentagon, and within each chamber a host of major and minor players compete for that coveted title of "Mr. Military." In 1981 it fell nominally into the hands of Republican Senator John Tower of Texas, after having been firmly in Democratic hands for most of this century; but for years before that it was a constant source of dynastic struggles.

"MR. MILITARY"

The congressional preeminence of the military clan dates from World War II. For a while after V-J Day, it appeared that the clan might break up as America brought the troops home, disbanded the military, and returned to George Washington's sacred command that the nation avoid entangling foreign alliances. Although America had joined the Allies in fighting Germany and Italy, it was not at all certain that this alliance with England and the Soviet Union needed to continue after the war. Strains in the Soviet alliance and the general threat which America perceived from communism indicated even before the war ended that the relationship of convenience would not survive long after the war. As tensions heated up between the two former allies, the military powers in Congress were sustained. Despite some significant opposition in Congress, the United States signed a new set of treaties that created the NATO alliance, and by the end of the 1940s America was gearing up for war in Korea. The congressional opponents to these foreign involvements had either been converted or banished to the outer fringes of the club as reactionary isolationists and communist dupes. Next to the presidency, the title of "Mr. Military" was the most coveted political job in the government.

During most of those postwar decades, the leadership of congressional military affairs remained in the House, passing from Georgia's Carl Vinson to South Carolina's Mendel Rivers, and finally, Louisiana's Edward Hebert. Prior to the loss of the Vietnam War, there was hardly a shade's difference in either style or substance within this military triumvirate. Had Mendel Rivers's "Geechie," as the Charleston accent is called, not contrasted with the Cajun tones of Edward Hebert, the change in leadership would probably have gone unnoticed by everyone. Each of the three seemed to blend into the others.

The head of the Senate Armed Services Committee during this time was another Georgian, Richard Russell. As the most powerful man in the Senate, there is little doubt that, had he wanted to assume a major voice in military affairs, Russell could have done so. Instead, he chose to be the "Dean of the Senate" and the "maker of Presidents" rather than attend to the minutiae of defense matters. In those days the Senate was still what William White called "the Club," and in the inner sanctum of that group reigned the unchallenged Richard Russell. As mentor to Lyndon Johnson, Russell was too busy directing national Democratic and Senatorial politics to be overly concerned with the military. When Russell died in 1969, the Club died with him, and the Senate divided into a handful of co-equal political chiefs as the House had had for decades. With Richard Nixon and the Republicans in the White House and neither Lyndon Johnson nor Richard Russell around as a single individual strong enough to unite power in one fist, the power was fractured into roughly the same set of clans still evident in the 1980s. The military part of that inheritance fell to John Stennis, second in seniority to Richard Russell on the Armed Services Committee.

Shortly after Stennis assumed the chairmanship, the ruling Military Clan in the House came under unprecedented attack. In the ensuing unpopularity of the Vietnam War and the political paroxysms of Watergate, Edward Hebert was toppled. The Watergate Babies elected to the House in 1974 not only ousted him as chairman of his committee; they also destroyed the clan base, to prevent a new "Mr. Military" from taking over. The power of the committee devolved to semi-autonomous subcommittees, each with a different chairman. To prevent that authority's being reunited, a relatively weak congressman, Melvin Price of Illinois, was given the chairmanship of the whole committee. Price lacked the political skills of the old triumvirate, and he was not particularly interested in the military, being fascinated instead with the uses of nuclear energy.

While the House was preoccupied with these internal

changes, Senator Stennis grabbed the military crown for himself, thus moving the heart of the clan from the House to the
Senate. Stennis broke ground on his canal and consolidated his
authority over both the appropriations and authorizations parts
of the military jurisdiction. During those years of military disre-
pute, Stennis was not able to expand the military jurisdiction,
but the fact that he preserved it largely intact was a considerable feat. In the relative calm of the Senate, protected from the
excesses of voter sentiment that shook the House in the 1970s,
Stennis resisted the military critics. He did lose an occasional
vote, but by and large he held the line on military funding. The
clan also had to sacrifice its intelligence-gathering domain, but
in throwing the CIA to the wolves, pressure was relieved from
the core of the military establishment. Tearing apart the spy
network distracted the younger senators long enough for Stennis
to get his canal under way and to avoid fighting over major
parts of the Pentagon budget.

As the 1970s drew to a close and public interest flip-flopped
from spies back to military preparedness, Stennis's reign was
also drawing to a close. The potential range for a replacement
was limited. Senator Russell had died a childless bachelor, having spent his fatherly love and help on Lyndon Johnson. Edward Hebert's fall from power had destroyed his political organization and left the district prey to a series of vicious election
campaigns, court cases, and convictions. Mendel Rivers left his
Charleston, South Carolina, seat and his Armed Services Committee seat to his godson and namesake, Mendel Davis, but
young Mendel quit Congress in disgust in 1980. Even if he had
devoted himself to military affairs as arduously as Big Mendel
had done, it would take a lifetime to reunite the scattered pieces
of House jurisdiction blown apart in the cataclysm of '74.

John Stennis did have an heir in the form of his own son, but
young John was even a less likely replacement than young
Mendel. The junior Stennis was unable to muster public support in Mississippi; despite his father's name and political success, young John lost his 1978 campaign for Congress by an
overwhelming margin. Although the Stennis candidate out-
spent all the others, he drew only 27 percent of the vote. So, if he

ever got to Congress, it seemed unlikely that young John could fill big John's shoes.

The solution to the inheritance dilemma seemed to come from Georgia in the form of Sam Nunn, grandnephew of old Carl Vinson. Back when Vinson bore the "Mr. Military" title, he enticed young Sam to Washington to work as a staffer on the House Armed Services Committee. With his interest in military work and his ability to stay on good terms with his seniors, Nunn quickly took shape as the most likely successor to his Uncle Carl. His first chance for a seat in Congress came when the heirless Richard Russell died. The Russell legacy was also claimed by the Georgia Mafia of Governor Jimmy Carter. In his official capacity, Carter was able to make an interim appointment to the Senate seat for his own protégé, David Gambrell. When it was time for Senator Gambrell to face the constituents, Nunn, as well as thirteen other Georgia politicians, challenged him for the prestige of Russell's seat. Those thirteen, including former Governor Vandiver, were defeated in the primary election. The legacy of Carl Vinson defeated the Carter appointee by 4 percent in the run-off election. Nunn then went on to defeat the Republican candidate in the general election with a narrow, but sufficient, 54 percent of the vote.

Having thus established himself as the rightful heir to Senator Russell's seat in the Senate, Nunn also managed to take Russell's old seat on the Armed Services Committee. Ancient Carl Vinson left his Georgia retirement home to escort his nephew to the Capitol, where he formally presented thirty-four-year-old Nunn to the care of Senator Stennis. Stennis, who had been in elective office over a decade before Nunn was born, accepted the charge with some reservations. At the time he was beleaguered by those young senators who were trying to reduce his jurisdiction and military appropriations. Taking another one of these youngsters into his fold was not necessarily a wise strategic move, even if the young man did have Vinson and Russell connections and even if he had defeated the forces of Jimmy Carter.

Nunn could have combined his military legacy and that special legitimacy which it gave him together with his youthfulness to take command of the young critics in the Senate. If the anti-Stennis forces had been led by someone like Nunn, they might have been able to do in the Senate what similar young politicians had done in the House. Instead, Nunn worked as an ardent assistant to the old man and as go-between representing him to the younger members. When Stennis was recuperating from gunshot wounds suffered in a 1974 robbery on his home, Nunn remained steadfastly loyal to the senior man, even when many assumed Stennis might never return to politics. After his return, Stennis, often busy with the details of his canal, allowed Nunn to fight many of his clan skirmishes for him. When it was decided that the congressional military establishment would not submit to Jimmy Carter's Salt II Treaty, it was Nunn who fired the opening shots against treaty negotiator Paul Warnke. When the treaty was finally presented to the Senate, Nunn again led the attack on it until Carter gave up on it in 1979.

In 1980, Nunn was given responsibility for seeing the Draft Registration Bill through Congress. In his capacity as chairman of the Subcommittee on Manpower and Personnel, Nunn was assigned primary responsibility for working out the details of the new military that was to lead America through the 1980s. All of this, combined with the persistent rejection of young John Stennis at the Mississippi polls, slowly made Nunn into Stennis's heir apparent. By assuming the heritage of John Stennis and adding it to his already rich legacy from Uncle Carl Vinson and Richard Russell, Nunn gave every indication of providing a peaceful and uncontested transfer of the "Mr. Military" title on Stennis's abdication or death. When young Mendel Davis decided not to run for reelection to the 1981 Congress, Nunn became the uncontested Democratic Dauphin of the Military Clan.

The struggle for control of the Military Clan took a totally unexpected turn when the Republicans won the Senate in the 1980 election. Both Stennis and Nunn had to step aside for the senior Republican John Tower, who had hoped to become President Reagan's Secretary of Defense but had not expected to become chairman of the Armed Services Committee. As with all Congressional Chiefs, Tower moved his own staffers into the controlling positions within the committee, and Stennis was demoted to leader of the Democratic minority delegation and staff. Stennis and Nunn, however, remain poised to regain their positions should the Democrats win back the Congress any time in the 1980s.

Even though each of the Congressional Clans has its own unique style and flair, the struggle to assume control after the death of a leader seems basically the same in all of them. The political personae of men like Vinson, Stennis, and Nunn may be diametrically opposed to the image presented by the likes of Kennedy, Rogers, or Culver, but despite these superficial differences, the underlying processes of their respective clans are largely the same. The jockeying for clan territory and for the preservation of the group is the same game, no matter who the players are. The political territory may consist of only a small congressional district controlled by a single Southern family or Northern machine. It may be a major clan as extensive, discrete, and durable as the military. Still, the principles of power remain the same. The continuity of the group depends on the preservation of its personnel and its jurisdiction under a central leader. This leader is someone who was closely associated with the last leader, and if possible, connected to him by either blood or a long-standing staff affiliation.

Throughout the world, local clans survive over many generations. The very concept of the clan implies historical continuity and constancy. This depends largely on biological kinship, with new members being born into the group to replace those who die. In Congress, membership in the clan is maintained through a mixture of recruitment and biological kinship, arising from the same need for clan continuity. As the Clan Chief ages, he wants to ensure that something remains of his group and of his work—that it is not just a flash in the political pan or an ad hoc network which survived only one generation to wither away with him. A politician who spends his career building an organization wants it to endure; it is his life's work. Just as he does not want it to dissolve, neither do his clients and staffers. The advantages which they personally derive from the group affiliation are greater than they would have acting as single individuals, and they resist the group's destruction when the leader dies or retires. A staffer without a patron is without a job.

Whether through the foresight of the departing chief or the efforts of his surviving clansmen, some plans for continuity are usually enacted. The group may attempt to fortify itself in the bureaucracy behind legislative walls erected to preserve its sovereignty; the leaderless clan may take refuge in a lobby for a while. In addition to these strategies, however, if the group survives the loss of a leader by more than a few years, the real focus of continuity must be within Congress itself. A bureaucratic stronghold can endure intact for a few congressional terms, but without a champion in Congress, it cannot last much longer. By the same process, an independent lobby eventually allies itself with some new patron if it wants to do anything more than carp on the political sidelines.

Kinship organizations such as clans are remarkably malleable institutions in most societies of the world; rarely are they confined by the constraints of mere biology and blood relationship. Membership is usually a hazy blur of blood members and incorporated relatives. Politically powerful or rich men are always able to attract skilled younger men to their following through a combination of marriage alliances, adoption, or long-term patron-client bonds. This is as evident in the following of a New Guinea Big Man as in that of an American senator today or a Roman senator two thousand years ago.

When Julius Caesar took over the control of the Roman Senate, he instituted a family dynasty that lasted over a century and an empire that lasted over a millennium. Yet no emperor in Caesar's family ever inherited his title from his biological father. Caesar himself took young Octavian as his legitimate heir. Octavian assumed the power under the name of Augustus and appointed as his own heir Tiberius, and so forth. From Caesar to Nero, the Julio-Claudian family ruled uninterrupted, but the heirs were recruited from amongst a host of blood relations, adopted relatives, and in-laws. Not until the Flavian dynasty when Titus followed his father Vespasian as emperor in A.D. 79 did a biological son follow his father to the throne. The Romans were always careful to preserve the form of inheritance from father to son, but the process was more cultural convenience than real kinship.

The difference between those older examples and the political families of today is a small but profound one. In the Roman Empire, as in the later kingdoms of Europe, legitimacy in the eyes of the people was ensured by the appearance of proper succession. Thus, each new ruler, even if he were a usurper, had to convince the populace that he was in fact the legitimate heir. If necessary, history could be made to show that his father was the illegitimate offspring of the last king or that his mother should have been the proper conduit of power. By contrast, in contemporary American society legitimacy is assumed to accrue through individual effort, which is sanctified in the votes of an election. Thus, most politicians try hard to maintain the fiction that they have made it on their own with little help from parents; they make it appear irrelevant that their fathers also happened to have been senators.

The exceptions to this are in the Old South and New England, which have older aristocratic sympathies that can help young politicians. An Edward Kennedy, Russell Long, or Herman Talmadge may bask in the public light of his family's contributions to the state, but a Jerry Brown or Alan Simpson from the West plays down his political inheritance. The result is that one region appears to be more family-oriented than another, just as America appears so much less aristocratic than the Roman Empire. But in all of these instances there is an interwoven fabric of blood kin and adopted, or adapted, institutional kin who combine to form political nuclei of major importance.

For the most part, this discussion has centered on the congressional families rather than broadening into the larger question of the political elite in America. But at least passing mention must be made of this larger context of relationships, for the same kinds of kin and staff relationships that are described here for the Congress stretch out to include all of the major political institutions of the United States. Many members of Congress who are not the children of congressmen are still a part of the large political families of the country.

Nancy Landon Kassebaum is not included in the senatorial kin, but that does not mean that she just sprang, self-propelled, from the American heartland. She was greatly assisted by her father Alf Landon, former Governor of Kansas and presidential candidate in 1936. Similarly, Charles Percy, Republican Whip of the Senate, did not come from a congressional family, but his daughter is married to Jay Rockefeller, Governor of West Virginia. The Rockefeller family itself is a prime example of these political families. The family has provided the recent governors of Arkansas and West Virginia as easily as it provided Nelson Rockefeller as Governor of New York and as Vice President of the United States under Gerald Ford. Thus, when Nelson Rockefeller presided over the Senate (in his capacity as Vice President of the United States), the Minority Whip before him was Charles Percy, father of Rockefeller's niece by marriage. Both Rockefeller and Percy were Republicans, but both Jay Rockefeller and Sharon Percy were Democrats, showing how little political parties need influence political families. The multiple memberships never hurt any of them and allow at least some of them to be always in office.

Former Senator Talmadge of Georgia was not strictly within the definition of congressional kin as used in this book, but as the son of four-term Georgia Governor Eugene Talmadge, he was not exactly a self-made man either. The same could be said of Adlai Stevenson III, son of Illinois Governor and presidential candidate Adlai Stevenson II. Similarly, the 1980 election brought two more gubernatorial sons to Congress, Representative Judd Gregg, son of former New Hampshire Governor Hugh Gregg, and Representative Dennis Smith, son of former Oregon Governor Elmo Smith.

Congress is equally a source of political power for family and staffers seeking local office. No doubt Massachusetts Lieutenant Governor T. P. O'Neill, Jr., was not hurt by being the son of House Speaker Tip O'Neill, any more than California Governor Jerry Brown was hurt by being the son of Pat Brown. Similarly, in 1980, three former congressional staffers had left Congress to become governors of their home states. These were Governor Lamar Alexander of Tennessee, Governor Charles Thorne of Nebraska, and Governor Richard Riley of South Carolina.

The extension of Congressional Clans through family and staff into other political arenas outside Washington seems to be an increasingly common phenomenon, but it is still a relatively new one. In this regard, the older and more traditional bonds of kinship have been supplemented by staffers as the vehicle for such extensions, thereby making kin and staff functional equivalents. With the election of a staffer or a family member to office, the Congressional Clan has come full circle. The entering freshman builds his organization, extends it throughout the congressional organization, branches out to include both bureaucrats and lobbyists in it, and then presides over the formation of subclans. With the election of his replacement, the cycle continues.

PART III

⋞§⋟

THE CONGRESSIONAL MYSTIQUE: RITUAL, MYTH, AND MAKEUP

The often chaotic feuding of clans, Big Men, and classes is held together by an arcane culture. Some of the congressional customs, such as the hazing of newcomers, were mentioned in discussing social organization; but the wider scope of Capitol Hill culture needs closer examination for a full appreciation of the legislative system. All too often the seemingly archaic procedures, odd speech forms, and quaint rituals of Congress are noted and then dismissed as nothing more than trivial bits of information. They are treated almost as a part of the scenery, picturesque background material not worthy of serious consideration. Marked as empty forms surviving from an earlier era, they seem inappropriate in understanding the real dynamics of contemporary politics.

Most of the rituals of legislation, however, are more than mere holdovers from the distant past: they are fairly modern inventions designed and inserted to play significant parts in the distribution and execution of power. The tedium and awkwardness with which they repeat, time and again, the same ceremonies, belie the function which these rituals supposedly embody. In the final analysis, the rituals form the warp and woof of the legislative tapestry, and around them the whole fabric of clans and subclans is woven into the strange dimensions and distorted hues of American politics and government.

8

⋖§⋗

The Ritual of Legislation

In the final years before the Aztec Empire fell to Hernando Cortes in 1521, the capital city of Mexico witnessed the sacrifice of untold thousands of Indians. Warriors, maidens, prisoners, and children were forced up the steep stairs of the numerous pyramids and sacrificed to gods with names such as Tlaloc, Uitzipopochtli, and Tlatecuhtli.

Upon entering the shrine chamber on top of the pyramid, the victim was grabbed by four priests. With one priest pulling each limb, he or she was then spread over a small stone altar in front of the jewel-encrusted idols. A fifth priest, his hair and fingers matted in dried blood and his face streaming with the fresh blood of the last sacrifice, approached, raised a flint knife, and inserted it into the chest of the victim. Being cautious not to harm the heart or to kill the victim prematurely and thus spoil the rite, the priest slit open the ribcage with surgical skill. With the beating heart exposed and the victim still conscious, the priest plunged his experienced fingers into the cavity, grasped the palpitating heart, and ripped it from the body. As the victim finally died in a paroxysm of pain and the twitching body was tossed down the stairs, the pulsating heart spurted out its last drops of blood and was thrown into a burning brazier of copal, a fragrant resin, where it slowly sizzled in honor of the god.

Depending on the occasion and the god to whom the offering was made, the procedures varied slightly. Sometimes the victim was slowly roasted almost to the point of death before the heart was extracted. For the awesome Tlaloc, who provided rain for the staple corn crop and was especially responsive to tears and screams, the sacrificial children suffered tortures even longer and more horrible than those of the normal victims. On other occasions sacred fires were kindled in the open hearts of victims, and carriers rushed torches ignited from the flame to other villages in the area.

No matter what the mode of execution, the victim's body rolled down the great pyramid steps and was seized by butchers, who carried it to a corner of the temple compound to be cut and cooked in huge vats. The limbs were consumed in ritual feasts or sometimes sold in the market square. The torso was used as animal food, particularly for the sacred rattlesnakes, which were hatched and raised in large number in the temples and the imperial zoo. The bones and skulls were hung up for decorations or sometimes used as building material.

Ritual human sacrifice has been practiced at one time or another in nearly every part of the world, including Europe. What is particularly unique about the Aztec example is not its gore, or even its cruelty, but its frequency. The level of sacrifices increased from the occasional execution of a prisoner of war or the periodic tossing of a virgin into a well to a continuous ritual affair. So many victims fell under the ritual knife that, according to Bernal Díaz, one of the few Europeans ever to witness it, the temple walls "were so splashed and caked with blood that they and the floor too were black." The exact number of sacrifices in Mexico each year is debatable. Estimates run from as low as 10,-000 to 15,000 to as high as a quarter of a million. What is certain, however, is that in the final decades of Aztec rule, the slaughter rate escalated to an unprecedented level. It was a ritual process gone amok. A mere ceremony had become a perpetual massacre industry, with the efficiency and monotony of an assembly line.

This industry employed over five thousand priests in the vicinity of the imperial capital of Tenochtitlán. Aiding the priests were the butchers and processors who cut and dressed the flesh, builders constructing ever larger pyramids on which to sacrifice, and artisans carving new images and decorating new shrines. The need for victims sent the army on repeated forays into enemy territory to capture the required thousands. Supporting the soldiers were more craftsmen making weapons, weaving cloth, cooking food, and raising the crops to feed them. Human sacrifice became the dominant activity of the capital city as an increasingly large horde of priests, warriors, and artisans engaged in some part of the ritual or practical tasks necessary to supply the thirsty Aztec gods with blood and hearts.

In the end, this ritual process helped to destroy the nation. When Cortes arrived on the Mexican coast, towns of subjugated and enemy Indians were quick to join him in the quest for liberation from the priest's knife and the tax collector's lists. The fabled Aztec troops fought with strategy developed for capturing the victims live rather than slaying them on the battlefield. With weapons meant to maim but not kill, they were no match for the booming cannons and the glistening steel of Spanish swords.

After the final conquest of Tenochtitlán and the suppression of human sacrifice by the Spanish, almost all the records and documents of the Aztecs were put to the torch by the zealous Christian priests. Today, we have little direct information to tell us how or why the empire changed from occasional sacrifice to perpetual slaughter. We can only make calculated surmises as to what made the ritual process whirl out of control until it ensnared the whole of Aztec life, society, and culture. According to some anthropologists, the volume of sacrifice arose from the need of the Aztecs for protein. They argue that the lack of large domestic animals such as pigs, cows, or sheep in the New World and the over-population of the Mexican plateau were the root causes of the escalation of sacrifices and cannibalism. A less materialist theory claims that the ritual process was simply a product of the religious and cultural beliefs. As Peter Farb puts it:

Once the Aztec religion initiated the practice of human sacrifice to forestall the cataclysms awaiting the people, it was trapped in a cycle of events. Sacrificial victims could be obtained only through war, yet war could be waged successfully only by sacrificing victims; and to obtain those victims, the Aztec first had to go to war. The loop of necessity thus expanded to include increasingly greater sacrificial offerings.

It is tempting to ascribe the Aztec sacrifices to the barbarism of American Indians, to some inexplicably bloodthirsty or cruel streak peculiar to the savage mind; but the facts of Indian life refute that claim. With its highly developed agriculture, detailed astronomy, heroic architecture, and meticulously precise mathematics, the Indian civilization in many ways surpassed that of its conquerors. How then could such a sophisticated nation fall prey to this cycle of rituals?

Oddly enough, some light may be cast on this puzzle by the two hundred years of ritual in the American Congress. In a far less dramatic fashion than the bloody sacrifices of the Aztecs, the American Congress slowly evolved a series of ceremonies that have recently escalated into a nearly all-consuming activity. More than just an idle exercise in the syntax of ritual, an examination of how this happened illuminates deep shortcomings and growing problems in contemporary American government. But before accounting for the results, we need to look at the roots of congressional ritual in the eighteenth-century Congress.

THE SEEDS OF CEREMONY

Congress convened for the first time on April Fool's Day, 1789, after an idle month waiting for a quorum of thirty out of the fifty-nine congressmen to arrive. Congress was a small, almost intimate affair, hardly larger than a contemporary congressional committee; indeed the whole Senate of 1789 could sit down to dinner together at the same table. Elaborate ceremony would have been completely out of place in such a small group, especially in light of the fact that many of the members were good friends with long working relationships, hardly a condition likely to foster ceremony or formality.

The first members of Congress had worked together in state

legislatures, in the Continental Congress, or the Constitutional Convention. Others had served together in the military campaigns of the Revolution and developed the fraternal bonds common to men who fight together for the same ideals. Many of them were related to each other by blood, coming from the same merchant and planter families of the Eastern Seaboard. Congressman Fisher Ames of Massachusetts called them a lot of "sober, solid, old-charter folks," who were definitely not "men of intrigue." Such men, with their various ties to one another, could assemble, speak plainly, and do the business at hand with minimal fanfare.

Meeting at first in New York City, and later in other towns on the East Coast, the Congress did not have a permanent home or space suitable to ceremony, even had one been desired. It convened in whatever cramped rooms were available, increasing the proclivity to proceed in an informal manner like a board of college trustees gathered for discussion in the back room of the student union building. The cramped quarters put them largely beyond the public eye and beyond the need for dramatic displays to the galleries or to reporters.

Nor was there much reason for the public to be very interested in what Congress was doing. The major decisions affecting the lives of the average citizen took shape in the state legislatures or town councils of the time, not in the Congress. Congress had less direct impact on them than the United Nations or the deliberations of the Organization of American States have on the average American today. Congress was a novelty, but not very significant. Even in novelty it ranked far below the presence in New York of George Washington, Revolutionary hero and the first elected President of the United States. An individual personality like Washington was certainly much more capable of inspiring interest or curiosity than an institution made up largely of unknowns. The business of those early congressional years was chiefly of a domestic nature—setting up house, so to speak. They were looking for a home, fixing rules for debate and procedure, establishing a judiciary, electing doorkeepers and clerks.

In the secluded, somewhat isolated environment of that early Congress, the legislative procedure was a simple one. Issues were raised in a meeting of the whole chamber. With participation open to everyone, the perimeters of the issue were sketched, the major direction of the legislation decided upon, and the primary points to be in the legislation agreed to. Having, in a few broad strokes, decided the thrust of the issue, a committee was chosen to draft all of that into a bill. After it accomplished the mission, the committee returned the drafted legislation to the whole body for inspection. If the bill was in agreement with the original instructions, the House passed it and the committee was disbanded. Operating in this fashion, the first session of Congress produced twenty-six bills from the House and five from the Senate. In effect these bills created an operating federal government, and their import is still highly visible in the contemporary Congress, courts, and the executive branch.

Thus was born the American government, but within it were some small seeds of ceremony that were to grow and blossom in the decades ahead. For the most part these early seeds were planted in the Senate. While the House performed the legislative duties involved in setting up a government, the Senate was pondering the metaphysics of its existence. No one in the country, least of all the members of the Senate itself, was quite sure what the Senate was supposed to do. Should it just revise bills from the House? Should it initiate its own bills? Or should it just confer with the President as a council of advisers? Some grounds for any of these options seemed to be in the Constitution, but the members were divided on the relative importance of each.

In the meantime, the Senate had more pressing business at hand. If the House was busy setting up the framework of federal government, then the Senate needed to set about decorating that framework with appropriately awesome majesty. Under Vice President John Adams, a committee of senators was established to decide on appropriate titles and ceremonies for the nation. They already had the constitutional title of "Senator," a name that sparkled with the pristine glory of Rome, but what about the word "President"? Adams found this much too common and prosaic, being a name he insisted the people would despise "to all eternity." After weeks of deliberation, the best title they could envisage was "His Highness, the President of the

United States of America and Protector of the Rights of the Same." It had a ring to it, reminiscent of the king of England's title as "Defender of the Faith" or the title of the Ethiopian emperor as the "Lion of Judea," but it did not seem just right.

As has since often been the case with important congressional decisions, the debate continued so long that before it could be decided, the problem dissolved. In this case the people began calling George Washington "Mr. President," a very simple, even pedestrian title, but one that took root. Though congressmen, senators, judges, and even state legislators and traffic court judges have the title of "Honorable," the President of the United States never received a proper title, a shortcoming that haunted Adams to his grave. The President is also the only constitutional official in America who can be addressed directly, in the second person, without the circumlocutions of third-person phrases such as "Your Honor," "If the bench will permit," or "The chair decrees."

The title of the President was not the only pressing problem entertained by the Senate in those early sessions. The whole matter of official protocol had to be decided. If they were not to use the court procedures of Europe, so loved by Adams from his lengthy sojourn there, how then were official acts to be undertaken? Should the Vice President stand when the President entered the room? How should messages be sent to the Senate from the House of Representatives? Should the messenger bow? Should the President have a small throne installed in the Senate?

Most of these issues and precedents were decided by happenstance and not by the decisions of Adams or the other senators. The messengers from the House barged in, but did bow, as they still do today. The President simply arrived and was announced; no trumpets were necessary. The upshot of Adams's concern was that he was dubbed "His Rotundity" by Senator Ralph Izard of South Carolina, and pushed over to the White House as the second President of the United States, confronting him with the perplexing problem of who should walk first in the inaugural procession. Washington himself decided that issue by proclaiming that as the new President, Adams definitely had to take priority over the past President. For the four years of his term, Adams then fretted over who should call upon whom and in what order their appearances would be made. Even though most of Adams's ideas were never adopted by the Congress or in the practices of the citizenry, they did begin the ceremonial process in Congress—a process that has grown and flourished ever since.

Despite the assiduous admonitions of Adams, the early Congress remained inimical to ceremony, pomp, and formal procedure. Not until it moved to Washington, D.C., did this attitude against ritual soften and give way to a more stylized approach. The change originated in the altered composition of the Congress in the nineteenth century and in the growing attention of the voters.

After the novelty of having a government and a President had worn off and it slowly became apparent that the decisions being made in Congress did have import on the lives of the citizens, there was increasing demand to open the proceedings. The House, even in cramped quarters, was generally open to the public, but the Senate was resolutely closed. The closed doors raised public suspicion and at least some desire to watch the ceremonial antics of John Adams in person as he presided over the Senate. These suspicions and jokes were fed by a constant trickle of rumors and reports seeping from the cloistered Senate. Some senators, of course, found it expedient to add to the gossip as a way of fortifying public opinion behind their own political positions.

Despite severe precautions to keep it secret, the entire text of John Jay's treaty normalizing American relations with England was leaked to the press by Senator Pierce Butler, thus initiating another government tradition. Butler had strong reservations about the impact of the treaty on the trade from his home city of Charleston, South Carolina, to the Caribbean. By making the treaty public, he rallied support from commercial interests around the country. Other senators were quick to grasp the expediency of such a tactic, and selected parts of every issue were swiftly leaked and published in the newspapers. It was difficult for two dozen politicians to keep anything secret, and the difficulty only increased with each new state admitted to the union.

After several years of public pressure and the repeated requests of state legislatures, the Senate, rather cautiously, opened its sessions to the public in December of 1795. The galleries of both houses of Congress have remained open almost continuously ever since. As recently as 1980, the House did have a closed session to consider funding of the Panama Canal Treaty. Except for the most sensitive issues, however, the proceedings are conducted in full public view. Beginning in 1979, the proceedings of the House have been televised and available to various parts of the country on a full-time basis, with expectation that the slower Senate will eventually follow suit.

The new-found interest in congressional activities increased when the migratory Congress stopped wandering up and down the northeastern corridor and settled on the banks of the Potomac. As of 1800 the Congress fixed itself on Jenkins Hill in reasonably sized, though temporary, quarters. Thus situated, with its public galleries, Congress was easy to watch. Petitioners always knew where it was, and newspapers could arrange to have permanent coverage of its activities.

By the time Congress settled in Washington, the House had already grown to 150 members, but it was trying to operate under the same easygoing procedures as when it had only half that number. Not only had the number of members increased, but the number of bills rose even more rapidly, thus necessitating ever more ad hoc committees to deal with each one. The 3rd Congress alone had over 350 select committees in operation to write and process these bills—four times as many committees as congressmen.

A DANCING ELEPHANT

The combination of increased size and increased publicity had a profound impact on congressional procedure: it became markedly more cumbersome. Particularly in the House, a meeting of over a hundred congressmen surrounded by even more onlookers was not conducive to careful legislative thought. There were more members to speak on each issue and there were more issues, as well as diverse constituencies needing representation. No longer were the congressmen speaking just to each other; they had to weigh the potential impact their words or their silences might have on the audience in the gallery and, more importantly, on the unseen voters watching through the eyes of newspaper reporters. This awkward state of affairs was criticized by Massachusetts Congressman Fisher Ames (1758–1808), who served in the first four Congresses and wrote that in floor proceedings, "a great, clumsy machine is applied to the slightest and most delicate operations—the hoof of an elephant to the strokes of mezzotinto."

A dancing elephant aptly described the chaotic atmosphere of floor proceedings: "Major debates and contests for oratorical preeminence were played to a packed house in a carnival atmosphere, supplies of popcorn and candy being dispatched from the floor to the galleries in slings attached to fishing poles." Members wrote letters, ate lunch, or met with constituents all around the floor. Even the hunting dogs of Congressman John Randolph (1772–1833) were given the run of the chamber. Randolph represented Virginia intermittently from 1799 until 1827, going progressively insane throughout the period, and thereby adding to both the comedy and the pathos of floor proceedings with his antics, babblings, and duels. In the midst of all this, vendors roamed selling refreshments, souvenirs, and political advice.

Throughout the nineteenth century Washington remained a frontier town, and the biggest show of interest remained the Congress. As it grew, most of the increase in members came from the frontier states such as Ohio, Kentucky, and Mississippi. These rough-and-ready types in coonskin hats contrasted greatly with the founding fathers who had met in the cosmopolitan and sophisticated atmosphere of Philadelphia and New York. Gentlemanly debate and discussion were more likely to become a fist fight or pistol duel in the frontier culture of Washington politics. Piercing arguments could give way to Bowie knives and leisurely debate to ludicrous brawls. Rome had its Circus Maximus; Washington had its Congress.

In such an atmosphere, legislating was impractical. Gradually the business of government slipped outside the public eye, away from the chamber floor. Increasingly, congressmen met in small groups off the floor to reach a consensus or to plan strategy for directing a bill through the chaotic chamber. The floor show continued, but the decisions were made backstage. Federalist Congressman Josiah Quincy (1772–1864) of Boston complained that the House "acts, and reasons, and votes and performs all the operations of an animated being, and yet, judging from my own perceptions, I cannot refrain from concluding that all great political questions are settled elsewhere than on this floor." Under such conditions, Quincy chose to leave Congress in 1813, returning to the Massachusetts Senate and eventually becoming president of Harvard University far from the maddening politics of Washington.

This anarchy on the floor and politicking off the floor were particularly criticized by the anti-Jefferson faction. Connecticut Congressman Roger Griswold said that the supporters of Jefferson, "finding themselves unable to manage their business on the questions in the House, have adopted the plan of meeting in divan and agreeing on measures to be pursued and passed." Griswold went on to charge that the "wickedness of such a course has never been equalled but by the Jacobin Club of Paris."

The "elsewhere" referred to by Quincy and the "in divan" of Griswold were anywhere that the members could find refuge from the galleries. They fled to dining rooms and boarding houses in the area, to caucus rooms, or to the ad hoc committees. Gradually, they formalized the committee system as the most convenient way to make decisions offstage. Since the issues could not be resolved on the floor, they would be referred to a committee where, out of the limelight, rational politics could be pursued. In time, the importance of committees surpassed that of the parties, caucuses, state delegations, and boarding-house cliques as the decision-making structure within Congress.

With the legislative activities safely isolated in the committee rooms, the floor was free for full-time theatrics. No longer need members address their remarks to one another—they could do that in the committee rooms while making real decisions. Their floor performances could now be addressed solely to the audience in the gallery and the newspaper readers throughout the nation. The importance of the audience to this performance was so obvious that even a visitor from czarist Russia recognized it. In his 1857 report, Alexander Borisovich Lakier stated that "most of the orators are verbose and it seems that more often than not their purpose is to satisfy the expectations of their constituents and the party to which they belong." Similar feelings were expressed by the British observer Lord Bryce:

> The speeches are made not to convince the assembly—no one dreams of that—but to keep a man's opinions before the public and sustain his fame. The question at issue has usually been already settled, either in a committee or in a "caucus" of the party which commands the majority, so that these long and sonorous harangues are mere rhetorical thunder addressed to the nation outside.

Thus, the showmanship of Congress separated from the actual decision making. Members were free in the public arena to play to their audience without interfering with the substantive work backstage. The floor became the political arena in which public reputations were cultivated and presidential ambitions were nourished. Through their performances on the floor of Congress, men such as Calhoun, Lincoln, and Clay became figures of national renown, and debating skills became the key to turn an unknown local politician into a respected statesman and presidential contender.

Congress changed from a circus to a continuous drama. It was the stage on which the national myths were enacted. In a sense, Congress was the prototype of the soap opera Americans have since come to love. Something dramatic is always about to happen, but nothing is ever resolved; old crises merely fade out of attention as one emotionally laden episode supersedes another. The issues of slavery, tariffs, and war were the dramatic themes for these shows, but little was actually being decided. The superstars of the era were the great congressional orators Webster, Calhoun, Clay, and Hayne, but as orators they were acting, not legislating. Slavery, the greatest issue of all, was decided on the bloody battlefields of the South and by presidential fiat, not by the debates of Congress. In six decades of passionate debate, Congress produced only the pitiful Missouri Compromise. Not until after the war and emancipation of the slaves did Congress add its assent to a fait accompli by passing not one, but two constitutional amendments.

While the committees churned out laws on taxation, expenditures, canals, pensions, and the details of bureaucratic administration, the bigger issues of the day thrashed irresolutely on the floor. There, the drama acted out the abstract themes of states' rights, individual liberties, and national pride, since these topics provided more dramatic shows than budget overviews and technical questions. As Lord Bryce described it, "Most of the political work is done in the standing committees while much of the House's time is consumed in pointless discussions where member after member delivers himself upon large questions, not likely to be brought to a definite issue."

Long before Americans became enthralled by the spectacles of professional sports and of Hollywood, they cut their teeth on the spectacle of the Congress. This dramatic arena made superstars, Presidents, and heroes, but not laws. The Civil War ended the era of great dramas on the floor. Ritual fights and verbal duels held little interest for a people savaged by the real blood of fratricidal war. Just as importantly, the war settled the more emotional issues; slavery, states' rights, and even the Indian threat were non-issues by the second half of the century. Until the rise of populism in the 1890s, there were few dramatic vehicles for the great orators. Floor proceedings sank into relative obscurity as committees concentrated on the details of reconstructing the South, conquering the West, building railroads, and opening markets everywhere.

Throughout the nineteenth century the legislative process operated on two tiers—the public arena of the chamber floor and the political arena of the committee rooms. By the time of Reconstruction, after the public arena had lost most of its public, Congress was no longer a stage from which members could play to the nation as a whole. Instead, they used it for small performances aimed at their local constituents. Members would use the floor as a platform on which to introduce special bills that had no chance of passing but pleased some segment of their constituency. They would deliver speeches as a way of supplying excerpts from the *Congressional Record* to impress the home voters. The form of legislative drama was maintained, but without any dramatic content. These political phenomena of empty actions and meaningless strings of words designed to appear significant to a small, distant audience necessitated a new word.

The new word coined in Congress was "bunk." The name derived from the otherwise unknown career of Felix Walker, congressman from the mountains of North Carolina. His home county was Buncome, and Walker was forever rising to "say a few words for Buncome." Eventually the phrase became synonymous with meaningless rhetoric designed to impress a small constituency. In time the phrase was reduced to "bunk" and passed into general parlance as an appropriate description of politics.

In the darkness of public inattention, the empty dramas of the floor proceedings became ritual bunk. The dramatic form of debate and legislative procedure was maintained as though it really were a decision-making process, but it was only a facade. As Woodrow Wilson described it: "The House sits not for serious discussion, but to sanction the conclusions of its Committees as rapidly as possible. It legislates in its committee-rooms." The floor sessions were only shadowy images on the wall of a Platonic cave: "even the speeches made in the Senate, free, full, and earnest as they seem, are made, so to speak, after the fact—not to determine the actions but to air the opinions of the body." The same description was painted by Lord Bryce when he said that each senator "brings down and fires off in the air, a carefully prepared oration which may have little bearing on what has gone before." Alexander Lakier, the Russian observer, did not think that the speeches were particularly well prepared. As he described these attempts at oratory, "their speeches are not distinguished by either profound thought or elegant style."

Congress had passed from being the forum in which decisions were actually made to being a stage in which great public dramas were enacted, and finally became a ritual arena in which only the form but not the substance of the two prior eras remained. Cold and moribund, the floors of Congress continue today to witness the needless parade of legislative ritual. Still couched in the archaic language of the eighteenth century, the floor is the final stopping point in the inaugural parade of a bill—full of pomp and circumstance, but void of anything more.

The floor consideration of a bill in the chamber of the Congress is merely the bestowing of legitimacy on a bill, the fate of which was decided elsewhere. As Woodrow Wilson said: "The voting and speaking in the House are generally merely the movements of a sort of dress parade." Congressman Sydney Anderson of Minnesota denounced the system even more severely in 1913:

> It is true that I am still permitted to cast my vote, but I do so with the foreknowledge that it will not count. The votes are counted and the return made up before my vote is cast.
>
> It is true that I may still offer an amendment, but though that amendment was suggested by the Apostle Paul it could not be adopted.
>
> It is true that I may still lift my voice in argument, but though my logic were as irresistible as the tide of human progress itself, and though I spoke with the voice of the angel Gabriel, I could not change a line or sentence of the bill.

In this way, Congress preserves the format of legislative procedure—the appearance of debate and decision without any of the substance. It is as much a ritualized act as was the sacrifice of prisoners on the pyramids of the Aztecs. Often, even the Aztecs allowed a prisoner the right to defend himself in something like a mock battle, but the outcome was never in doubt. In the end, the predetermined course was completed and the valiant warrior was sacrificed.

Occasionally, on the floor of the House or Senate a fight may actually erupt, and the public in the galleries gets a glimpse of a real political struggle. In much the same way, an occasional Aztec prisoner probably fought hard, with all his might, and may have wounded or even killed a priest in the process; but in the end his fate was no different than if he had willingly laid across the altar stone. The whole process was a breach in the decorum of sacrifice, a dramatic interlude in the ceremony, but of little more importance.

In some regards, occasional outbursts, whether from a victim going to slaughter or from a junior congressman, can actually help to reinforce the power of the ceremony and the ritual power of Aztec priests or Congressional Big Men. As the anthropologist Georges Balandier explains, the "supreme ruse of power is to allow itself to be contested ritually in order to consolidate itself more effectively."

The powers-that-be are reinforced in their power, yet the semblance of dissent is tolerated, in the end reinforcing the legitimacy of the ones in power and fostering an appearance of democratic process.

THE CREEPING VINE OF RITUAL

During the second half of the nineteenth century the committee system was firmly ensconced in the legislative process; for most practical regards, it was the legislative system. Senator George Hoar described it as rule by a handful of "little legislatures." Each of these was in turn ruled by the chairman.

Political analyses such as those of Woodrow Wilson and James Bryce helped stir American awareness of the committee system and the abuses of their chairmen. In the generation following the Civil War, Americans grew especially suspicious of secret deals and political cabals. The corruption of the Grant administration, the excesses of Reconstruction, the spectacular rise of the robber barons, and the inexplicable economic fluctuations, all fed the anxieties of an already mistrustful public. Observers were not fooled by the empty dramas of the congressional process and they soon demanded access to the back rooms where legislative power was exercised.

Congress effectively prevented such access. All stages of the committee process were closed to outsiders, including most of Congress's own small staff. Records were not made of bill drafting, amendment consideration, or votes cast. The press and the public had access to the bills as they were reported out on the congressional floor, and nothing more. The leaks and charges of unfair tactics or undue influence heightened public mistrust of the proceedings, but were not informative enough to illuminate the backstage machinations.

To insulate the working sessions of committees even further from the public spectacles of congressional politics, Congress opened two new office buildings in the first decade of this century. These marble fortresses, one for the House and one for the

Senate, moved the working sessions out of the Capitol and across the street. Now, rather than acting solely as backstage areas to the big show on the chamber floor, the committee sessions took place in their own private edifices. This left the Capitol as a public showplace and temple of democracy, but without the clutter of political action. Tourists and citizens could have the run of the building, and the great Drama of Democracy could be enacted relatively unimpaired by the messy work of legislation.

The office buildings were connected to the Capitol by underground tunnels, so that the members could dash across to the chamber floor for their appropriate appearances, and then return quickly to their work rooms. The office buildings were very much the private realm of the committees. There were neither signs nor door plaques to assist the unwanted visitor, nor were there any toilet facilities for the public—a clear indication that the public was not invited.

Rather than insulating committee work, however, removing it to a side building served to magnify public awareness of the committees and suspicion about their doings. It increased the pressure to open the meetings, and at the same time it vitiated one of the Congress's primary excuses for not opening sessions: lack of space. When the committees met in small back rooms of the Capitol, there was some truth to the argument that there simply was no room for the public in the crowded little cubicles; but in their new location, this argument did not hold. Each committee had built for itself a monumental hall in the new building—stages waiting for their own dramas to be enacted. The wait was not long.

On the floor of the chamber each senator may be just another face in the crowd, but in the committee room, each senator can be a king in his one-room Versailles. At first these public audiences were rare, but with public demand to see all the committees at work, Congress passed the Legislative Reorganization Act of 1946. After that, all committee hearings were to be open to the public and press. This allowed the public into one phase of committee activity. They could observe the committee taking testimony from the people interested in the bill: the government bureaucrats, lobbyists, voter groups, and a few constituents from the members' home districts. During these hearings, the members of the committee questioned the witnesses, but for the most part the members did not discuss the issues with each other. This was not the part of the process in which they voted, considered amendments, or engaged in substantive acts of legislation. The hearing was merely an exploratory session, an inquiry into a problem.

Immediately, however, the hearings became more elaborate affairs. In 1947, the year following the Reorganization Act, the full potential of these events burst forth on the American public. The House Caucus Room was outfitted with klieg lights and HUAC entered American history. The House Un-American Activities Committee under Chairman J. Parnell Thomas became the star attraction of every newspaper and Movietone news in the nation. Under the guise of a search for America's enemies, Thomas united in one grand show the glamor of Hollywood, the suspense of espionage, the excitement of Weltpolitik, and the majesty of the United States Congress. Movie stars, producers, writers, and musicians marched before the peering eyes of the committee, revealing not only their political beliefs but their sexual practices and everything else that Thomas wanted to know. When one witness balked at this invasion of privacy, Thomas barked: "The rights you have are the rights given you by this committee."

Not to be outdone by the House, the Senate opened its own show in the Senate Caucus Room. Under Senator Owen Brewster and the Senate War Investigating Committee, a similar scenario was enacted on the themes of war profiteering and, in particular, of any possible collusion between millionaire Howard Hughes and President Franklin Roosevelt. In place of FDR was his son Elliot, who had to answer charges about his deceased father. Brewster brought forth to the committee room all that HUAC had to offer on the other side of the Hill—Hollywood sex parties, bribery, treason, and war. But Brewster surpassed the HUAC show by combining all of that with the themes of high finance, big money, and the mythical aura of the Roosevelt White House. Brewster's superior performance in putting together his show was capped when his hearings became the first set of congressional hearings to be televised live from the Capitol.

Brewster and Thomas inaugurated the era of committee hearings on the air. They set a format that was to be followed for the next three decades. Hearings became public dramas reminiscent of the floor proceedings before the Civil War. The nation was shocked, titillated, and fascinated as one committee after another tried to outdo the last show. Estes Kefauver brought the nation Mafia dons and the terror of organized crime. Joseph McCarthy combined the techniques of Brewster (on whose committee McCarthy had served) with the subject matter of Thomas's HUAC committee and gave the nation several years of congressional spy trials. Nixon took on Alger Hiss; John McClellan took on business management. Not since the days of Webster, Clay, and Calhoun had the nation been so intrigued by the goings-on in Congress.

Just as the chamber floor had been the public arena in which national politicians were fashioned from local ones in the nineteenth century, now the committee hearing became the forum in which to nourish presidential ambitions. Radio and television brought the proceedings into every home, and it provided the politicians with an even better forum than the moribund floor. On the chamber floor, members could only play off one another in "debate," but in televised hearings, they could bring forth the full panoply of their acting and entertaining talents. It may be difficult for a senator to come out as the unquestioned white hat in a floor debate with another senator, but in confronting a Mafia don or a communist spy, there is no doubt as to who are the good guys and who the bad. Senators could arrange a whole performance with all the special effects of television— not just the dry facts and occasional charts of a floor presentation, but real live criminals, suitcases of blood money, dying cancer patients, children, and animals. The whole committee could be whisked away to the far corners of the globe for on-the-spot investigations or confrontations. The potential spectacle was limited only by the imagination of the members of Congress and their staffs.

The era of committee drama coincided with the public career of Richard Nixon. It was Thomas's HUAC committee hearings that launched Nixon before the public eye in 1948, and it was Sam Ervin's Watergate Hearings that finished his career in 1974.

The era could have easily been called the Kennedy era. The Kennedy brothers received their first national attention during the McCarthy hearings, in which young Robert Kennedy worked as counsel to McCarthy and John Kennedy was a fellow committee member. This was followed by the Kefauver hearings, in which Robert Kennedy also popped up after switching to Kefauver's Democratic staff. Edward Kennedy abandoned his brother's role of Cold War Warrior against crime and communism to become the Beneficent Benefactor of the Huddled Masses, but the format was essentially the same. Instead of communists and criminals, Ted Kennedy brought forth the crippled and cancerous. Even after their assassinations, both Robert and John were symbolically dragged forward for the gruesome travesty of the House Special Investigations on Assassinations in 1978. This gory postmortem over a decade after the murders failed to excite much more than disgust in the public, and none of its hearings was televised.

In their heyday, committee hearings inspired a sense of drama matched only by the concurrently popular Perry Mason. Spies and traitors were exposed in live legislative theater, just as Perry Mason exposed criminals with his daring courtroom antics. Fact and fantasy, truth and fiction were as intertwined and inseparable in congressional hearings as they were on television.

The public is gullible for only so long, or perhaps they are willing to watch the same television series for only so long. In any event, interest in the congressional hearing waned, and the public turned to doctor programs and situation comedies. The last great spectacle of the era, the Watergate Hearings, showed the whole system for what it was—an orchestrated performance. The degree to which the hearings were planned in advance was apparent to everyone who could read in the morning newspaper what "dramatic revelations" would be forthcoming in that afternoon's hearings. Just as the newspapers published a summary of the evening's detective and medical dramas, the reporters summarized the testimony of each witness before his or her appearance.

The sole dramatic revelation to unfold publicly was Alexander Butterfield's testimony about the existence of the Nixon tapes, but even this apparently spontaneous confession was preplanned and scripted. The entire story had already emerged in closed sessions with the staff, who had decided it would be more dramatic to reveal it in "question and answer" format rather than in the written testimony. Like the floor in the nineteenth century, the committee hearing had passed from an action arena where decisions were made to a theatrical arena in which shows were performed. And once the drama had been thoroughly milked, Congress was left with another ritual proceeding.

In form if not in substance, the hearings still resemble those of the McCarthy days. An outraged senator spews forth a series of "spontaneous" comments for a sixty-second spot on the evening news. Another member tosses out a series of epithets and *bon mots* in the hope that one might be picked up in a newspaper headline. A third poses with pencil fiercely pointed at the accused in hopes of getting a picture in the local paper. To aid in the process, all manner of witnesses and props are still brought forward. Senators troop out to visit a hazardous waste dump, bring in geiger counters to take radioactivity readings in Congress, drive around the parking lot in alcohol-powered cars. Every hearing begins with the regular appearance of a star witness to capture public attention and highlight the work of that committee. Whether it is Elizabeth Taylor testifying on why Congress should award John Wayne a medal, Rosalyn Carter on mental health, or the Reverend Jesse Jackson on education, each hearing begins with the media personality and slowly works through a list of lesser knowns.

The hearing is only one stage in the committee phase of legislation. Even after the hearings had been made public, members could still work together behind the scenes in bill-drafting sessions and in mark-up sessions where bills were amended. The privacy of this domain held for a quarter century after hearings had been opened to the public. As the public became saturated with drama that showed no relation to legislative product and bored with the hearings, there were greater demands for access to these back rooms as well.

This too was changed in the Watergate episode. With the public demand for more openness in government and the public realization that the Watergate Hearings were not a real look behind the scenes, both chambers opened the entire committee process of bill drafting and mark-up to the public. First in the House in 1973, and then in the Senate in 1975 immediately after the Watergate Hearings, the entire process was exposed. By and large, however, the general public was not captivated by this behind-the-scenes look. The committees were already playing to small audiences, and for the most part opening the other phases of consideration did not greatly expand these audiences. What public attention there was on committees did change from the hearings to the mark-up sessions where decisions were "being made." In the House, consideration of the Nixon impeachment basked in the public limelight for a few days, but no other mark-up session received quite the same following. The mark-up of the Panama Canal Treaty was broadcast on public radio and the mark-up of the Salt II Treaty was broadcast on public television. But they played to small audiences, and none of the commercial stations was interested.

Without passing through a period as a dramatic arena, mark-ups went quickly from the real decision-making phase to being only another part of committee ritual. Amendments were proposed, debated, withdrawn, and passed with as much predictability as they were on the chamber floor. The busy public hardly noticed that there was a difference between the hearings they had seen on television and the mark-ups.

With the meetings of the committees fully public through all the steps of legislation, only the conference remained as a private forum in which members of Congress could sit down together and hash out legislative decisions. The conference is the stage in consideration that comes *after* a bill has passed both houses. The conference is composed of a few members from the relevant committees in each House meeting together to iron out any differences in the two houses' versions of the bills. Conferences have been a part of legislation since the 1st Congress, but before the 1960s they were little understood outside of Congress. Even though it occurred after the bill had supposedly passed, the conference became increasingly important as the juncture at which legislation was being written.

In the late seventies the conference committees were opened to the public. For the most part, conferees tried to resist public exposure, mainly through the technical considerations of calling conferences at the most inopportune times and in the most remote and smallest rooms of the Capitol, with space for only a few reporters and a handful of lobbyists. Bulky camera equipment and lights are inappropriate. Nevertheless, the conference is a public forum reported by the newspapers, and members cannot pass the opportunity to make their publicity plays. The nation has been treated to ever-lengthening scenarios of standoffs between conferees, particularly with regard to appropriations.

By the time Congress completed its second century, the entire legislative process had been ritualized. As each arena in the long procedure was opened to the public, it went through a brief flurry of attention and high drama, but with the exposure, the essence of politics retreated further backstage. The public quickly tired of the repetitive dramas and followed the decision making further backstage to turn another political arena into a dramatic stage, leaving the neglected arena an empty shell. The transition from action to drama to ritual was repeated in each congressional arena until the entire process had been ritualized. The procedure is redundant and ceremonial, yet it is still the path each bill follows in becoming law. It is the path, but no longer the process. For the real process of legislation has once again escaped beyond the klieg lights.

In a far more prosaic and pedestrian fashion, the creeping ritualization of Congress portrays much the same process as that of the escalating sacrifices of the Aztecs. What began as a minor affair involving the occasional sacrifice of one or two prisoners grew to become an all-encompassing, never-ending cycle of ritual sacrifices. What began as a minor issue in the Congress of 1789 about what to call the President and who should walk in front of whom grew in the intervening centuries to an all-encompassing, never-ending cycle of ritual politics. The process is so long that even a bill such as that to create the Department of Education may have a majority of all the senators co-sponsor it and still take several years to work its way through the sequence of rituals.

For the Aztecs, the ritual process contained the seeds of their own destruction and eventually brought their civilization crashing down around them. The results of the civic rituals of America may not be as spectacular, but the ultimate results are profound and far-reaching.

9

Tower of Babel

At the end of a long day sacrificing virgins and warriors, when the Aztec priest finally wiped off his knife and put it down there was the very practical problem of what to do with all those bodies. The mutilated, heartless corpses piled up by the hundreds, and then there was that blood all over the pyramid, as well as the excrement and urine released by terrified dying victims.

The Aztec solution for getting rid of all the flesh was fairly straightforward: the bodies were butchered and eaten or fed to the animals in the imperial zoo. Even when the meat was gone, however, there was still a large residue of bones—thousands of skulls, femurs, and countless ribs and finger bones. Such a vast number of bones was not easily disposed of. To bury them would take up a great deal of important land space in a country already pressed for both farming land and residential property; nor could they be used for many practical purposes, in the way that the bones of smaller animals could be rendered into tools. Occasionally, bones could be used as filler in building a new temple; but overall, bones do not make good construction materials, certainly not as appropriate as stone or wood.

The Aztecs never found a very good solution to that vast residue of their sacrifices, but they had to do something with the bones. So they used as many as they could for decoration. Skulls hung from rafters and filled niches in the temple walls; they were piled around doorways to the sacred chambers. But still bones and more bones spewed out of the temples at a rapidly increasing rate. The bones piled up in the courtyards and temple squares and spilled out into the market squares. Sometimes they were neatly stacked; other times they just piled up in growing heaps. The piles of bones became small towers and eventually large towers. Bernal Díaz described one such pile in the plaza of Xocotlan: "[There] were piles of human skulls so neatly arranged that we could count them, and I reckoned them at more than a hundred thousand. I repeat that there were more than a hundred thousand of them."

At another site in Mexico City, there was an even larger pile. Díaz described one compound as being filled with "skulls and large bones arranged in an orderly pattern, and so numerous that you could not count them however long you looked." A later chronicler, Andres de Tapia, with the help of Gonzalo de Umbria, used modern math to count the number of layers or sticks on which the bones rested and multiplied by the number of skulls on each layer. By this count they came up with the total of 136,000 skulls in that one tower.

All of these towers and heaps were eventually destroyed and removed by the Spanish, but their existence brings up one of the many problems of rituals. Ceremonies produce a by-product, a ritual residue left over after the excitement. Whether it is a thousand tons of confetti and ticker tape on the streets of New York after a parade, wreaths of dried flowers after a funeral, or the hundreds of thousands of Aztec skulls, something must be done with this ritual residue.

The ritual residue of Congress was dramatized by West Virginia Senator Matthew Neely at the end of the 82nd Congress in 1951. He hauled on to the floor of the Senate and stacked up all of the *Congressional Records* for that one session. Congressional loquacity filled 100 pounds of paper, each page of which was covered with three columns of very small print. Neely called this construction a virtual "Tower of Babel," and insisted that its true dimensions were many times what was displayed, if the committee reports and records of hearings were added. Lacking the strength or the staff to bring all of it in, he decided to make his point with only a portion of the total *Congressional Record* for that session.

This stack of records points out a major difference in the ritual residue of a highly literate society such as the United States and societies with lower literacy rates. Once a society becomes literate, it seems compelled to record rituals in increasing detail. Ceremonies become events performed more for posterity and the historical record than for the immediate benefit of the participants or spectators. This record may begin as a simple document, such as a certificate of marriage or baptism, or a tablet containing the words of a law voted on by the tribal assembly. Invariably, it soon leads to detailed descriptions of the entire event and mounds of accompanying speeches. Just as the simple marriage certificate gives way to scrapbooks, lists of guests, registers of gifts, and in the twentieth century to albums of photographs and home movies, so too do legislative rituals become memorialized in an ever-growing Tower of Babel, which records far more trivia than substance.

TABOO AND MANA

Ceremony operates best in a symbolically rich setting that calls for special seating arrangements, particular forms of dress, and various ritual accoutrements such as crosses, thrones, flags, and maces. The full panoply of these objects marches around the congressional chamber in the process of legislation, but it is in the peculiar use of ritual language that the real nature of congressional ceremony emerges. Because of the sanctity of words, special speech forms are often used in many different societies to separate normal human interaction from interactions with particularly powerful beings such as gods or emperors. In European nations, God is addressed in the archaic "thee"; emperors, kings, and popes use the royal "we" and must be addressed obliquely as "your highness," "your excellency," or "your holiness" rather than directly.

Taboos on the use of personal names and certain pronouns reach an inordinate level in the American Congress, where neither the words "I" nor "you" are proper. Nor can the legislators address one another directly by name, as in "Edward Kennedy," "Ted," or even the more formal "Senator Kennedy." A simple phrase such as "I would like to ask you" becomes "Mr. President, the Senator from Texas would like to ask the Senator from California." The speaker must always act as though he were speaking to the presiding officer, or, in congressional parlance, to the "chair," never directly to another person. In simple statements the odd form of speech is easily understood despite its awkwardness, but it quickly disintegrates when a member really tries to say something. This is evident in a classic attempt of Senator Lyndon Johnson to say to Senator Knowland of California: "I want you to know that I did not feel criticized by your statement." In congressional parlance it came out as: "The Senator from Texas does not have any objection, and the Senator from Texas wishes the Senator from California to know that the Senator from Texas knew the Senator from California did not criticize him."

Such forms of address rather clearly separate congressional discourse from the more common varieties. The practice is so difficult to understand that in recent years members have been allowed to use an occasional "I" intermittently with their titles, but the ban on that three-letter word, "you," endures as strongly as ever. The more simplified version of the 1980s is evident in this excerpt from House debate, in which members refer to one another as "the gentleman" rather than "the Senator":

MR. KAZEN:	Mr. Chairman, will the gentleman yield?
MR. BAUMAN:	Mr. Chairman, will the gentleman yield?
MR. RUDD:	I yield to the gentleman.
MR. KAZEN:	I think the gentleman has yielded to the gentleman from Texas. Has the gentleman from Arizona yielded to me?
MR. RUDD:	Did I answer the question of the gentleman from Texas?
MR. KAZEN:	No.
MR. BAUMAN:	Mr. Chairman, will the gentleman from Arizona yield to the gentleman from Maryland?

Mr. Rudd: I yield to the gentleman from Maryland.
Mr. Bauman: I thank the gentleman for yielding.

The introduction of the word "I" has rendered congressional speech much simpler, though still rather convoluted. Even in the bewigged and aristocratic House of Lords, such elaborate circumlocutions are not used. The Lords actually address one another directly as "My Lord," eschewing the indirect mode of speech "through the chair."

This manner of speech poses an even greater problem when written down for the record. Some use of personal names must be used in the published forms, otherwise it would be impossible to know which of the two senators from Nebraska or the forty-three gentlemen from California is being referred to. The names of the speakers are therefore written to the side of the speech, as in the above example. If a senator must be referred to when he is not in the room, his name is then placed in parentheses next to the title:

Mr. Cranston: I announce that the Senator from Massachusetts (Mr. KENNEDY) and the Senator from Florida (Mr. STONE) are necessarily absent.
Mr. Stevens: I announce that the Senator from Tennessee (Mr. BAKER) and the Senator from Pennsylvania (Mr. HEINZ) are necessarily absent.

Personal names are taboo in speech; and even in writing they must be handled with special care, written in capital letters and enclosed in parentheses. They become *nomina sacra,* which cannot be written in the normal fashion. Just as the names of Egyptian royalty were enclosed in a cartouche when written, the names of congressmen and senators are set off in parentheses in a different form of type. Such practices were common among the ancient Hebrews, who could not write the name of Jehovah, but used a special set of abbreviated symbols to refer to it, or among the Greeks and Romans, who often used analogous special forms for indicating the name of mythical gods or the Christian God. The names of normal mortals who appear in the *Congressional Record* are written in the normal fashion, as in: "I would like to congratulate Mr. John Doe of Gitler's Knob on his one-hundredth birthday." Only members of Congress qualify for the *nomina sacra* form.

The name taboo encourages the proliferation of titles in an almost Teutonic fashion. Senators become "my distinguished colleague and esteemed friend, the Senior Senator from Massachusetts" or "the respected Ranking Minority Member of the Judiciary Committee." This use of titles in preference to names occurs in tribal councils throughout the world, from Africa to the South Pacific, and even among Indian tribes in North America. A close parallel to present congressional usage comes from the Iroquois councils of New York. The Council of the League of the Iroquois was composed of five Indian nations—Mohawk, Oneida, Onondaga, Cayuga, and Seneca. These were divided into fifty groups, or sachemships. As in the United States Senate, each sachemship had equal representation, regardless of its size, and the representative was known by the name of the sachemship, not by his own name. In 1851, Lewis Henry Morgan described the Indian system:

> When an individual was made a sachem, upon the death or deposition of one of the fifty, his name was "taken away," and the name of the sachemship held by his predecessor was conferred upon him. Thus upon the demise of the Seneca sachem, who held the title *Gä-ne-o-di'-yo*, a successor would be raised up from the Turtle tribe, in which the sachemship was hereditary, and after the ceremony of investiture, the person would be known among the Iroquois only under the name *Gä-ne-o-di'-yo*. These fifty titles, excepting two, have been held by as many sachems, in succession, as generations have passed away since the formation of the League.

In much the same way that these Sachems took the name of their sachemships rather than personal names, American members of Congress take the name of their state, as in "the Junior Senator from Massachusetts" or "the gentleman from California."

In the Congress, the name taboo extends much further than among most tribal councils. Even the names of the parties are taboo in congressional debate, being replaced by the euphemistic "Majority Party" and "Minority Party." Thus the party head in power becomes "Mr. Majority Leader," rather than just the Republican Leader or the Democrat Leader.

All of these name taboos create one of the major congressional fictions employed to sustain the appearance of Congress as an unchanging, eternal body. Under this fiction, it is not just a council of men. As engraved in marble on the Senate building, it is "the living symbol of our union." Consequently, it is composed of offices, not people. The senators from Nebraska may come and go, but there is always "the Junior Senator from Nebraska" and "the Senior Senator from Nebraska." In much the same way, parties may change from Whig or Federalist to Democrat or Republican, but the Congress is always presided over by "the Majority Party." This sense of the eternal and immutable state was expressed in a speech by Robert Byrd, Majority Leader in the 96th Congress:

> One hundred Senators do not make up the total of the Senate. In addition to those 100 Senators who come and go, while the stream of the Senate goes on forever, there are the traditions, the customs, the rules, the precedents, the history, and the role that the institution plays under our constitutional system. All of these things, and more, make up the Senate.

As Byrd said, "It is greater than the sum of its parts." By avoiding the use of all names referring to particular people at a particular time and place in history, the fiction persists that the legislative assembly never varies.

At the same time that each chamber of the Congress affirms the fiction that it exists unchanged and eternal, it tries to deny that the other chamber of Congress exists at all. By rule, no member of the House of Representatives may mention the existence of the Senate, any member of the Senate, any words spoken in the Senate, or any acts of the Senate. Any direct acknowledgment of the other's existence is strictly proscribed. By tradition (although not by rule), the same applies in the Senate regarding the existence of the House of Representatives. This makes for even more awkward speech patterns since the other half of Congress can be referred to only as "another body" or "some other chamber." This difficulty is evident in a 1903 speech by Representative Joseph Cannon, who served intermittently in Congress from 1873 to 1921. In 1903 he wanted to denounce the Senate for tampering with one of the appropriations bills he had written. The culprit in the Senate was South Carolina populist Benjamin Ryan Tillman who, as usual, was demanding more money for his home state. In denouncing him, Cannon could not mention Tillman's name or the Senate, or attack the state of South Carolina. He had to focus his furious words on the methods and procedures in "Another body":

> Another body, under these methods must change its methods of procedure, or our body, backed by the people will compel that change. Else this body, close to the people, shall become a mere tender of the pregnant hinges of the knee, to submit to what any member of another body may demand of this body as a price for legislation.

In a similar fight over the Appropriations Bill for 1980, Barry Goldwater of Arizona expressed his sentiments a little more directly by actually mentioning the name of the other body. Goldwater sent the Senate into near panic when he said that "the real scoundrel in this act, the dog in the manger, is the House of Representatives." By breaching the taboo and actually naming the other body, he underscored the severity of the crisis.

Taboos against attacking other members of Congress and the other chamber also extend to the various states of the Union. Senate Rule XIX specifies that "no Senator in debate shall refer offensively to any State of the Union." Of course, for Senate rhetoric that prohibition does not include Washington, D.C., which is not a state. Consequently, much verbal furor is directed against the hapless citizens of the nation's capital. New York may have its financial crises and dens of iniquity, Mississippi its racial problems and poverty, but neither can be criticized or maligned directly. Much of the pent-up regional hostility is then directed at Washington. This situation alone is enough for the citizens of the District of Columbia to work so ardently for statehood, and thereby come under the verbal protection of Senate Rule XIX.

RITUAL AND THE RECORD

Ritual prevents interaction. Even when a rite takes the form of interaction—as in responsive readings in a church service, congressional debate, or the exchange of marriage vows—it is certainly not interpersonal behavior in the everyday sense. In such ritual acts, the activities are aimed at an audience that may be present literally or may be unseen. These invisible observers may be gods, spirits, saints, ancestors, the voting public, or the muses of history. When a man and a woman exchange marriage vows before the altar, they are not just speaking to each other, they are making vows before *God,* the *State,* and the *Community,* of whom the assembled guests are only witnesses.

In the same way, members of Congress are not just speaking to one another or for the benefit of the spectators in the gallery; they are addressing the Nation at large and History. They are speaking "for the record." The oratory aims beyond those present within the sound of the speaker's voice: it aims at the permanent record of history. Those records are seen first by the readers of tomorrow morning's newspaper, and then by the bureaucrats and the judges who use the legislative record to interpret the law, and eventually by historians researching the issues and personalities of the day or writing political commentaries.

The arcane speech patterns, the name taboos, and the strange verbal circumlocutions all keep that fact constantly before the legislators. They are not allowed to address one another or to use the word "you" because the comments are directed toward the record, not toward another living human being in the same chamber. When they speak, they are not just speaking for themselves but for the whole district or state that elected them. They are states speaking to one another, and like kings who used phrases such as "I, England, and my dear brother, France," congressman, too, are more than mere mortals. They are historical entities interacting rather literally on the stage of history. Ritual creates and enforces this mythical type of interaction, constantly reminding them of their status and the importance of what they are doing.

This was not always the case. Members of Congress actually talked with one another and made decisions together on the chamber floor in the earliest years of the Republic. But how did the record assume such importance in this process? What is the connection between ritual and record? To answer these questions, we need to look back briefly at the development of the *Record.*

At least since the time of Hammurabi, the keeping of a written record of law has been acknowledged in most literate societies as a proper way of ensuring the continuity of their civilizations. Even the preliterate societies went to elaborate trouble to ensure that the words of law were memorized by expert reciters, marked down in pictographic form, read into wampum beads, or preserved in quipos—knotted strings used by the Incas to record information. Without records, the very distinction between a government of law and a government of men becomes impossible to sustain. By the time the United States Constitution was drafted, the importance of records was firmly established in the nations of the literate world. The Constitution specified that Congress would maintain a list of laws that are found in the United States code. Then it added: "Each House shall keep a Journal of its Proceedings, and from time to time publish the same, excepting such Parts as may in their Judgment require secrecy."

Faithfully since April 1789 that "Journal" has been kept. Contrary to what many people assume, however, it is not the *Congressional Record.* The two are completely distinct creations. The *Journal* records the official acts of the body: the introduction of a bill, the vote on an amendment, the vote on a quorum call, and similar parliamentary steps. It contains the official acts of the chamber, but not the various acts and speeches of the members. In the *Journal* the content of a bill is important, but the comments about it are largely irrelevant.

This accorded with the doctrine that it is important what the law says, not what politicians say about the law—a position in keeping with the tradition of Anglo-Saxon legal theory inherited from England. Judge Lord Wrenbury ruled on this in 1769 in the case of *Millar* v. *Taylor* well before the beginning of colonial independence: "Neither the debate nor the outcome of the debate is admissible to explain the words which are found in the Act as passed." That point of jurisprudence was in effect as English law at the time the American Constitution was written, and it has stayed in effect in Great Britain, but somewhere along the way it changed in the United States.

In the early days of the Congress, not only was there no legal need for keeping a record of debate, but there was no practical or political advantage to doing so. Indeed, many politicians thought it highly imprudent to affix permanently on paper their fleeting thoughts and comments. Such permanence has always been a bane to uninhibited discussion. It was largely to preserve spontaneity and openness in debate that the republican Senate of Rome did not record its proceedings. One of the earliest champions of a written record was the Roman orator and senator, Cicero, who wanted all of his remarks preserved for posterity. He explained that most of his colleagues, and in particular Marcus Antonius, did not agree "because if one of them happened to include some statement he might later prefer to have left unsaid, he would then be at liberty to deny he had ever said it." That line of reasoning would not be lost on a contemporary American politician, and it holds for any context in which the free exchange of ideas is mixed with the exercise of authority.

Making a record inhibits this free flow of ideas and decision making, but it is no longer a problem once ideas are not flowing freely and decisions are not being made. Once the legislative process was removed from the congressional floor and lodged in the caucus and committee rooms, there was no longer any reason *not* to record the proceedings. And, in fact, there was a good reason to do so. If the legislator's appearance on the floor was nothing more than a performance for the gallery, why not write out that performance beforehand, practice it, and then have it printed up and distributed to the larger audience of the constituents? If the words impress the gallery, why not use them to impress the voters back home? Why have the speech reported only through the critical eyes of newspaper reporters, when the whole thing can be made available directly from Congress? Thus was born the *Congressional Record,* on March 5, 1873, nearly ninety-four years after the first meeting of Congress.

Unlike the *Journal,* which was ordered by the Constitution and contains only the acts of the chambers, the *Record* contains the acts and words of the individual members, omitting the words of most of the bills. In this way Congress achieved a compromise between the positions of Cicero and Marcus Antonius. The privacy of real politics could be preserved in the back rooms where politicians like Antonius could speak freely and deal practically. A modern-day Cicero, however, could put on his senatorial toga and march to the chamber floor assured that his political oratory would be preserved for history. The making of legislative history continued unhampered in the committee rooms, while the ceremonies of legislation were being recorded in ever greater detail. Only after the chamber floor had been thoroughly ritualized and cleansed of the messy decision making and political dealing were its proceedings finally recorded and presented to the public. This division of labor between a public and a private sector ensured that the appearance of openness would in fact serve to obscure what was actually occurring.

Such a solution was hardly new; it was adopted in Rome in the last years of Cicero's life when his enemy Julius Caesar came to power. Caesar's first act as Consul was to institute regular recording and dissemination of the *Proceedings of the Senate* of Rome. By sending out copies of the debate to all the libraries and officials in the nation, Caesar increased his following and fame. The record also sustained the appearance that the Roman Senate continued as a live, deliberating body, thereby obscuring the fact that Julius Caesar himself was arrogating all of the real power. Decisions were not being made in the chamber of the Senate, they were being made in the back rooms of Caesar's villa. The record gave the appearance of open legal procedure while serving as a screen to hide Caesar's machinations.

After Caesar's death, when Augustus Caesar wanted to revive the moribund Senate as a real legislative body rather than a ceremonial chamber, he instituted two reforms: he suspended publication of the *Proceedings of the Senate* and he did away with seniority. Both practices he claimed kept senators from actually doing or saying anything of substance. The reform did not last. By the time of Tiberius and Caligula, the record was once again in full production, being dispersed to the remotest corner of the empire. While Tiberius and Caligula ruled as absolute tyrants, the Senate went ahead with the ceremonies of state in a lavish display of open democracy.

In the United States Congress, the *Record* began when power was safely behind the scenes in the hands of a dozen Caesars acting as committee chairmen. The *Record,* coming in 1873, arose at the precise moment in history when the committees were at their greatest power, conducting the Reconstruction of America after the Civil War. As long as the committees kept their proceedings out of the public eye, they remained strong. As recently as 1963, Senator Joseph Clark complained on the Senate floor about this extensive secrecy:

> The minutes of the Democratic Steering Committee are under lock and key in the office of Mr. Robert Baker, the Secretary of the Majority . . .
> When I want to ascertain what happened in the Steering Committee in 1913 . . . I have to go to Mr. Baker's office and get books unlocked, before I can read what happened at the time Mr. Wilson was in office. It makes no sense.

But as long as the records were locked and could not be seen by public, press, or even staff, the exercise of power was safely protected in obscurity.

When liberals in the House tried to revitalize the caucus in the late 1960s and early 1970s, one of the first steps they took was to close the records of the caucus from the public. Like Augustus Caesar, they knew that politicians would vote their consciences freely only in privacy; and to ensure forthright discussions, the proceedings should not be recorded or published.

For nearly a century, from the 1870s to the 1970s, this system worked fine. Members of Congress could go to the floor, deliver a great harangue against government spending, communism, or whatever the issue of the day was, throw in a few good words "for Buncome," and return to the committee room to write laws and distribute money. Behind committee doors they were secure in the knowledge that what was said there would never be known to the public. But by 1980, this system had changed. Beginning with the opening of committee hearings to the public in the 1940s and then the opening of executive sessions, mark-up sessions, and conferences in the 1970s, the whole process became part of the public—and therefore the recorded—arena. The Legislative Reorganization Act of 1946, which opened the committee hearings, also provided for the publication of these hearings. In addition to the printed bills, the committee reports on the bill and the floor comments of legislators were added to the committee hearing. In each of these instances, record followed ritualization. Only after an arena of Congress became public was it recorded for posterity. The *Record* is not an account of the decision-making process; it is an account of the ritual process.

A RECORD OF NON-EVENTS

The *Congressional Record* is a smokescreen behind which politics is conducted. The few pieces of real information, such as how a politician votes, lie buried in arcane little passages. Even on important issues for which a rollcall vote is published, the information is often nearly impossible to understand. In the closing days of the 1980 session, the Senate recorded rollcall vote number 507 on the Fair Housing Bill. The vote was announced as follows:

> The question is on agreeing to the motion to lay on the table the motion to reconsider the vote by which the motion to lay on the table the motion to proceed to the consideration of the fair housing bill was rejected.

After listing how each senator voted, the result of the vote was then announced:

> So the motion to lay on the table the motion to reconsider the vote by which the motion to lay on the table the motion to proceed to the consideration of the fair housing bill (H.R. 5200) was rejected was agreed to.

Even a superficial look at the *Congressional Record* shows that it is not a real record of anything. The record begins as a verbatim account of what is said. Stenographers follow senators around the floor noting every syllable. As soon as a speech is recorded, one of the stenographers races off the floor to transcribe it. The written account is then available for the senator or his staff to *correct*. This right to correct does not mean that the senator looks for errors in order to make the record reflect more accurately what was actually said; it means that he can correct it to reflect more accurately what he should have said. A grammatical error is changed, a poor choice of words improved, a mistaken number corrected, an unintentional slip omitted, a nasty innuendo erased. Senator Richard Neuberger wrote that after debates, he has frequently seen senators

> virtually rewriting the speeches and retorts just delivered on the floor of the Senate. Some will totally expunge comments made in the heat of debate that may seem indiscreet or unwise in the cold, gray light of the next dawn, and in the inflexible type of the *Congressional Record.* Others will be adding after-thoughts, which may furnish an extra fillip to a reply that was flat or ineffective when uttered under the duress of argument in the Senate Chamber.

Just in case *the right to correct* is insufficient for the changes the legislators want to incorporate, they have *the right to extend and revise* their remarks. This is a process which, according to columnist Jack Anderson, changes "absentees into prime movers and verbal clubfoots into gazelles."

The revision of the record is shown in Senate consideration of the controversial Supersonic Transport (SST). Liberal Senator Birch Bayh of Indiana gave a rousing speech against the continued funding of the project. On the same day he made seven additional speeches on subjects as varied as voter turnout, consumer class actions, health care, and arms control, thereby covering the whole litany of liberal concerns. Such performances earned him his label as one of the movers of American politics. What does not appear in the record is that Birch Bayh was actually skiing in Colorado on that important day. Although he tried to get back to Washington in time for the SST vote, he missed it. Nevertheless, the *Congressional Record* shows what should have happened, in the eyes of Birch Bayh. He should have been a prime mover, an oratorical gazelle, playing an important role in the defeat of the SST.

Bayh's phenomenal ability to legislate from the ski slopes of Colorado, however, is nothing compared to the supernatural powers of former House Majority Leader Hale Boggs. In the closing days of the session just prior to the November elections of 1972, Boggs is noted in the *Record* as making a speech before the House of Representatives. The striking thing about the speech was that Boggs died several days earlier in an airplane crash in Alaska. The newspaper mockery of this episode was too much for even the high tolerance of unreality allowed by Congress. Henceforth, speeches "delivered" by members not actually present were to be marked with a small dot beside them in the *Congressional Record.* Still, as long as a member gave one line of the speech, it would appear in the *Record* "as though delivered in its entirety."

According to the law, the *Congressional Record* is supposed to be "substantially a verbatim report on proceedings." By tradition, however, a very nebulous definition of "substantially" is used. The rationale for this liberal definition is explained in Cannon's *Procedure in the House of Representatives:*

> Especially important, though often derided, is the right to extend remarks in the record. In large legislative bodies where time is necessarily at a premium, it affords members opportunity to explain their attitude on pending questions and so give constituents a basis on which to approve or disapprove, and at the same time apprises colleagues and the country at large as to local sentiment the member is elected to represent.

Speaker Champ Clark phrased it a little more directly in 1920 when he said: "I concluded that it was preferable to let them be printed rather than be compelled to listen to them."

Just what constitutes apprising "colleagues and the country at large" is well understood by anyone who has taken a look at the *Congressional Record.* On a randomly chosen day in 1980, the *Record* contained a speech by Representative Henry J. Hyde on "swallowing goldfish," which attacked those who attack big business. On the same page, Congressman Joseph Addabbo gave a moving tribute for the "Woman of the Year Award at Bellevue Hospital" in his home state of New York. From the same state came Norman Lent's endorsement of the "proposed plank of the Irish National Caucus for the 1980 political platform." New Jersey's Representative William Hughes delivered a speech on "a distinguished resident of New Jersey's Second Congressional

District, one Morris 'Snooks' Perlstein, a man with an international reputation for his expertise as a player of the artful game of pocket billiards." A tribute to Adolph Leuzinger High School on its fiftieth anniversary was made by Charles Wilson of California, while Representative Edward Derwinski delivered a stirring oration on all the great Ukrainian athletes.

Not all entries that day were on the local level. Congressman Richard Cheney of Wyoming introduced two columns on "Eisenhower as an Activist President"—a timely topic for the 1980s. On that day no bills were passed by either House of Congress, but thirty-three new bills were introduced, as well as seven resolutions.

Few, if any, of these speeches were actually delivered. According to Wisconsin Congressman William A. Steiger, 70 percent of all the material contained in the *Record* was never spoken on the floor. Steiger cites a study by David F. Quadro in which he says, "Until Congress takes action to either prohibit the practices of revision and insertion, or clearly identify them when and where they occur, the *Congressional Record* will continue to be a less desirable source of speech texts than it might otherwise be." Steiger immediately introduced the whole text of the article, footnotes, tables, and all into the *Record,* along with a set of his own introductory remarks which were, of course, printed, but never spoken.

Sometimes Congress can avoid completely the task of coming in to work by relying on the provisions of "revision and extension." A pro forma session may be called for a few minutes and immediately adjourned for lack of a quorum. One such session in the Senate lasted for only eight seconds, just long enough to gavel the Senate "in" and then "out" again. The record of that day's activities and speeches took up 112 pages of fine print. Technically, the eight-second session constituted a work day, and should anyone doubt it, there are all the speeches and comments.

The record is by no stretch of the political imagination an account of what actually happens in legislative reality. It is a record on a mythical plane appreciated only by members of Congress. It represents reality as it should have been, if everything had worked out—if the members had arrived from the ski slopes on time; if the plane had not crashed; if they had not been at an embassy reception; if there had not been another pressing engagement.

This mythical plane stretches to include within it the committee rooms scattered all over the Hill. If the *Congressional Record* is a mythical fabrication, so too are the committee records with their thousands of pages of testimony. Since the hearing is only a ritual parade of mandatory witnesses, it is much simpler and less demanding on the legislators if the record can be compiled with as little demand on their time as possible. Witnesses are "encouraged in the interests of time" to submit their testimony in written form "for the record." Their testimony may be expanded to whatever length they desire—fifty to a hundred pages being not unusual. The actual testimony of the witness consists of a cameo appearance in which one of the senators entertains the audience by recalling an amusing anecdote. Of course, the record does not show the ad-libbed anecdote; instead, it gives the formal testimony, which was written down but not spoken.

The senator also asks a few questions that were written down on index cards for him by his aide. After a thirty-second answer, the senator interjects to say that he realizes the matter is too technical to be answered on the spot, so he suggests that the witness prepare answers at his leisure and "present them for the record." In the weeks and months after the hearings, staffers who think of other questions can submit them to the witness through the mail. Or, simpler still, the staffer can write the question and the answer and just telephone the witness to get his approval for the comments going to press under his name. This practice allows senators who were not present that day to add their own questions, make little speeches in the transcript, and generally appear as one of the prime movers of the legislative episode.

This process reached a climax in the hearings for 1976 appropriations for the Department of Labor and the Department of Health, Education, and Welfare. The transcript of testimony stretched to 4,500 pages. Senator Magnuson, the committee chairman, welcomed witnesses representing every conceivable interest for and against the various items on the budget. The witnesses answered the questions and expressed their positions with great skill. The committee then voted out an appropriations bill of nearly $60 billion, an average cost of approximately thirty dollars to every man, woman, and child in the United States. The only unusual thing about the hearings was that not one word in the 4,500 pages had been spoken in hearings. Each page had been created *ex nihilo,* as it were, by the staff. The hearing was the quintessential non-event put together under the auspices of Magnuson's assistant, Harley Dirks. In gratitude for Dirks's good work, Magnuson even wrote at the beginning of the hearings a special citation for the excellence and speed with which the staff had made available the printed copy of the hearings. Of course, that expression of gratitude had been written by the staff.

Investigative columnist Jack Anderson exposed the committee to great embarrassment by making this farce public knowledge. Like the episode of Hale Boggs speaking from beyond the grave, this one resulted in a minor change. At least one senator had to be present to call the hearings to order. Otherwise, the hearings could still be fabricated events, but staff could not do it without token appearances by senators.

Suspicion should have been aroused by the shortness of a set of hearings only 4,500 pages long. Hearings that are actually held may run to ten times that length. One of the all-time great hearings was the two-year affair of the Senate Select Committee on Improper Activities in the Labor Management Field. Meeting under Chairman John McClelland in 1957-59, the final tally noted that "the committee heard 1,726 witnesses, whose testimony consumed 46,510 pages, and its staff filed 19,000 investigative field reports."

With hearings like that it is no wonder that Congress has become the world's largest producer of printed matter, spewing out more material than the largest daily newspapers. To the nascent publication of the United States Code and the *Journal* that are required by the Constitution, Congress added the *Congressional Record* in the nineteenth century and committee records of all descriptions in the twentieth. As each step in the congressional process was ritualized, another form of *the record* was added to the growing flood of words. So important was this activity of publishing the record that Congress established its own mechanical scribe in 1861—the Government Printing Office (GPO)—as an arm of Congress, not part of the executive branch. Even though the GPO today publishes for the federal government as a whole, it is still directly under the supervision and control of Congress. By law, the GPO can be located no farther than one mile from the Capitol, thus facilitating the rapid transfer of transcripts and prints. Each morning before the work day begins, copies of the previous day's *Record* are delivered to every congressional office. The copies—equal in size to a couple of paperback books bound into one volume—are then "corrected" once again by staff before being printed for the general public. The total number of pages yearly stretches to almost 50,000 for the *Congressional Record* alone, not counting the committee hearings and copies of the bills.

Most of the GPO's work for the executive agencies of the government is allotted to subcontractors, but the work on Congress's personal Tower of Babel is done by the GPO itself. In 1980, the GPO printed an estimated $0.5 billion worth of records, forms, books, and pamphlets. Congress's share of this was officially listed as only $36.6 million, but a congressional aide on the House Printing Subcommittee put the total at closer to a quarter of the total GPO budget, or $125 million. Twenty-four hours a day, in three shifts of workers, the GPO continues turning out the millions of pages of political rhetoric and meticulously recording every detail of the many legislative non-events purported to have happened that day in the halls of the Capitol.

Producing the ritual record has become the real business of Congress. Slowly but persistently through two centuries, the demands of ceremony, ritual, and the accompanying record have crept through the Congress like a kudzu vine, taking over one legislative forum after another.

The normal work day of a member of Congress is spent making a series of cameo appearances in the various ritual arenas. Early in the morning he bangs the gavel calling a committee hearing to commence and, reading from a sheet, announces the subject, which is always of grave importance, and welcomes the visitors, who are always distinguished and dedicated experts. While the expert rambles on about this issue, the senator listens to an aide explaining about the upcoming meeting with a 4-H Club and at the same time signs a batch of documents thrust at him by his secretary. As soon as another senator stumbles into the room with his handful of question cards, the presiding senator turns the hearing over to him and excuses himself. He then dashes over to the Senate floor, where he presents a one-minute oration on the need to increase widget exports to Third World countries, the national importance of the upcoming peach festival in his home state, and why he favors another round of disarmament talks as a way of solving the energy shortage. Having been delayed on the floor by a long line of other one-minute orators, he is late for another committee meeting that is supposed to mark up and report a bill. The amendment his staff drafted is not presented because the bells ring and the lights flash in the committee room, calling him back to the floor for a vote. Running out of the room with all the other senators, he asks if anyone knows what the vote might be on. Before they can decide, they are in the crowded hall in front of the chamber. Surrounded by lobbyists and by aides trying to find their masters, he barely catches a glimpse of his own legislative assistant pinned against a fluted column on the far side of the room. Unable to get closer than twenty feet to one another, the aide gestures a set of prearranged signals to his boss telling how they need "to go on this one." Still not knowing the topic, he hurries into the chamber, registers his vote, and tries to get back to the subway before most of the other senators leave the chamber. Sitting with two other senators for the ride back to the office building, he asks if anyone knew what that vote was all about. One thinks it was a motion to table the motion to reconsider the addition of $5 million to build halfway houses for abused spouses. Another insists he heard something about a medal of honor commemorating John Wayne's heroic services to the American nation. Before a consensus can be decided, they arrive back at the office building and each rushes off to his next appointment.

Even though our senator wants to return to the committee mark-up of the farm bill and propose his amendment, his aide tells him that he must go back to the original committee hearing because two teachers from his home state are about to testify as representatives of the huge and politically active State Education Association. As he arrives back at the hearings, the teachers are almost finished, but he interrupts to welcome them, restate the importance of the grave subject and distinction of the witnesses, and to beg their forgiveness, for he has an appointment at the White House. The White House bill-signing ceremony is not for another four hours, but such excuses sound much better to hometown folks than telling them that he has a photograph appointment with the 4-H Club. Leaving the 4-H on the Capitol steps with an aide to give them a personal guided tour through the building, he runs back into the chamber, where he must introduce three bills that his staff has worked on for the past several weeks. Then comes a reception for the President of Italy, but he stays only long enough for a friendly photograph to be used in the hometown Italian newspaper. Finally getting back to the committee mark-up, he finds that the meeting is almost over, but his clever assistant has managed to get another senator to sponsor the amendment in exchange for his voting proxy, which the aide rapidly drafted and signed with the senator's name.

Each day for a member of Congress resembles the schedule of a film actor, which indeed a number of politicians may have been prior to entering public service. An actor plays in several different productions at once and must rush from one shooting scene to the next. The politician enters one scene, is coached by a waiting assistant for a few moments, and then performs the role. His particular performance may have no relation to that of the actors who appeared just before or after him, but the pieces will be edited together in a coherent fashion afterwards by the staff. The important point is simply that he should get his appearance on record. He voted, he came for the quorum call, he asked the question of the witness, he introduced the bill, he co-sponsored the amendment, he spoke the sentence. The staff can issue all the press releases and printed speeches to show that this made him a prime mover. The one question can be turned into a probing inquisition on paper, the one-minute speech into three speeches of oratorical grace spread out throughout the day's record. The picture with the President of Italy can be released to the press with a long explanation of the senator's active participation in Italian-American concerns. The film clip of his welcoming the members of the State Education Association in the ornate committee room can be shown on local television as proof of his sincere concern with local issues. In each of these scenes, the politician uses only enough time to act out an abbreviated symbolization of what he appears to be doing.

Politicians have become specialists in ritual—ceremonial figures who preside over and invest each session with the appropriate dash of authority. They bestow on it a patina of official mana.
Symbolically, the legislator occupies center stage as the star of
the event, but the real decisions occur backstage. The member of
Congress, however, has too many of these public appearances
each day for him to get backstage where the decisions are made.
His day is too filled with the rites of legislation for him to be very
involved in its actual substance.

"DECORATED LEAVES"

The spread of the ritual record descends from Capitol Hill
through the bureaucratic offices of Foggy Bottom, and from
there out to the most remote sections of the nation. Congress
passes the laws, mandates numerous bureaucratic forms, and the
filing of various reports. In implementing these congressional
policies, the bureaucracy heaps on additional regulations, new
forms, and another layer of reports. The whole burden, in the
end, comes to rest on the shoulders of local governments, business
enterprises, and ultimately the private citizen who must fill out
all those papers. The papers then work their way back through
the long chain to be deposited in a committee room as dramatic,
tangible proof that the bureaucracy is doing its job and needs
additional money to maintain a high level of efficiency. Like
other ritual objects of respect, the papers may be fondled and
paraded, but they may not be folded, spindled, or mutilated.
Along with the lengthening and thickening tentacles that origi-
nate from the Congressional Clans and reach out to control the
nation, Congress reserves the greatest care and attention for this
cultural record.

Americans are ensnared in a written record that documents
even the most intimate parts of their lives. The newspapers and
commentators often point with pride to the fact that Americans,
unlike the citizens of communist and totalitarian states, are not
compelled to carry special identity passes or to register with the
police. That observation implies a relative independence for
Americans which other people do not enjoy; yet closer examination reveals that the American mania for the written record

probably exceeds that of any civilization known to humankind.

The poor in America fill out government forms in quadrupli-
cate and quintuplicate for every kind of government assistance
they receive. All of their possessions, family details, and even the
kinds of food they buy are regulated. For the middle-class and
upper-class Americans who are exempt from these forms of the
poverty record, the same effect is achieved through congressionally mandated tax forms, which demand an official record of
such things as where business lunches were eaten and what they
cost. Meticulous records are maintained of even the smallest
business transactions. This obsession with forms makes every
American home into an office with its most sacred and important
objects locked away in a file box. Nothing is real unless written
down as a part of the record. The demands of the income tax and
social security procedures alone require volumes of family papers
stored for years.

At the behest of government and in imitation of the government, this practice has fanned out from the bureaucracy and
business to invade ever more arenas of public life and pull them
into the record process. The record, especially when it can be
codified into statistics as a higher level of abstraction than mere
words, becomes the sine qua non of public arenas as diverse as
churches, sports, and entertainment. The number of worshippers
and the amount of money they give now compared to last week
or last month is posted prominently in the front of the church or
listed in the program. The record of events assumes primacy over
real work and the passion to record becomes the chief activity.
The record of each sports team and player blares from the screen
of television sets during ball games, and the climax comes when
some former record is broken. Even the daily weather forecast
gives the record high and low temperatures, snowfall, rain, or
barometric pressure, and somehow a day that breaks the record
or a town that gains the highest or lowest temperature assumes
an importance on a higher plane of dramatic reality.

So deeply preoccupied have Americans become with records
and documentations that the social distinction between a legal
resident and an illegal alien is personified in the phrase "undocumented worker." America defines itself in terms of papers,
documents, and records. Just as the undocumented alien is at the

lowest end of American social life, the highest form of honor the nation pays its modern Presidents is not in building monuments to them like the Washington Monument or Jefferson Memorial but in building libraries to house all their presidential papers. The Truman, Johnson, Kennedy, and Carter libraries form the memorials to those administrations, each boasting ever larger quantities of paper.

The importance of documents has become so ingrained in Americans that even rebels and nonconformists use them as the focus for their deviations. Many young couples pride themselves on living together without a certificate of marriage. They preserve the forms of marriage as any other couple, but by not having that certificate they see themselves as living on the fringe of society, free from bourgeois morality. Yet in their rebellion they often draw up contracts of relationship and documents of agreement that specify all of their rights and responsibilities, down to who takes out the garbage and who bathes the dog. The ultimate act of rebellion has become the making of one's own documents, forms, and records.

The Yanomamo tribesmen of Venezuela and Brazil, who have neither paper nor a written language, call the documents that westerners find so important "decorated leaves." In that concept lies a naive truth about the use of written documents and records, which have become the talismans of modern life, replacing the crude fetishes of primitive cultures. These documents are revered as barriers against evil, and they are the proof that the bearer is a full, participating member of society.

Supplying the constant demand for decorated leaves employs ever-increasing portions of the American work force. Companies spend time keeping these elaborate records, individual families spend greater amounts of time on similar practices in the home. To help both businesses and individuals, whole new industries have grown up. Ostensibly part of the tertiary arm of the service-oriented society, they specialize in making and filling out forms. These document experts supervise every major activity an individual may undertake: one set of experts fills out the tax forms, another set handles the papers accompanying the sale or purchase of a home. Already in the City of Washington some private agencies specialize in nothing but filling out the civil service employment forms of prospective bureaucrats.

America is becoming a culture of paper rituals. Like the Aztecs whose whole society was enmeshed in the ritual requirements of their religious ceremonies, Americans have become ensnarled in the civic rituals of keeping the record. In this regard, Congress throbs not just with the social and political power of the nation but with the heartbeat of its culture as well. Ultimately, all of the long paper chains extending throughout the country begin and terminate in the action of the Congress and its clans.

10

⋞§⋟

Choreographing
the Congress

THE FRENCH COURT at Versailles endures in history as persistent evidence of just how complex and labor-intensive
civil ceremonies and rituals can become. The pageants around
Louis XIV, and particularly around his successors in the last
century of the French monarchy, required the participation of
the assembled aristocrats of the country, and their families, mistresses, and friends; they necessitated an army of retainers as
well. Servants, valets, and pages fluttered constantly about the
lords and ladies of the plush court, while coachmen, footmen,
and grooms adorned the already ornate carriages outside. Because fashions in clothing, jewelry, and hairstyles played a central part in court ceremony, whole villages of ancillary artisans
worked to produce decorations and baubles. These artisans included tailors and haberdashers, seamstresses and lacemakers,
jewelers and goldsmiths, wigmakers and hairdressers, as well as
dozens of subsidiary specialists. The complex ceremonies surrounding the daily acts of eating, dressing, hunting, and
promenading required thousands of other servants to cook and
serve the meals, dress and powder the leading actors, plant and
prune the elaborate gardens, and train and groom the hunting
dogs, falcons, and horses. The evening balls required musicians

and dance teachers, as well as actors and singers.

In its own way the French court showed the same degree of ritual hypertrophy as the Aztec Empire. In both cases a series of perpetual ceremonies stretched out to include ever more people and to absorb ever more resources of the nation. The ceremonial complex finally contributed to the destruction of both societies, the Aztecs falling to outside conquerors, the French to internal turmoil and revolution.

So far, we have examined two of the primary components of congressional ceremonialism—the growth of ritual and its concomitant, the record. Now we must turn to the third feature of this phenomenon: the increased need for retainers, assistants, and craftsmen. Because the rituals of Congress focus on the written word, they require specialists adept in the latest fashionable use of words, both oral and written. The rituals of Congress induce an insatiable appetite for speech writers, public relations experts, secretaries, clerks, and artisans with related verbal skills. The fashions in word usage and the changing manner in which they are presented vary as much as the hair arrangements and styles in silk stockings at the French court, but in each instance the emphasis remained on imagery and public appearance. The difference consists primarily in that the congressional image was designed for paper and videotape, while that of the French court was for the immediate audience.

To understand the present significance of the 25,000 people employed by the Congress, we need to look at the historical background of staffing practices in Congress. Once their origins are clear, the contemporary nexus linking staff with both ritual and the record becomes clearer too.

FIRST STEPS

Congress began without staff. The legislators themselves managed the posts of Clerk, Doorkeeper, Sergeant at Arms, and assorted assistants to these offices. Because the chamber floor was still the legislating forum, members vied with one another for election to these important positions.

The first Clerk of the House, Congressman John Beckley of Virginia, dominated the House more than any other representative of the time. House Speaker Fredrick A. C. Muhlenberg (1750–1801) from Pennsylvania presided in the impartial and apolitical stance of the Speaker in the British House of Commons. As Clerk, and later as Librarian after the establishment of the Library of Congress in 1800, Beckley played a more partisan role than the Speaker. With the combined offices of Clerk and Librarian, Beckley knew all the issues under consideration, the details of bills and amendments, and the disposition of each. He also positioned himself to keep close surveillance on individual voting performance. The Congressional historian Alvin Josephy, Jr., describes Beckley as "a fountainhead of gossip and a master of trouble-shooting and dirty tricks for the Republican cause." Serving the political interests of his two fellow Virginians, Thomas Jefferson and James Madison, Beckley operated as "a combination campaign manager and communications center."

During the tenure of Beckley, the House floor gradually lost its legislative function. He and his fellow Republicans (or "Jacobins," as Congressman Roger Griswold called them) relied increasingly on off-floor caucuses and clandestine meetings in back rooms, thus shifting power away from the floor. By the time Beckley gave up the clerkship, the floor had become the dramatic but non-legislative arena described earlier. It was in Beckley's new role as party leader that his real power was being exercised, and his duties as Clerk became largely ceremonial. Consequently, when Beckley was replaced, it was his position as party leader and campaign manager that was coveted, not the office of Clerk. Gradually through the nineteenth century the positions of Clerk, Doorkeeper, and the floor offices were filled with hired personnel rather than elected congressmen. Frequently these clerks were and still are chosen from among ex-members who have lost their seats, but because they are familiar with congressional procedure are retained as employees.

As floor proceedings increased in drama, more bills were introduced, more speeches given, more amendments considered, and more parliamentary motions entertained. These shows required additional clerks to record the bills, copy the debates, and maintain the *Journal.* Since legislation was decided upon in committees and caucuses that excluded staff, these clerks were processing the non-essential bills, the bunk items. While their staff aides attended to the ceremonial chores of legislation, they were carefully barred from the substance. With more legislative bills in Congress, the committees' workload increased. The members of the committees were, for the most part, too busy writing legislation to pay attention to the bills of other legislators. Consequently, these more routine tasks of handling unimportant bills went to clerks. In 1856, the first full-time clerks were hired for the Senate Finance Committee and its House counterpart, the Ways and Means Committee. Staff growth in the nineteenth century remained minimal, however. According to a report compiled by Senator W. A. Peffer of Kansas in 1898: "The total number of persons employed in one capacity or another in and about the Senate is over three hundred. An investigation recently discovered 353, among whom were 121 clerks, 57 messengers, 52 skilled laborers, 23 pages and 18 folders." This comparatively small staff for the Senate sufficed to handle Senate duties so long as the chamber floor was the sole ritual arena forming part of the official record. The power-exercising forums—the committees—did not require much assistance. Politicians rarely need help exercising power, only in displaying that power.

The quantum increments in the number of retainers followed the opening of committee rooms to the public. Suddenly dozens of ceremonial stages sprouted all over the Capitol. During 1946, that first year of open committees, only 181 committee staffers worked in the House of Representatives. Over the following thirty years, this figure escalated by 1,000 percent to 2,014 in 1977. Apologists for this rapid growth blame the increasing "legislative load" of modern government. During those same three decades, however, the actual number of laws passed in each session of Congress declined from 1,739 to 968. A 1,000 percent increase in staff produced a 45 percent decline in the number of bills passed, confirming the 2,000-year-old observation of Aristotle that "a greater number of servants often does less work than a smaller."

Although fewer bills were passed, many more were written and introduced. Accompanying these was the usual panoply of speeches, hearings, and investigations. Between 1947 and 1977, the number of bills in the House increased from 7,611 for the 80th Congress to 16,982 for the 94th. Resolutions correspondingly increased from 950 to 2,389. Most of these were electioneering bills, never intended as anything more than public relations vehicles by the sponsors; nevertheless, hearings had to be held on them. The total number of hearings doubled, the quorum calls trebled, and the number of votes quadrupled. Thus, there was a significant increase in the formal activities that gave the appearance of legislating, but without a corresponding increase in substance. The ceremonial motions of government escalated, but without a corresponding increase in results.

Staff growth in the 1970s received an extra push from the rather unlikely source of President Richard Nixon. The Democratic Congress initially increased staff as a way to fight the Republican White House more effectively, but a significant boost to congressional staff came from the Watergate tapes. A conversation between John Dean and President Nixon on February 23, 1973, particularly piqued congressional self-importance:

> D: I spent some years on the Hill myself and one of the things I always noticed was the inability of the Congress to deal effectively with the Executive Branch because they never provide themselves with adequate staffs, had adequate information available—
>
> P: Well, they have huge staffs compared to what we had.
>
> D: Well, they have huge staffs, true, as compared to what they had years ago. But they are still inadequate to deal effectively—
>
> P: (Expletive deleted) Don't try to help them out!

Congress, of course, assumed that the Nixon White House knew something about organization which they didn't, and interpreting Dean's comment about "adequate staff" to mean more staff, immediately increased the payroll. From this era came the Congressional Budget Office, established to help Congress match the executive branch in complex financial analyses; the Office of Technological Assessment to aid Congress in such technical areas as solving the energy crisis; and, of course, a few more staffers for each of the members of Congress.

Some members of Congress, even among the Democrats, strenuously resisted the urge to add more staff. They claimed that it was all a matter of pride and the desire to improve the appearance of legislative sophistication without improving quality. In working against further staff increases in 1975, Senator Herman Talmadge of Georgia pointed out that "when you get more staff and more clerks they spend most of their time thinking up bills, resolutions, amendments. They write speeches for Senators, and they come in here on the floor with Senators."

Only a fraction of these bills is ever passed. Lord Bryce noted that "American statesmen keep their pockets full of the loose change of compliments and pompous phrases, and become so accustomed to scattering it around the crowd that they are surprised when a complimentary resolution of electioneering bill, intended to humor some section of opinion at home, is taken seriously abroad." In the intervening century since Lord Bryce's analysis, the practice has flourished with increases in clerical assistance. During the nineteenth century it was usually considered sufficient for a member simply to introduce the bill and give one supporting speech; he could then ignore the issue in committee, where it was destined to die through neglect. Once the public invaded the committee sessions, however, a convincing political performance was extended to include hearings on the bill and the full application of political ceremony. Electioneering bills required electioneering investigations and hearings. A short speech inserted in the *Congressional Record* may have satisfied a constituent group in the last century. Today, these groups want a complete show to be convinced that the legislator is really pursuing their interests.

Staffers act as ritual experts managing all of these ceremonies. They write the non-bills and the non-speeches that accompany the bunk issues. Staff arrange the hearings, coach the witnesses, furnish questions for the senators and congressmen, and sometimes even furnish answers for the testifying experts.

Staffers no longer bury themselves in legal research or typing pools. They are not the ones copying down the debates and committee hearings—new clerical reporters have been added to perform these more mundane tasks. Stenographers and reporters for debate are acquired mostly through contracts with private companies (and thus do not count as part of the Congress's payroll). Similar contract agencies provide newspaper clipping services, while mail handling has become computerized.

Other clerical duties are performed through the congressional support agencies. In addition to the seven thousand employees of the Government Printing Office, Congress controls another six thousand through the Government Accounting Office, the Congressional Budget Office, the Congressional Research Service, and the Office of Technological Assessment. These people provide research analysis on almost any topic. They can even write speeches and compile committee publications when the regular congressional staff is too busy; the support personnel includes experts in law, economics, science, and arts, as well as most languages of the world.

The extreme growth in congressional staff springs directly out of the growth of ceremony and ritual. Staffers function as ritual accoutrements, constantly ministering to the needs of the record and fluttering around their boss like bees around the queen. Just as the court retainers at Versailles produced elaborate costumes and ornate wigs, the courtiers of Congress produce volumes of speeches and investigations. Much of the work is done in the back rooms, but it can also be seen in the gaggle of staff surrounding each member of Congress as he moves through the corridors. Behind him flows a trail of aides clutching reams of paper, striking out a word here, adding a comment there, like the Versailles retainers following their patrons and constantly readjusting clothes, adding a stitch here or straightening a curl there. All power centers, like all ceremonial centers, use a large number of retainers to play the supernumerary roles in the pageants of public life. Sometimes, however, the process reaches the point, as it did in Versailles and in Washington, at which the throngs of bit players conceal a subtle but important shift in power relations.

Just such a shift occurred in France when the real power of state moved away from the throne and into the hands of a select few of those fluttering retainers. The government came into the control of a succession of cardinals, dukes, and madames. While the king remained as the ceremonial focus of state, decisions were actually made by the duc d'Orléans and the duc de Bourbon. Appointments to offices were influenced by Madame de Pompadour and later by Madame du Barry. Cardinal Fleury exercised the power of the purse, and other decisions were made by the ducs de Choiseul and d'Aiguillon. Concealed from public view by the attentive retainers orbiting around the king, and by the conspicuous execution of public rituals, the machinations of lords, mistresses, and prelates behind the scenes constituted the real government of the mightiest nation on earth.

It would be easy to dismiss the lacy puffery of French courtiers or the preppy preening of congressional retainers as mere vaudevillian humor, irritating but not important—a moment of comic relief in the serious business of state. But to treat them as flippantly as they appear overlooks the power of a potential Pompadour or Cardinal Fleury. The occasional sex scandals of Capitol Hill notwithstanding, the powers behind the scenes in Washington are not likely to be mistresses, any more than they are priests or ministers. The hidden authority of today is much more likely to be the undramatic lawyer, policy analyst, or media expert in a three-piece suit and wire-frame glasses. These are the ones who have worked their way up out of the typing pool or lawyer pool and into the decision-making roles within Congress.

The role of these individuals is obscured from public view by the blizzard of papers and the blatantly ceremonial function of a large number of them. But just as we must distinguish between the dukes helping the king dress and those who wielded the powers of state, so too must we distinguish between the congressional aides who serve as ceremonial props and those exercising genuine power. Not all staffers are taking shorthand notes, running to the library to look up a legal reference, or fanning the congressman with a sheaf of papers. Some of them are back in the office running the congressman's clan, administering his control over the bureaucracy, cajoling or neutralizing the lobbies, and in general politicking. The first group of aides to make the transition from ceremony to power were the ones in the oldest arena of Congress—the ones working the chamber floor.

POWER OF THE DANCE

As the ceremonies enacted on the chamber floor grew in complexity and left the hands of elected officials such as Beckley to move into the hands of hired staff, the legislators paid decreasing attention to the management of floor activity. The politicians specialized in public appearance, but they understood less and less what the arcane rituals really meant. They were good role performers, but had less control over the scripting of the part. The clerks on the floor became choreographers arranging what Woodrow Wilson called "the dance of legislation."

The indispensability of floor personnel hinged on their sole possession of the knowledge to run the elaborate rituals. The House Parliamentarian, for example, is in theory an appointee of the Speaker. As all staffers, he serves at the will of the appointing officer and leaves office when his sponsor leaves. The Parliamentarian assists the Speaker in handling floor activities by means of expert knowledge about the rules and precedents of the House of Representatives. In practice, however, the Speaker needs the Parliamentarian more than the Parliamentarian needs the Speaker. An experienced expert such as Lewis Deschler, who held the office of Parliamentarian from 1928 to 1974, was indispensable because only he had access to all the rules and precedents. Deschler was first appointed to his office by Republican Speaker Nicholas Longworth, the son-in-law of President Theodore Roosevelt; but even when the Democrats gained control of the House, they found it more expedient to reappoint Deschler to his position than to have him work for the minority Republicans. The Democrats probably could have kept control of the body without Deschler, but they could not have done so against him. Deschler working for the Republicans would have created a parliamentary snarl capable of bringing the Congress to a halt. Deschler stayed in office under nine successive Speakers until his retirement in 1974 during the tenure of Carl Albert. From the presidency of Calvin Coolidge until that of Gerald Ford, Lewis Deschler remained one of the most powerful individuals in the House of Representatives; he then passed his position on to William H. Brown, his hand-picked assistant and heir.

Deschler kept his information literally under lock and key. Although thousands of precedents are published, the printed volumes are always from five to thirty years behind the times. Trying to figure out the precedents without the personal guidance of the Parliamentarian is like trying to practice law with antiquated law books. The Parliamentarian is the only one who knows all the rules; and in a legislative body where rules have paramount importance, that knowledge is power. The difference between being the only one who knows the rules and the one who makes the rules becomes a trivial distinction.

It may well be that long after historians have forgotten Speakers such as Henry Rainey and Joseph Byrns, Lewis Deschler will be remembered as the first congressional staffer to have achieved and maintained independent power in his own right. Nicholas Longworth may be recalled as the man who married Alice Roosevelt, but Deschler will be remembered as the man who wrote the book on how to have power as a master of ceremonies. As military chief Mendel Rivers said, "He is the image of Congress."

The two current Parliamentarians of the Congress have not yet achieved the eminence Deschler had during his half century of rule, but they are not too far behind. The Parliamentarian has the power to refer bills to committees that appear proper to him—a task with tremendous leeway, which can mean survival or neglect for the bill. He advises the committees on legislative procedure, telling them in effect what they can do, how they can do it, and when. Especially in the House, where a new rule is written for every single bill that comes to the floor, the power of the Parliamentarian is steadily increasing.

Other floor officers have built up their own bailiwicks with increasing autonomy from the masters they supposedly serve. They have their own staffs and sometimes limousines; some have independent franking privileges to send letters with their signature in lieu of a stamp. Because of those innocuous sounding names like "Doorkeeper" and "Clerk," people outside of Washington visualize some nineteenth-century office continuing as a sinecure of patronage. Instead, these anonymous staffers are becoming patrons of their own. The Clerk of the House exercises primary responsibility for handling the House budget and defending it before appropriations hearings. He operates the finance office and controls the increasingly important computer system. The Clerk is responsible for "the handling of bills throughout their passage in the House, the preparation of daily calendars of business and taking of roll calls." Assisting him in these duties are a Deputy Clerk, three Assistant Clerks, a General Counsel to the Clerk, Journal Clerk, Reading Clerks, Tally Clerks, Enrolling-Digest Clerk, Bill Clerks, Finance Clerks— and most of these positions have their own layer of assistant clerks, as well as secretaries, messengers, and office helpers.

At times the Clerk and even the Doorkeeper have acted as presiding officers over the House of Representatives, a symbolic statement of their power and prestige within the body. Occasionally, one of them may be booted out, just as a Speaker or powerful chairman has sometimes been dismissed. Doorkeeper Fishbait Miller was ousted in just such manner as part of the housecleaning reforms of the Watergate Babies, and Senate Secretary Bobby Baker lost his position when his criminal activities came to light. But these changes have the aura of a palace coup more than the simple dismissal of a House employee. Most of the officers are so firmly ensconced in their positions that they verge on becoming independent Big Men. Their powers rank them with the other Congressional Chiefs in surpassing the authority of the lowly junior members.

The floor is the largest and oldest of congressional arenas, and its staffers have achieved the highest level of independence of all congressional employers. The numerous and much smaller committee areas have only recently become ritualized public forums, and their staffs have not yet freed themselves from the masters' control; but they seem to be following the path toward autonomy and increased control over the part of the government and private business which their committee legislates.

Part of these staffers' power is analogous to that of the floor officers. Since each committee has its own set of rules, the staffers for any particular committee are usually the ones who know those rules best. The rules vary as to what constitutes a quorum for different kinds of business, which voting proxies are applicable to which situations, what requires majority consent, what necessitates unanimous consent, and what kinds of

amendments may be introduced at various points in the procedure. Such questions are the heart of the legislative process and
determine the fate of many policy issues. Because each legislator
serves on several committees—each with a different set of
rules—it is difficult for him to know or remember which rules
apply in which situations. To a great extent he must rely on the
word of the staff. Should a junior member try to contest a staff
decision, the staffers can pull all kinds of rules and precedents
out of the file to prove that "this is the way it has always been
done"; the member has little ground on which to argue unless
he can persuade the whole committee to change the rule.
Usually it is easier for the younger members to go along with
what they are told.

While the legislator stars as a ritual actor in a succession of
legislative dramas throughout the day, the staff exercises the
real power of his office. He is trapped by the ceremonial calen-
dar. "Not having enough time to think" is the bane of legislators, according to Senator Charles Mathias of Maryland: "We
all put in 12 to 18 hour days that leave us panting. Whatever
creativity and wisdom we have is fragmented by the incessant
demands upon our time—all legitimate perhaps individually,
but taken together, devastating and debilitating." This description was borne out by the 1977 research of a special House
commission, which found that on the average a congressman
has only eleven minutes a day in which to read. These official
findings indicate the difficulty even a conscientious member of
Congress has in trying to keep watch over his staff. He simply
cannot keep up with all the materials they prepare in his name,
the decisions they make for him, or the statements they issue.
Their relationship rests more on trust than on oversight. The
legislator depends on one-minute briefings from his staff as the
legislator enters the arena in which he must perform. The legislator may not know what the issue of discussion is: he knows
only what he is supposed to say.

The extent to which a member may not know what is going
on was illustrated in the confirmation hearings of Ambassador
Harvey Feldman to represent the United States to Papua, New
Guinea, and the Solomon Islands. Senator Claiborne Pell, the
second ranking Democrat at the time, looked at the ambassador

and asked: "The Solomon Islands. You hear a lot about them. Where exactly are they?" This was asked by the same Senator Pell who was heir to three hundred years of family involvement in foreign relations. The chagrin of his staff was only increased when the senator tried to give a little foreign policy advice of his own to the ambassador: "Don't let the people like you so much they eat you up."

What is unusual about Pell's episode is not his lack of knowledge, but his inability to hide that lack. Most senators are more skilled at "winging" such episodes without showing their ignorance. If caught in a situation without a staffer beside him, the senator should be able to avoid saying anything substantive at all.

A senator's plight without his staffer is frequently embarrassing. Former Senator John Tunney of California once left his office suite to go chair a subcommittee hearing without a staffer to escort and brief him on the way. He showed up at the wrong room to chair the wrong hearing. It took half an hour for his staff at the right hearing to notice that he was missing. Like interchangeable actors in a play, it does not really matter which one of them chairs which of the sessions, as long as the staff keeps the government operating.

Members are the specialists in the performance, not in the substance. "Although decisions technically remain the responsibility of the House or Senate Members," explains former staffer Margaret Boone, "much of the daily workload is carried by committee staffers." This situation prompted columnist James Reston to call the staff a "hidden legislature." Senator John Warner of Virginia used much the same language to praise the staff as a valuable "third house of Congress." But whether the power of staff is applauded as professionalization or denounced as usurpation, no one denies that the power is lodged increasingly with them.

According to Congressman Morris Udall, the typical congressman's day "is now dominated by the staff." Senator Ernest Hollings denounced the situation even more vehemently when he said that all senators do is run around responding to their staffs—"Everybody is working for staff, staff, staff." This present situation was foreseen by Senate Majority Leader Michael

Mansfield nearly two decades ago when he tried to stem staff power by denying aides access to specific parts of the legislative process. On the Senate floor in the winter of 1963, Mansfield argued vociferously:

> As far as concerns allowing a staff member of a Senator to look at confidential matters, based on what I have seen in my service in the Senate, all too often the assistants or members of the staff of a Senator are as important and influential as the Senator himself is. Those people are not elected. They do not go before the people. I think what is open only to a Senator should remain available only to the Senator himself. . . . I repeat, the staff members are not Senators who have been elected. They do not have the responsibilities which Senators have.

Mansfield could have been whistling in the wind for all the impact he made. Congress was just beginning its major expansion of staff, and with that growth came added authority for the aides. In the intervening years since Mansfield's warnings, the staff has become more entrenched in its specialized domain, while politicians have spent more time in televised hearings, on the campaign trail, and trapped in their round of rituals.

If the power of staff continues to grow at its present rate, the nation will have more Lewis Deschlers presiding as the unknown and unelected decision makers in American government. With them will come a proliferation of bureaucrats like J. Edgar Hoover who run their fiefdoms independent of the President, but protected by their close association with the Congress. Just such a possibility was raised by two clerks of the British Parliament, Kenneth Bradshaw and David Pring, who wrote in their analysis of the American Congress: "there is the bureaucratic danger that staffs who are given or receive too much freedom of action may come to dominate the people whom they ostensibly serve." This is especially true, they note, "in the Senate where members have to sit on more committees than do members of the House." In time, however, this danger may come to threaten both chambers.

The increasing power of staff in Congress reflects a political theme common to many societies throughout world history. As the titular rulers become embroiled in ceremony, power flows to their assistants. At first the assistants merely act "in the name of" the powerholder, but in time they come to exercise that power in their own right. Egyptian sultans in the thirteenth century lost power to the Mamelukes, their former slaves. Nineteenth-century emperors in Japan ruled as ceremonial heads of state while the Shoguns exercised dictatorial powers. The harem eunuchs of the Ottoman Empire took over control from their sultans and pashas, just as Byzantine eunuchs and bureaucrats ended with control in the preceding empire. The monarchs of England lost power to their privy councils and chamberlains. The Frankish kings were thrown out by the Mayor of the Palace who headed the domestic staff, and popes lost power to the Vatican Curia.

Just as often, the whole system simply collapses when there is too great a disparity between the appearance of government and the realities of its exercise. The heavy ritualization of aristocratic life in the French court gave rise to a series of cardinals, mistresses, and ministers acting as the real powers behind the throne, and eventually the entire system fell. Louis XIV was able to control much of the ceremonial life which he himself helped create, but his successors were not able to do so. French affairs fell to such people as Cardinal Fleury, Madame Pompadour, Madame du Barry, and Ministers Turgot, Malesherbes, and Vergennes, ending with Finance Minister Calonne under whose administration Benjamin Franklin received assistance for the American Revolution. Throughout this time the kings and aristocrats of the court continue to appear as rulers of state, signing documents, granting audiences, issuing proclamations, and going through even more elaborate rituals of government.

The American Congress is not yet as ritualized as the old French court, but the process is analogous. The elected legislators have become specialists in their roles as ceremonial actors, but increasingly these ceremonies are choreographed, written, directed, and produced by the staff.

11

⋐§⋑

Battling Guerrillas
and Swatting Gadflies

A<small>N ACUTE SHORTAGE</small> of women developed recently in a village of the Yanomamo—the exceptionally fierce tribe inhabiting the jungles of Venezuela and Brazil. According to the anthropologist Napoleon Chagnon, the Yanomamo men sought to relieve this dearth by strategy that combined their traditional ferocity with some tricks learned through dealings with Christian missionaries. Taking some pots, machetes, and other trade goods acquired from the westerners, the Yanomamo paid a visit to a more remote jungle village which had an ample supply of females. Displaying their metal wares to the rustic villagers, the Yanomamo explained that they had been taught by the white man to pray to a new god who supplied these treasures. As an act of camaraderie and amity, the Yanomamo were willing to teach the unenlightened men of the village how to do the same thing.

The first step in praying to this new god was for all the village men to get down on their knees, bow their heads, shut their eyes, and put their hands together. As soon as the villagers complied, the Yanomamo attacked them with their steel machetes, butchering the whole lot. They then herded together the hysterical widows and daughters and marched them back to their own village.

Even by the rather loose and violent standards of Yanomamo culture this was an act of treachery, what they called *nomohoni,* the ultimate form of violence. The Yanomamo allow for a wide usage of both trickery and violence; in some ways they even encourage them. Nevertheless, the deceit does have boundaries, and the violence is often highly ritualized in a variety of duels between individuals or village groups. The ruse of teaching another village to pray and then massacring them while in this defenseless position went beyond the culturally prescribed perimeters of normal deceit and tolerated violence. In the opinion of the Yanomamo men themselves, only the extreme exigency of not having any marriageable women justified such a bloody violation of their own standards.

A similar raid to steal women also worked in ancient Rome. In need of women to populate their newly founded city, the Roman warriors attacked the neighboring Sabines, slaughtered the males, and abducted the women and girls to become their wives. Although this episode has been repeatedly romanticized in stories and paintings as the rape of the Sabine women, the general culture of the Romans by no means condoned rape, kidnapping, or murder.

Striking by surprise in violation of the unwritten rules of warfare is a standard strategy of opponents who are weaker or fewer in number. Such tactics worked as well for the American revolutionaries under General Francis Marion, the legendary Swamp Fox, fighting Great Britain as they did more recently for Ho Chi Minh and the Viet Cong fighting first the French and then the Americans. With lesser success they have been used by Afghanistan tribesmen against the Soviet Union, by the Palestinian Liberation Organization against Israel, and by South Moluccans against Indonesia. But guerrilla activities need not be confined to revolutions; on a smaller, more circumscribed scale, they can be used within institutions as well. A sudden coup by a minority of stockholders can overthrow a board of directors, or students refusing to obey the rules of their university can storm the administration building.

Within Congress, too, there is usually a minority that deems it helpful to violate many of the unwritten norms and occasionally some of the written rules of the organization. Like guerrillas throughout the world, these people proceed with stealth and cunning, striking in unusual ways at unexpected targets. To round out our present analysis of congressional politics, we need to look at the actors who deliberately violate the patterns outlined so far.

THE TERRIBLE H'S

Senate Bill 210 to create the Department of Education arrived on the chamber floor just before Easter 1979. Carefully scripted and choreographed by the staff through several years of committee hearings and investigations, its passage appeared routinely imminent. Senator Abraham Ribicoff, who had been Secretary of Health, Education, and Welfare under President Kennedy, was the primary sponsor and, as leader of the Governmental Affairs Committee, he directed a large clan working on the bill. They had already lined up a majority of the Senate as co-sponsors, including prominent committee Republicans Charles Percy and Jacob Javits. Jimmy Carter had been cajoled into supporting the bill by the politically active National Education Association as a 1976 campaign promise to them, and with him Carter brought the cooperation of his cabinet.

Ribicoff's clan worked out a scenario whereby the bill would be on the floor for two days. After a series of supporting speeches by the long list of promoters, a few amendments would be made, and the bill would be forwarded to the House of Representatives. For the first few hours the proceedings followed the script. Opening praises were lavished on the bill by its sponsors, and all the committee-sponsored amendments attained approval without dissent. Senator John Melcher of Montana, not a member of the committee, introduced an amendment adding rhetorical phrases about rural family education, and, as already worked out by the staff, those words were added by voice vote. As planned, both Ribicoff and Percy praised it as "an excellent amendment" and thanked Melcher for helping them to improve the quality of the bill.

The most controversial point of discussion that day centered on setting a time for the Easter recess to begin. Most senators wanted to start on the Tuesday before Good Friday, and in order to book their airlines reservations they needed to know the time precisely. United Airlines was on strike, other airlines were booked with heavy holiday travel, and by adjourning on Tuesday before the weekend rush, senators hoped to take a full two-week break. Since the Education Bill was not expected to take long, they agreed on a Tuesday afternoon adjournment. With that pressing issue resolved, Senator Helms announced that he had a few amendments he would like to attach to the Education Bill.

Even though Helms's staff had not arranged this with the Ribicoff clan ahead of time, no one appeared overly alarmed. Helms, it was assumed, either had some special clause he wanted inserted as a gesture to his constituency or else he would raise one of his easily defeated diatribes against school busing. Helms rose in the back of the chamber and introduced Unprinted Amendment 69 to remove the issue of school prayer from the jurisdiction of the United States Supreme Court. The couches buzzed with incredulity. What did that mean; was it constitutional to remove something from Supreme Court jurisdiction? No one had ever heard of such an amendment or law.

Sensing that whatever it meant it was bad for the bill, the Ribicoff team immediately moved to table the amendment. At this point Helms was expected, by the rules of Senatorial courtesy, to lose gracefully. He had made his move, which would please the backers who donated that $6 million in the last campaign; and if he allowed himself to be gracefully defeated, he would have appeased them without causing any real trouble to his colleagues in the Senate. Helms, however, demanded a roll-call vote; he was going to the mat on this one.

The buzzers sounded, lights flashed, and bells rang through the complex signaling senators to rush to the chamber floor. With police clearing the hallways of gawking tourists, one senator after another stumbled into the Senate to find out why they had been called so unexpectedly. Although it was still a week and a half before Easter, only eighty-six of the one hundred senators were present, and at the end of the fifteen-minute voting period, they stood evenly divided: forty-three voted to table and forty-three not to table. Without a majority, the motion to table was denied, thereby permitting a vote on the Helms amendment. Senators George McGovern, Lowell Weicker, and Donald Stewart suddenly disappeared from the floor. The Ribicoff forces were able to locate only one more senator, Daniel P. Moynihan, to pull in for their side. The amendment passed. Ribicoff's clan was falling into disarray, for the amendment would kill the bill, which was exactly what Helms intended it to do.

Ribicoff made a motion to reconsider the vote, and by prearrangement Majority Leader Byrd then stepped forward to move for adjournment until the following Monday, allowing Ribicoff four days to scrape up enough votes to defeat the amendment. Over the weekend, the Ribicoff and Byrd forces worked together to devise a counter-strategy. Bringing in Vice President Walter Mondale to preside and thereby avoiding another tie vote, they would bring to the floor a bill relating to the courts, attach the Helms amendment to it, and then return to the Education Bill. Senator Dennis DeConcini, the sponsor of the Court Bill, approved the plan; but as soon as Senator Kennedy, the chairman of the Judiciary Committee, heard of it, he objected. Kennedy did not want any such issue attached to a bill coming out of his committee. By Monday afternoon, the unexpected problem had become a legislative snarl, and the Senate was a free-for-all with a five-way clan war going on among the forces of Ribicoff, Byrd, DeConcini, Kennedy, and Helms. In the words of Senator Helms, "comity is in disarray"—a parliamentary euphemism meaning that all hell has broken loose. Like sharks smelling blood, other senators were rushing to the floor to join the fray. Two bills were on the floor, two versions of the prayer amendment were under consideration, and five clans argued over it all. Finally, Majority Leader Byrd flaunted his ultimate weapon. Seizing the microphone, he announced: "I thought the Senate would be recessing tomorrow night, but it does not appear that it will be." Raising his voice like an irate school marm, Byrd repeated: "I say I thought the Senate would be recessing tomorrow evening but it does not appear it will be."

Byrd paused as his words quieted the room and their import was weighed—missed airplane reservations, the airline strike, no vacation, no fact-finding mission to China, no parliamentary union meeting in Paris. Byrd then softened his tone. "I would still hope that we could have a vote on this amendment and this bill." Faced with the united disapproval of the other senators, the warring clans were forced to be quiet. Then under a series of "unanimous consent" orders, Byrd waived all the remaining rules that had not been broken, attached the prayer amendment to the Court Bill, passed the Court Bill, returned to the Education Bill, and removed the prayer amendment from it. The ordeal had taken up nine votes, five days, and had ruined a whole day in the schedule of Vice President Mondale. If the Senate were to recess in time for Easter, the remaining ceremonies necessary to pass the Education Bill would have to be postponed. It was almost a month before the Senate finally got back to the Education Bill and passed it; and it was not until May 1980 that the Department of Education finally opened its doors for business.

The episode contradicts most of the normal congressional patterns. Helms struck by surprise, forcing senators to vote on an issue their staffs had not had time to analyze. The senators themselves had to become the political actors: in the process they violated all of the unofficial rules of congressional etiquette and many of the official rules of parliamentary procedure. The real decisions were being made "live" on the Senate floor, where senators were speaking without a written text or a list of staff-approved talking points. In the ensuing confusion, Helms had managed to get his prayer amendment passed (on the Court Bill) and he had substantially delayed the start of the Department of Education. By tossing his ideological bomb into the public arena of the Senate, Helms blew apart the ceremonial decorum. Committee hearings and all the other rituals of Congress were suspended for several days while the Senate repaired itself.

At the time of this incident, Helms was the leader of a band of Senate guerrillas who specialized in just such disruptive tactics. The group was often called "The Terrible H's" in reference to the initial letter of the names of its most outspoken members—

Helms, Hatch, Hayakawa, and Humphrey. In 1981 the group was expanded to include newly elected Paula Hawkins and John East, a Helms protégé who, because of his confinement to a wheelchair, was dubbed "Helms on Wheels." They did not strike often, for to do so would have made them too predictable; but when they did attack, it was with enough force and panache to generate sustained publicity and crippling damage to the liberal establishment of the Senate. They did not draw up detailed strike plans, plot long strategies, fire warning shots months ahead of time, or try to approach the opposition through neutral mediators. As with the Yanomamo raid on their neighbors, the Terrible H's depended on total surprise and exceptional cunning. The Yanomamo did not try to bargain or trade for wives, nor did they challenge the other village to a duel or battle. They attacked. So, too, Helms simply attacked, without warning.

When the conservative Republicans assumed control of the Senate in 1981, the Terrible H's were no longer guerrillas attacking the system from outside—they were the inside powers. Helms became chairman of the Agriculture Committee and moved his clan into all the appropriate staff slots. The decimated liberals of the Senate became the minority, forced to think up their own guerrilla tactics to fight the conservatives. As Senator Helms explained in the confirmation hearings for Secretary of State Alexander Haig, he had to surrender the title of "Jesse the Bombthrower" because "now I'm catching them."

The new liberal guerrillas in the Senate initially attempted to use some of the same techniques that had worked so well for Helms, but in due course they tried out new kinds of "bombs" to throw. Helms and his group had such a lengthy apprenticeship as the minority that they knew how to thwart the liberals in their neophyte play at guerrilla warfare. The exact membership of the guerrilla bands changes over time with the varying sentiments of each election, and the methods also vary according to which group is in power and how vulnerable they seem to be on specific points. But there is always a group in whose interest it is to violate the normal rules of procedure.

The House, too, has its guerrilla bands, which play with the rules and wreak havoc with the plans devised by the Speaker in conjunction with the other Big Men. For a while this House guerrilla band was known as "Bauman's Gang," in recognition of the vocal leadership of Representative Robert Bauman of Maryland. Bauman, who worked his way up to congressman from his original position as page and later, as a staff aide, knew the House rules and procedures intimately, put his knowledge to use against the more liberal leadership of his own party as well as the Democrats. Overall, Bauman's Gang was less effective than the Terrible H's in the Senate, in part because the House Whips of both the Democratic and Republican parties were themselves former staffers and as well informed on House procedure as Bauman. Helms, who was also a former congressional staffer, did not have to face another staffer in the Senate leadership he was battling.

Bauman was defeated in the general election of 1980 after being charged with soliciting sex from minors, but the guerrilla band he had formed continued to operate under the old cadre plus the conservative recruits supplied in the same election. Bauman himself was subsequently hired by the party leadership as a consultant to help them in their rules fights against the weakened yet still substantial liberal minority.

GUERRILLA LOBBIES

Working in tandem with the congressional guerrillas is a new breed of lobbies using essentially the same techniques. In the episode over the prayer amendment of Jesse Helms, the strength of these lobbies appeared in a torrent of telegrams, night letters, and telephone calls that inundated the Senate between Thursday afternoon and the following Monday. The volume of constituent responses was not unique, but the speed with which it was generated was unprecedented.

In the slower legislative pace pursued by traditional lobbyists, just getting the word out to the interested supporters takes several weeks or possibly even months. These newsletters have to be carefully researched and then phrased in such a way as to win approval by a committee of affiliated lobbies. The guerrilla lobbyists, however, had little need for carefully crafted rhetoric or lengthy analyses of the technical legalities of their position.

Even before the Friday newspapers were on the stands announcing Senate passage of the prayer amendment, the guerrillas were in full operation. Through a vast network of personal contacts, relying on the telephone rather than newsletters, they passed the word to key figures in communities throughout the country. These religious and civic activists just as quickly informed fellow sympathizers, and all of them went to work sending off individual messages to their senators. By Monday morning, over five hundred religious and civic groups had passed resolutions or signed statements in support of Helms's proposal.

Like the guerrilla senators, the prime tactic of these lobbies is to move with great speed, with surprise, and then to generate the maximum publicity. They do not bother to sponsor a parade of witnesses to Capitol Hill committee hearings; nor do they fine-tune their operations to concentrate on one strategic committee one month and a related committee the next month. They forego the sophisticated computer printouts of hard data that the traditional lobbies use in appealing to the scientific and statistical training of the congressional staff. Instead, they go straight for the political soft spot—the votes. They aim to hit the politician in his home district among his own constituents. If the congressman or senator does not respond to the position of the group, they target him for defeat, as they did a number of politicians in the 1978 and 1980 elections. Unlike the traditional lobbyists, who try to play ball with everyone, these guerrilla operators are only interested in whether the politician is for them or against them. If he is against them, they will waste little effort trying to convert him or persuading him to compromise with them.

The guerrilla lobbyists show an equal lack of enthusiasm for cooperating with other lobbyists outside a narrow ideological range, and do not work on extraneous issues as political favors to their congressional supporters. Because of this unwillingness to play politics in the broader sense, they are labeled as special-interest lobbies, in contrast to the generalized interests of traditional lobbies willing to take on any issue. They support only their own, and do not try to hedge their bets by giving even token support to politicians or groups that disagree with them.

A good number of these guerrilla groups ascended into the Washington establishment with the election of Ronald Reagan and many of the conservatives they had supported for Congress. In the election of 1980, the National Conservative Political Action Committee (PAC) raised $4.5 million, a substantial portion of which went to support twenty-two Senate candidates targeted as allies. Of that number, sixteen won election and in the process defeated a whole rostrum of established Democratic committee chairmen. Using the same grass roots methods, direct mailings, and personal contacts that had worked so well in Jesse Helms's campaign of 1978, they nearly swept the Congress in 1980.

This novel set of techniques and these guerrilla tactics became institutionalized very rapidly. Literally overnight, on election night in 1980 to be exact, the conservative groups changed into *the* establishment. This transition was not just a definitional one prompted by the victory of their candidates; the change to being establishment showed in their switch to establishment strategies. Three days after the election (on November 11, 1980), the group called a press conference in Washington to announce that it was beginning to raise funds for the 1982 election and that it had a preliminary list of liberals targeted for defeat. These included such senators as Kennedy of Massachusetts, Harrison Williams of New Jersey, and Howard Metzenbaum of Ohio.

The primary change was that rather than working quietly at the grass roots level as they had done so successfully in 1978, the group was firing loud and clear warning shots a full two years ahead of the next election. In making public a list of senators, they were letting them know that these now tested and proven methods would be used against them. There was no element of surprise or playing cards close to the chest. None of the characteristics of the earlier guerrilla strategy was evident—the group was no longer a guerrilla band. Its methods had passed into the arsenal of all groups and were being emulated by liberal organizations wanting to regain office.

The change from guerrilla to establishment lobbies was evident in a more profound way as well. The National Conservative PAC put a large number of middle-of-the-road senators on notice that they, too, might experience the fate of the 1980 liberals. The conservatives did not presume that they could coerce old-style liberals like Kennedy into the conservative camp, but they did include in their list some not-so-liberal senators like Daniel P. Moynihan of New York, Lowell Weicker of Connecticut, and Paul Sarbanes of Maryland. These senators were being warned to cooperate with the new Senate powers like Helms and Thurmond or risk the demonstrated power of the National Conservative PAC to defeat them. In other words, the conservative lobbies were acting as conduits of pressure and information from the conservative leadership to the rank and file. In this sense they had moved inside Congress, so to speak, and were fulfilling the real role of lobbyists—to work for the Big Men in power.

Correspondingly, the establishment lobbies, including consumer groups and public action organizations that leaped from being guerrilla to establishment in the 1970s, were then kicked outside. They could still act as channels of power for a minority of legislators, but much of their function had been usurped by the new conservative lobbying groups.

BREAKING THE RULES

No matter how Congress is organized and what the current rules of political propriety demand as proper behavior, it is always in the interest of some group to violate those norms and aim directly at the weak point, the Achilles heel of the people in power. Just where this vulnerable spot is varies from generation to generation as the organization and political climate slowly change. The guerrilla tactics of one era will not be appropriate to another, but the strategies always focus on some form of obstruction.

It was in just such a fashion that the classic weapon of the filibuster first arose in the nineteenth century. In 1854, in a debate over the proposed Kansas-Nebraska Act, a minority of senators banded together to defeat the act by exploiting the tradition of unlimited debate. Since then the filibuster has been used alternately by both liberals and conservatives to block the will of the majority, but subsequent changes in Senate rules have made it much less potent. Although it is still a significant tool in the armory of any guerrilla band, it has been reduced to one of a number of equally obstructionist tactics, thereby lessening its original power.

The very term "filibuster" originally had the same connotations as the word "guerrilla." First used by Dutch sailors, *frij buit* (literally, free booty), as a term applied to pirates who raided Dutch merchant ships, was picked up by other European nations as *der Freibeuter* in German, *el filibuestro* in Spanish, and freebooter in English, all meaning pirate or vandal. In the nineteenth century when the Spanish no longer had pirates like Sir Francis Drake raiding their ships, they expanded the term to refer to American adventurers who were intent on fomenting revolution in Latin America against the Spanish crown. From this usage of the term, *filibuestro* was taken over by the Americans to describe willful hindrance and the insurrections of rabble-rousing politicians. In time the meaning of the word narrowed to that particular brand of obstruction known as talking an issue to death, and it is in this sense that the filibuster survives in Congress today.

The filibuster no longer carries the revolutionary connotations it once did; it has long since become an accepted, though modified, tool in the legislative game. In the same way, the original practitioners of that art themselves became part of the political establishment of the time. In many senses the history of the filibuster and its users presaged that of Helms and his guerrilla tactics. What was once an unusual set of tactics employed by nonconformist politicians was modified as both the tactics and the practitioners became accepted parts of the congressional machinery. Through this process the culture of Congress constantly, albeit slowly, drifts and changes. Those who foster the changes are usually the radicals of the day; but as they gain power, they become the new establishment. The process then repeats itself as a band of radicals enters the system under another name and develops its own variety of obstructionism. Whether they are called Young Turks, radicals, filibusterers, or guerrillas, the process continues in essentially analogous repetitions of the same scenario.

The congressional guerrillas and their affiliated lobbies provoke a splash of real, though fleeting, action in the ceremonial play of politics. The genuine sincerity with which guerrillas promote their causes, whether against the Vietnam War in the 1970s or school busing in the 1980s, infuses the system with a momentary life that shows just how moribund the normal procedures are. They contradict the usual rules and rhythms of Congress, but in so doing, expose the ceremonial and sterile politics of legislation.

As a consciously macho enterprise, even in the rather tame setting of twentieth-century industrial America, politics sparkles with the action metaphors of struggle and warfare. Like war correspondents covering the trenches of Verdun, journalists and television reporters sprinkle their assessments with the argot of battle—phrases like "marshaling the troops," "digging in for the siege," "sallying forth to fight," "duel of will," and "hand-to-hand combat." The congressional arena clamors in a primeval *bellum omnium in omnes* as one warrior struggles against another, as committee fights committee, and as the two chambers of Congress wage constant warfare on each other. In this glorified and gorified atmosphere there are no losers, only victors and martyrs; even the defeated have the honor of falling on a heroic field surrounded by eulogies to their noble struggle.

At a remote time in congressional history, these fights were real; but they have long since been tamed and ritualized into combative displays. The senators resemble those knights who, long after armor and lances were outdated on the battlefield, continued their stylized form of combat in jousting pageants. Attired in the full regalia of struggle, glowing in the romantic rhetoric of chivalry, they sallied forth to poke at one another in a harmless travesty of manhood. So too do the grand heroes of Congress confront one another in the daily assault of debate that has long since lost any resemblance to actual struggle of decision making. The point was noted by Lord Bryce a century ago when he wrote that the skirmishes of Capitol Hill cause tremendous concern and a seemingly life-or-death excitement in the City of Washington, but rarely are taken seriously by the citizenry outside. In the final analysis, "the country seems to be watching a fencing match rather than a *combat à outrance* [fight to the death]."

But because it is all so carefully staged, scripted, and choreographed beforehand, the pseudo-warriors make easy targets for real fighters. When the guerrillas strike, they do not just parry and thrust before bowing for applause; instead, they wreck the whole performance and unmask the legislative charade for what it is. Therein arises their greatest danger to the system and their greatest power. By violating congressional protocol and the normal confines of the legislative game, the guerrillas—whether the doves of the last decade or the neo-conservatives of this one—threaten to expose the system. In this regard it is not the explosion of the guerrillas' bombs that the other legislators fear so much as their exposure in the light thus emitted. As quickly as possible the whole system rallies round either to expel or to co-opt these forces.

FOOLS, SAINTS, AND OTHER GADFLIES

Guerrillas operate outside the normal boundaries of political action, but often they achieve some power within the system, as shown by practitioners of the filibuster in the nineteenth century and by the Terrible H's in this century. Further from the center of power circles a motley collection of nonconforming politicians who rarely manage to bring their orbits in line with the expectations of normal congressional culture. This idiosyncratic assemblage has been dubbed fools, saints, gadflies, untouchables, and nuts, and although the turnover in their ranks is high, every Congress seems to attract at least a few more. By normal standards, it may seem strange to lump together in one cognitive group individuals as disparate as a fool and a saint, but in the pragmatics of power the distinction between the two blurs. Even a buffoon in office usually has a cadre of supporters who view him as a hero. What both of them have in common is that aloofness from the system which marks them as outsiders, whether they incur respect or opprobrium for it. It does not matter that the uniqueness may be rooted in exceptional stupidity, perversity, or integrity. Their place remains on the outer fringes of the congressional constellation.

Although almost every member of Congress is labeled a fool at some stage in his career and almost all of them appear moronic in their first years learning the political system, a few stand out as classic examples of pure stupidity. They achieve fame within the narrow confines of congressional folklore as exemplary personifications of what a politician should not be or do. High on this list ranks Richard Kelly, the only Republican congressman convicted in the Abscam scandal. His 1981 trial for accepting bribes capped a totally inept career. After serving as the city attorney for Zephyrhills, Florida, he advanced to the office of judge, presiding over the state's sixth judicial district. Even though he was impeached for badgering court lawyers, witnesses, and even other judges, the Florida Senate did not convict him; the state judicial commission ordered him to undergo psychiatric evaluation, which he did voluntarily.

Despite all of this, Kelly was elected to Congress in 1974 as one of the few Republicans to win in that Watergate year. Bragging that because of his mental examination, "I'm the only member certified to be sane," Kelly frequently voted with Bauman's Gang, but even for them he was too erratic and strange to be admitted to their guerrilla band. Having been married four times, his was not quite the image they wanted. Undismayed, Kelly launched an independent campaign against government spending. He began by donating part of his salary to the U.S. Treasury, but quickly ran into trouble when he overspent his rather generous office allowance by $12,000 and had to pay back the money with bank loans. With such debts and alimony obligations, the $25,000 bribe offered him by the FBI agents posing as Arab sheiks seemed a godsend. According to FBI videotapes, Kelly stuffed the cash into every pocket he had and then, always concerned about his appearance, asked whether it showed. He kept the money in the glove compartment of his car, and when arrested, quickly returned the unspent portion, explaining that he took the money as a part of his own investigation into the shady associates of his staff. He spent part, he claimed, only to convince his bribers that he really was a crook; after all, if they could afford that large a bribe, they could probably afford someone to follow him and check to see what he did with the money. Although the Republican caucus immediately expelled Kelly, the irony was that many colleagues felt Kelly was so lacking in sense that his preposterous excuses might actually be true.

The closest intellectual rival to Kelly in the Senate was Virginia Senator William Scott, who served from 1972 to 1978. For most of his career, Scott worked as the typical Washington bureaucrat, holding various civil service jobs under administrations from that of Franklin Roosevelt through that of John Kennedy. All the while, he lived across the Potomac River in the suburbs of Virginia, where he established a private law practice after leaving government service. Following a quiet tenure in the House, Scott was elected to the Senate in 1972 largely on the basis of a quarter-million-dollar campaign contribution from an anonymous millionaire. His only public recognition came when the Fort Worth *Star-Telegram* revealed that in advertising for staff, he had demanded "white only." The only time he made the cover of a national magazine was when he appeared on the front of *New Times* under the headline: "The dumbest Congressman of them all: Sen. William Scott." In response, he indignantly called a press conference to deny the charges and thereby spread the news from that one publication to all the newspapers in the country. Scott threatened to sue for libel but then backed off, explaining: "I don't want to bring a suit and not win." Claiming that if he did lose, "People will think it's true," he dropped the issue.

Throughout this distinguished political tenure, Scott acquired a record as one of the best-travelled officials in the government, visiting twenty-nine countries in a single congressional term. Like all congressional junketeers, he explained his travel as being necessary to acquire personal knowledge about the pressing issue of legislation. As the most apt example, Scott cited his trip to the Panama Canal while the United States was preparing the new treaty with Panama. He claimed to understand in much better detail the function of the Canal after seeing ships travelling on it in both directions.

As so often happens with the truly stupid, they are eventually flushed out of politics by their own constituents, leaving behind a series of didactic anecdotes, but having made no substantial mark on the system. Such men often wind up as objects of public ridicule; they tarnish the image of Congress but do not inflict irreparable damage. Even while embarrassing other politicians, they siphon off some of the pomposity inherent in politics and serve as negative models for the public behavior of other politicians.

At the opposite extreme from men like Kelly and Scott appear the politicians whose personal demeanor, rhetoric, and actions place them half in the legislative world and half in the church. Former Senator Philip Hart of Michigan left such a reputation when he died in 1976. Hart was known as the conscience of the Senate and, as such, was one of the worst politicians. Whereas most senators jump at the opportunity to pick up one or two staff or even a thread of jurisdiction, Hart agonized over whether or not he should take the proffered chairmanship and staff of the Monopoly Subcommittee under the Committee of the Judiciary. After nine very public days of hand-wringing and advice from Hubert Humphrey, Hart reluctantly assumed command of the powerful organization. His indecisiveness over every issue earned him the nicknames of "Hamlet" from admirers and "Chicken Hart" from critics. Hart refused to go through with the ceremonies of political attack, always preferring instead to say something nice about his opponents. Even as chairman, he prevented his staff from aggressive questioning of witnesses. At one hearing when his aides were questioning representatives of Blue Cross, Hart stopped the proceeding, explaining that "it sounded too much like Kefauver"—the senator who had acquired a national following as the preceding chairman of the panel.

Unwilling to play the informed role so important to the charades of politics, Hart often admitted to not knowing much about the issues. At a press conference on one of his bills to regulate non-ferrous metals, he confessed to the startled audience: "I don't know what the hell non-ferrous metals are." After reading a staff-prepared speech on the Lockheed loan, he admitted on the floor of the Senate that although he did not understand what he was talking about, he thought his staff did. So unpleasant were the ritual duties of legislation and politics that Hart once admitted: "If I knew twenty years ago what I know today, I would have walked in front of a bus then." Hart displayed a

Jesuit's reasoning and erudition, but along with these came the concomitant proclivity for martyrdom—a fate that finally caught up with him in his agonizing death from cancer while he was still trying to serve in the Senate. His beatification into the congressional pantheon came when the Senate named its newest office building in his honor.

The revered position of Philip Hart in Senatorial folklore stands as a radiant example of the sincerity and sensitivity with which all politicians wish to be portrayed. At the same time, his ghost lurks as a reminder to the more pragmatic of just how ineffective a senator can be if he allows such sentimentality to interfere with his politics. In this way Hart, like Kelly and Scott, acquired a place in the cultural configurations of Congress without having had a significant impact on the social or political organization of the institution.

A figure who nearly succeeds in combining the pragmatic and saintly roles of politics emerges from the folklore about Congresswoman Barbara Jordan, who unexpectedly resigned in 1978 at the height of her popularity. As both a female and a black representing a Texas district, she was an anomaly from the time of her first election to Congress in 1972. Even though she maintained a liberal record on most social and domestic issues, Jordan persistently supported the major economic concerns of her district, including oil and gas. In the process she managed to work effectively with national and local leaders who were ideologically opposed to her, as evidenced, to the dismay of many liberals, by her support of conservative Senator Lloyd Bentsen, her fellow Texan Democrat. In addition to her acknowledged intellect, Jordan possesses those two other necessary traits of a good politician—she is a charismatic speaker and she knows how to wheel and deal behind the podium. After only four years in Congress, Jordan was chosen as a key speaker at the Democratic Party Convention that nominated Jimmy Carter. This propelled her to her first wide national exposure, but shortly thereafter she chose to resign.

Before her retirement in 1978, Jordan showed every indication of becoming a real political power within Congress and thereby the first Big Woman in the decisively male hierarchy of the institution. Yet this decision to retire, in spite of demonstrated abilities and her seemingly rosy future, raised Jordan to the awesome level of respect she acquired after leaving Congress. Had she gone on to become another Speaker or a powerful Warlord, she would not so readily have become a candidate for sainthood. Like the athlete dying young, Jordan departed in a blaze of highly regarded potential without sullying her record. In a body that so glorifies conquest and battle, such voluntary renunciation of power ranks with the enigmatic sacrifices of the Martyrs.

In between these saints and fools falls a kind of legislative outsider more difficult to categorize. While few observers would quibble over labeling Philip Hart a congressional saint or William Scott a less than inspiring figure, such characterizations are applied with equal conviction by the critics and by the admirers of gadflies such as William Proxmire and James Abourezk. Their respective careers illustrate the gamut of possible outcomes for such perverse politicians, and (at least in the case of Proxmire) illustrate how occasionally the system can adapt to include a nonconformist.

James Abourezk flamed through the Senate as one of the most colorful and outspoken legislators in this century. His far-left politics qualify him as the only true radical in the Senate since World War II and as the most controversial senator in the history of his home state of South Dakota. While his views seemed orchestrated to offend every group, he managed to build a constituency out of them. On the one hand he worked hard for Indian land rights in the West, hardly an issue popular with the Dakota farmers who battle in the courts with Indians today almost as doggedly as their ancestors did on the plains during the last century. Nevertheless, Abourezk sparked an affinity with those same farmers by the populist spunk and almost juvenile iconoclasm he maintained in all of his politics. As the only Lebanese-American in the Senate, he vociferously championed the rights of the Arabs and Muslims over Israel, burying the rivalries that his own Syrian Orthodox religion had with some of those same Arabs. Even while defending the Arab causes in international diplomacy, he persistently denounced the oil and gas industries and their role in the American economy. Indeed, he felt so strongly on the issue that he took to the floor in a filibuster in his last few days in office, thereby incurring the considerable wrath of his colleagues anxious for adjournment.

Abourezk left the Senate in as much controversy as he arrived. At his retirement press conference, he told the reporters that he was glad to escape the Congress, which he called a "chicken shit outfit," and in his last days he sported a lapel button with the same epithet. After his retirement in 1978, Abourezk went on to spark heated controversy in the Senate when he remained in Washington lobbying for unpopular causes. The most opprobrium was directed toward him for his role as legal representative for the Iranian government while the Iranian radicals held the fifty-two American diplomatic hostages.

Even when not defeated at the polls, politicians like Abourezk tend to quit Congress about as regularly as do the Scotts and Kellys. Their isolation within the congressional system usually corresponds to the degree to which they generate real controversy, as opposed to just political publicity. One senator who did manage to turn his role of gadfly into that of Congressional Warlord, however, is Wisconsin's William Proxmire, the former television commentator elected to the Senate in 1957. Together with his wife Ellen, he ended each of his programs by drinking a glass of milk on camera—a move that earned him the gratitude of dairy farmers, but struck his colleagues as rather weird. Proxmire's milk-drinking, however, was only one small part of his health fetish and an almost maniacal concern with his body. Every work day began with two hundred pushups and a four-mile jog to the Senate office building. He often worked standing up, ran through the congressional hallways, and talked louder and faster than almost anyone else. Proxmire not only watched his physique, but had hair transplants to combat his baldness.

It was not, however, his odd personal habits so much as his ruthless attacks on congressional sacred cows that earned Proxmire the dislike of his colleagues. On George Washington's Birthday in 1958, a day of great solemnity when Washington's Farewell Address was read to the Senate, Proxmire accused Majority Leader Lyndon Johnson of trying to "dominate" the Senate. This prompted one of his colleagues to report, "The Senate heard two speeches today: Washington's Farewell Address and the farewell address of William Proxmire." Despite this attack, Proxmire remained in the Senate and continued to attack every big spending issue from the financing of the SST and the M-X missile system to the loans for the Lockheed and Chrysler corporations.

Behind his unconventional outbursts, Proxmire carefully fabricated his own clan, carving out authority over the Department of Housing and Urban Affairs. Despite the pessimism of that department's bureaucrats when Proxmire assumed chairmanship of the committee over them, they continued to prosper even more than before. With this rise to power, however, Proxmire's style also underwent a related change. Under the auspices of his monthly Golden Fleece Award, he continued his apparently iconoclastic attacks on government spending, but they were severely moderated. He still fired an occasional salvo at the Pentagon, but his sardonic rhetoric was aimed chiefly at academic research projects. Satirizing studies examining why people fall in love, get angry, or clench their teeth, Proxmire maintained a high public profile, but minimized the antagonism from his colleagues. His style had been ritualized into a loud but harmless performance, which the other members of Congress, long conditioned to ceremony, could more easily understand. As long as he did not try to do any real harm to their domains, they were willing to leave his alone.

Proxmire's long apprenticeship as a gadfly before becoming a Warlord served him well when the Democrats lost control of the Senate in the 1980 election. With Ronald Reagan in the White House and the Republicans controlling all of the Senate committees, Proxmire emerged as the only Democrat with any guerrilla experience. The party leaders like Robert Byrd and Alan Cranston, as well as the deposed committee chairmen, had spent most of their legislative careers in more agreeable roles as mediators and facilitators pursuing consensus politics. The transition to outside critic was not easy for them; but Proxmire seemed to relish it, immediately attacking defense expenditures in the 1982 budget and voting against confirmation of some of Reagan's cabinet officers. Thus Proxmire's role as gadfly became institutionalized as he turned his Mau-Mau attacks away from his Democratic colleagues and toward the Republican administration, thereby promoting not just his 1982 reelection campaign, but the entire party as well.

Proxmire's case illustrates how even the most unconventional deviants, in times of change, can play a significant role in congressional politics. In the same way, other marginal types, such as the guerrilla warriors, represent persistent forces of change that, very slowly over a long number of years, do bring new methods and procedures into the political arena. In fact, guerrillas can be one of the few forces for change in an otherwise very conservative set of rituals. The changes induced by such guerrillas, however, take the form not so much of the ideologies that wash over Congress in rapidly succeeding waves as of more subtle changes in methods and procedure, which then become available to anyone pursuing any ideological cause. The filibuster is added, then modified. Other obstructive techniques are devised and eventually incorporated into the routine procedures, thus expanding the steps in the long ritual of legislation. As antidotes are developed to combat these new tactics, further preventive steps in the legislative process are added to make an ever-lengthening script. In violating the normal congressional standards, guerrillas add to the growing ceremonies that make up the ritual of legislation.

The majority of congressional gadflies, however, never make a change. Politicians like Scott, Kelly, and even Abourezk arrive on the scene, cause a tempest of one kind or another, and depart, leaving the body relatively unchanged.

AMAZONS ON THE POTOMAC

The ancient Greeks left voluminous texts on various peoples, both real and fictional. One of the most bizarre to intrigue the interest of subsequent generations derived from the legend of a female tribe that killed off its males and, except for procreation, lived, fought, and ruled without the aid of men. For centuries these Amazons were thought to live somewhere in the wilds of Asia Minor or in the Caucasus Mountains. The Greeks wrote about and searched for this mysterious tribe for centuries without success. The legend surfaced again when Columbus discovered the New World, and the hunt was resumed. So sure were the Spanish explorers that they had at last found the home of the fabled women that the river on which they were assumed to live was named the Amazon.

Anthropologists have fairly well recorded all the groups of South America, including the Yanomamo and the Shavante, yet they never did locate the tribe of women warriors. Good stories, however, die hard, and whereas the scientists abandoned the quest, others did not. The search for the Amazon women continued in many parts of the world, but nowhere more fervently than in Washington. Ever since the first woman was elected to Congress in 1916, articles and books have been regularly published about the newly emerging or about-to-emerge power of women in Congress. Somewhere lurking within the thick brush of Capitol Hill, the budding power of female politicians is about to burst forth and be recognized. The heralds of the new tribe jump at every shred of evidence they can find. If the proof were not in the election of the first woman to chair the Post Office Committee, then surely it must be in the first female to use profanity on the floor. If the new importance of women is not evident in the selection of the first woman for the armed services panel, then it must be in the fact that one of the women smokes a pipe. Despite these signs (always lurking behind the pillars or just beyond the next election), the real power of women never seems quite to materialize.

In 1981, the total number of women in Congress had not attained even 4 percent of the body; nor had the preceding years been ones of steady increase. The number of women in Congress hovered around a dozen from the end of the 1920s until the early 1950s, when it began growing again, reaching a high of twenty in 1962. Despite the increased concern over women's rights and female equality, the figure declined steadily throughout the 1960s. By 1970, it was back to the level of the early Eisenhower years, then increased to fifteen in 1972 when Elizabeth Andrews was elected to fill the term of her husband, and Governor Edwin Edwards of Louisiana appointed his wife to the Senate to fill out the term of deceased Senator Allen Ellender. Not until the Republican victories in 1978 and 1980 did the total number of women reach twenty, matching the old record set in 1962.

The declining number of women in office in recent decades coincides with the congressional rules against relatives being hired as staff. Service on their husbands' staffs had been in earlier decades the primary path for many women (Margaret Chase Smith is one example). At the same time that the rule against nepotism was established, non-relatives on the staff began running for those elected offices and winning. The rule against nepotism closed off one of the few insider roles that had been available to women, and in its place made possible the recent phenomenon of male staffers succeeding their chiefs. By 1981, only four of the women in Congress had begun as replacements for their husbands on the ballot. Another two, Senator Nancy Kassebaum and Representative Olympia Snowe, had been congressional staffers before their election. Generally, however, the exemption of Congress from the Civil Rights Act prevents women from rising to very high ranks on the congressional staff. Both Snowe and Kassebaum, who did manage to parlay their staff positions into elected offices, began with the advantage of having a husband or father active in other political arenas prior to their getting jobs on Capitol Hill. Most women who do not have those political connections have not been able to rise in the ranks of the staff and thus have been excluded from a major avenue to elected office.

Regardless of whether the women entered through the inside networks or fought their way up via city councils and state legislatures, their place within Congress consistently remained on the edge of power. For a while the lack of female power within Congress was attributed to their lack of service in secondary political arenas; but as ever more experienced women were elected and still failed to gain power, it appeared that the reason must lie elsewhere. It possibly derived from the women's lack of exposure to the peculiarly masculine styles of interaction in locker rooms and men's clubs. Women often find it difficult to engage in that particular type of ritual behavior so common to male interaction. Men, in turn, minimize such behaviors around women for fear of being ridiculed.

Although the Congress has never had a real female chief, much less a whole clan of Amazons, the role of women in their marginal capacity has at times been important. Not being a part of the clan politics, women have often been able to violate normal congressional standards and perform some extremely unconventional actions that no insider could have done. This was the case when Margaret Chase Smith took the Senate floor on June 1, 1950, and denounced Senator Joseph McCarthy. Warning that the Senate was being turned into a "forum of hate," she issued a Declaration of Conscience against the tactics of McCarthy. In so doing, she opened a floodgate of sentiment, first in the Senate and then throughout the country, which finally ended the McCarthy era and freed the government to concentrate on the real issues of the nation. Though a Republican, like McCarthy, she was not inhibited by the web of political relations that had prevented her colleagues and the press from denouncing so formidable a tribal chief as McCarthy.

In similar fashion, Jeannette Rankin had broken with congressional traditions a generation before. Rankin was the first woman ever elected to Congress, arriving in 1916 from Montana four years before the Nineteenth Amendment to the Constitution gave women the right to vote. Voting against America's entry into World War I cost her her reelection, but she finally returned to Congress in 1940. Once again she voted against American participation in another external war, but this time she was the only member of Congress to do so. So severe was the reaction of her colleagues and the public outside that she had to be escorted from the Capitol by armed guards. Again she lost her seat, but undaunted she continued campaigning against sending American soldiers to die in foreign wars in Korea and Vietnam.

The verdict of her constituency may have gone against the unpopular stand of Jeannette Rankin, just as it did for a while against Margaret Chase Smith's unusual action; but such episodes provided Congress with an alternative voice which its traditional members could not give. In many less spectacular ways the same principle continued in operation as roles were found for women that no one else could handle. This happened in 1970 when the exceptionally outdated procedures of the House

needed reform for the necessary realignment of some clan territories and modification of the seniority system. The committee
established to study the problem and write guidelines was
placed under the control of Julia Butler Hansen of Washington
State. Her efforts established the framework for the changes
that followed in House organization over the next five years, although many of the reforms were never approved by Congress.
As a respected person on the margins of power, she was able to
offer the objectivity and neutrality which the quarrelsome chiefs
lacked, even if she had little power to make the changes.

Being on the fringe means that often the women become professional gadflies, adding a great deal of color but little substance. Such was the case when the glamorous socialite and
playwright Clare Boothe Luce served in Congress at the close of
World War II. Her chic clothes and stylish good looks made fine
photographs for the picture magazines of the era, and her
barbed repartee with other politicians and acerbic wit made good
copy for the news magazines, but her presence was seen far more
that it was felt. The short tenure of Bella Abzug in the early
1970s caused another diversion, with her odd clothes and her
use of four-letter words. She provided amusing sidelights for the
television news and tested the abilities of reporters to find adequate rephrasing for her undiplomatic utterances. But like her
media predecessor Congresswoman Luce, Abzug's lasting imprint was one of style rather than content.

Whether or not the marginal role of women in Congress will
change, as is constantly proclaimed, is difficult to predict. Perhaps as more women find ways to work up the political networks of staff and inside politics, or perhaps as the masculine
style of political interaction changes, there may one day be a female chief among the tribal clans of Capitol Hill. So far, there
appears to be no concrete evidence and little historical precedent for such a development. The search for the Amazons continues.

CONCLUSION

12

⤙§⤚

Clan, Culture, and Nation

THE CONOY INDIANS who inhabited the Potomac three centuries ago are now largely forgotten. A few of their descen-
dants still live in the area and cling to the remaining threads of
their traditional culture, but the Conoy are generally ignored by
historians and unknown to most newer Americans. Their fate
provokes speculation about the ultimate destiny of the modern
tribes on the Hill and how anthropologists of the distant future
will look back on this era and judge its civilization. Archeologists may conclude that after several millennia of small settlements in the Potomac River area, the society suddenly
flourished, increased many times in size, and erected a huge cult
complex on and around Capitol Hill. As a religious center of
grandiose architecture, it obviously consumed the labor of tens
of thousands of workers over many decades, hauling granite and
marble blocks from as far away as Vermont and Georgia. Under
the names of Nacochtanke, Washington, or simply the Place of
the Hill, it could join the Mayan city of Chichén Itzá, the Cam-
bodian complex of Angor Wat, or Great Britain's Stonehenge as
one of the mysterious spots in human civilization. Conversely,
like Athens, Peking, Jerusalem, and Mexico City, it may con-

258 / TRIBES ON THE HILL

tinue with its ups and downs as a dynamic and seemingly permanent actor in world history.

We, today, will obviously never know the future verdict on our own time and way of life. We cannot foresee how long this present civilization will endure; how, if at all, it will be remembered; whether the present tribes will soon die out, or, like remnants of the Roman world, survive for centuries. Judging from our past and present, however, as well as from the fate of other peoples and their culture, we can speculate about some possibilities.

Many of the tribal societies examined so far are either extinct or on the verge of destruction from outside forces. The Shavante and Yanomamo survive in a perilous condition, threatened by the numerically greater and technologically more sophisticated invaders of their homelands, just as the original Indians on the Potomac were threatened. The social systems of the Hutu, Twa, and Watutsi collapsed under the twin transitions into colonialism and then an independent nation. Despite the enlightening parallels which some may draw between these societies and certain aspects of life in the United States Congress, these tribes and the Congress are ultimately quite different entities. The Congress is not literally a tribe in the sense that the Shavante or Watutsi are, and the Congress is not in danger of attack by another tribe sailing up the Potomac or scaling the marble terraces of Capitol Hill to lay siege to the community.

Nevertheless, though it may lack real enemies, Congress does have some rivals for power and some threats to its continuity. Within the federal system, Congress shares power and often competes with the presidency and judiciary. Within the larger scope of American society, Congress occasionally battles state and local governments or combats institutions such as business, the press, and the churches. But the greatest potential threat always seems to be the voters. Unlike the other tribes, Congress has to worry about what its constituency thinks of it, and steadily throughout this century, that opinion has been sinking ever lower. What kind of genuine threat do these other forces pose?

ENDANGERED TRIBES ON THE HILL

Congress may have fallen in public esteem, it may be the object of frequent complaint, derision, and editorial chastisement, yet it has little to fear from the public. Congressmen are reelected more often than ever before, they stay in office longer, and even though as an institution Congress may not be well liked, individual congressmen are held in high regard within their own districts. Occasionally, as in the Watergate election of 1974 and the surprise Republican victory in 1980, the voters seem to have finally risen up against the "establishment" Congress. But this is more an illusion of danger than any genuine threat.

The 1980 election returned 85 percent of the old Congress back to form the new Congress. Only 36 politicians out of the 535 in Congress failed to be reelected, while almost that number retired or sought a different political office. Without those voluntary retirements, well over 90 percent of the Congress may have been reelected.

Even in the Senate, which changed hands from the Democrats to the Republicans, seven of the new senators came out of the old House. Also included in the supposedly new face of Congress were as many of the old families as usual and an all-time number of congressional aides elected to full office. Amid much press speculation, the old political family of Herman Talmadge of Georgia was defeated after his misuse of public monies. With considerably less attention, however, Chris Dodd of Connecticut was elected to the Senate and brought his brother with him as an assistant, marking the return of the Dodd family after their father had been defeated a decade earlier for misusing public funds. The reemergence of other political families was marked by the election of Denny Smith, son of a former Governor of Oregon, and by one of his cousins, Steve Symms, of Idaho. A few of the staffers-turned-politicians were defeated— men such as Senator Culver of Iowa and House Majority Whip John Brademas of Indiana—but the dozen new staffers elected to office for the first time more than compensated to keep that trend alive.

If the 1980 election was an example of an especially hostile message from the voters to Congress, then the Congress has little to fear. Any group that can go into combat and lose only a handful of its oldest men in its worst years of fighting is in no immediate danger of extinction. If there were a message at all, it implied that Congress should continue as usual, but avoid getting caught in ethics or sex scandals. Were it not for such scandals, the only threat to a congressman's career would seemingly be old age and death.

When congressmen are not complaining about the terrible way their constituents are treating them, they bemoan the great threat posed to them by special-interest groups within the electorate. Single-issue politics seems to be the bane of a politician's existence. Yet by remaining divided, such groups ensure no united opposition and thus blunt its impact. They may be a petty annoyance, but they are not dangerous. When one group campaigns solely on abortion, another solely on nuclear energy, and yet another solely on school busing, the politician suffers only if he finds a way to alienate all of them at once. Occasionally in political history one of these groups has coalesced into a genuinely potent force, as happened with the prohibition movement and with the movement against the war in Vietnam. In such cases, Congress quickly surrenders on that one issue, the opposition dissipates, and then Congress continues its other policies unimpaired. Most such special interests, however, die out long before they reach such magnitude.

Having so little to fear from the general voting population or from any segment within it, Congress finds its major rivalry from within the government itself, from the White House just down the street from Capitol Hill. When the President appears to have united strong electoral approval behind him, this coalition of the President with the voters seems to pose problems for clan politics in Congress. Here again, the 1980 election supposedly was a good example of such a threat. The people rebuked a sitting President and elected one who promised to do something about the run-away government and economy. To do this, Reagan, in sharp contrast to his predecessor, immediately embarked on a strategy to win over congressional help in his enterprise. He made it abundantly clear that in tackling the problems of government he intended to work closely with Congress, observe their rituals, avoid breaking their taboos, and pay all the courtesy calls on the Big Men that were necessary to get the job accomplished.

Reagan's approach greatly pleased the tribal powers on the Hill, and they in turn pledged their mutual support, love, and comity. Getting the help of Congress in curing the nation's problems was tantamount to asking the Mafia to help the country fight crime and then telling them that if they would help, the campaign would be fought according to their rules and procedures and would not violate any of their ceremonial traditions.

With great alacrity, Congress came forth to help Reagan. Like recently allied chiefs who exchange wives, daughters, and a few other relatives to cement a pact, all of the Congressional Clans were ready to donate a few of their members to help Reagan run the government. Reagan already had as his Vice President George Bush, a former member of Congress, son of a member of Congress, and father of an unsuccessful candidate for Congress. For his cabinet he appointed former Senator and previous vice presidential running mate Richard Schweiker as the Secretary of Health and Human Resources, and for the first time two former congressional aides reached the pinnacle of cabinet-level appointments. David Stockman, who began his political career as babysitter for the Moynihan family, went on to become a legislative assistant in the House, and finally a congressman himself, was appointed to lead Reagan's budget fights as Director of the Office of Management and Budget. The new Secretary of the Interior, James Watt, was greeted in the press as a wild man from the Rockies sent to wreak havoc on the environmental programs. Far from being a stranger to Washington, however, Watt was the former legislative assistant to Senator Milward Simpson, whose son Alan Simpson had just joined the Senate himself in the election of 1978. Watt, Stock—man, and Schweiker immediately enlisted the assistance of a host of other congressional aides who had served with them and with some of the other Big Men on the Hill.

For the real outsiders in the cabinet without Washington experience, the Congressional Clans opened up their membership to provide assistance in administering the bureaucratic maze so difficult for the uninitiated to comprehend. Senator Paul Laxalt's daughter Mimi went to help at the Agency for International Development, as did an assistant to Senator Goldwater. Senator Mark Hatfield's son went to work in the White House, as did Senator Robert Dole's wife, who took with her one of her husband's top aides. Other staffers poured out of the offices of John Warner, Roger Jepsen, William Armstrong, and Jack Kemp. To show that the new administration was not overly partisan, they parceled out some of the high appointments to members of the Democratic clans of Daniel Moynihan and Scoop Jackson.

Although Reagan proposed to trim back the budget and thereby cut into the old clan territories in the bureaucracy, the willingness with which he embraced the traditional practices of clan politics had an exhilarating impact on Congress—so exhilarating, in fact, that Congress decided it must be safe to hire some of those congressmen defeated in the previous election. The Republicans in the House hired Robert Bauman, who had just been kicked out of office for soliciting sex from a minor, and Bauman's wife received an appointment in the Department of Energy. As soon as former Congressman Charles Diggs, Jr. was allowed to leave prison on a work-release program, the congressional black caucus returned him to the payroll as an aide.

The 1980s opened in Congress with a pronounced return to normalcy after the unpredictability of the Nixon and Carter administrations in the 1970s. Of course, there was the usual round of musical chairs that follows each election as some of the old Big Men departed and some of the juniors rose to the level of clan leaders. But the changes in faces and names hardly altered the game. The liberal Harrison Williams had been ousted as chairman of the Labor and Human Resources Committee; in his place was Orin Hatch, one of the charter members of the Terrible H's and a committed backer of Reagan's new austerity programs. As soon as Hatch assumed leadership of his old rival's clan territory, he began defending it with exceptional vigor. The Job Corps program, for example, had long been criticized as a waste of money, costing more to train a laborer than to send him or her to Harvard University. Hatch immediately defended it as a cost-efficient enterprise, and as one of the Reagan allies, he deflected the budget ax away from it and toward the weaker clans. Hatch then went on to defend OSHA (the Occupational Safety and Hazard Administration), which he had long been accustomed to attacking, but which was now in his territory. Under the protection of Hatch, the labor programs in general were much better off than had they remained under Williams, who lacked the clout with the new administration necessary to defend them so effectively.

Similarly, Charles Percy, who took over as chairman of Foreign Relations from defeated Frank Church, was able to protect that other traditional target of the conservatives, foreign aid. In so doing, it did not hurt him that a number of congressional aides and kin had been appointed to office in the Agency for International Development. Other programs from Headstart to Foster Grandparents fell under secure patronage, and there was never any question of cutting the traditionally conservative strongholds of Defense and Agriculture. It hardly mattered that the Agriculture clan had changed from Senator Herman Talmadge of Georgia to Senator Jesse Helms of North Carolina, or that Senator John Tower had replaced old John Stennis as the head of the Military Clan.

With their own territories securely protected, the clan leaders next had to deal with the serious business of how to parcel out the budget cuts among the territories of the less powerful. The first step for the House Budget Committee was a trip to Europe for five Democrats, five Republicans, nine aides, and two consultants. Beginning in London, the budget cutters sought advice in Brussels, Rome, and even in an audience with Pope John Paul II, before returning to Washington to settle their own priorities.

Some programs and pieces of turf, of course, did suffer, and to the extent possible both Reagan and the Congress worked together to share those cuts as equally and impartially as was practicable among the weaker Congressional Clans. Despite this suffering by a few individual parts of the system, and the more than usual publicity and speculation associated with it, the normal flow of clan politics and organization persevered undamaged. Congress was willing to sacrifice a chunk of the budget to the President, as long as he did not interfere with its clan territories.

Despite Reagan's promises to the nation to clean up the government, the 1980s opened with the specter of even greater latitude for the Congressional Clans in running their bailiwicks. In his inability to command Congress effectively, Reagan was not alone. Carter before him had tried to run the government by ignoring congressional protocol to the extent possible, by appointing his own people to the high offices in the bureaucracy, and even by interfering with the traditional patronage of senators in nominating federal judges. Reagan abandoned all of that in favor of the cooperative approach, just as Ford had tried cooperation in the face of the failure of Nixon's confrontation tactics.

Despite the much-touted power of the executive, Presidents have rarely been much of a match for Congress. On occasion a President such as Franklin Roosevelt, Abraham Lincoln, or Lyndon Johnson arrives on the scene and for a while appears to lead Congress, but in each case their successors in the White House forfeit much of the ground that had been won. After Lincoln, Congress impeached Andrew Johnson. Although it allowed him to stay in office, it ran the country directly without further interference from him. Again, after Lyndon Johnson Congress drove the next President from office and severely reduced his power over the budget, foreign affairs, and the bureaucracy.

In comparing the relationship of the American Congress and President with that of other legislative assemblies in history, Lord Bryce concluded that time and politics were always on the side of the assembly. Despite periodic leaders like Julius Caesar, Oliver Cromwell, or Napoleon, legislative bodies have the advantage in the long run:

> Men come and go, but assembly goes on for ever; it is immortal, because while the members change, the policy, the passion for extending its authority, the tenacity in clinging to what had once been gained, remain present . . . its pressure is steady and continuous; it is always, by a sort of

natural process, expanding its own powers and devising new methods for fettering its rival.

Even if a President should, in the final decades of the twentieth century, succeed where so many others have failed to harness Congress, there is little historical justification for thinking that the presidency as an institution will triumph for long. Occasionally the President can rival, but only rarely threaten, the political power and continuity of Congress. The tribes of Capitol Hill, therefore, are in little danger from the President.

THE LURE OF THE STAGE

The tribes on the Hill do not appear to be endangered from any external source, and the hold of Congress on the powers of government seems to be as strong, if not stronger, than ever. Yet Congress is slowly grinding to a halt before the eyes of the nation. Each year it takes longer to get through the session, although Congress produces fewer pieces of legislation. The bills that do survive the mill of congressional ritual show little potential for curing the major problems of the nation. They are compromised and hammered into pap designed to produce a little bit of everything, but nothing decisive.

The frequent excuse for not working on the major legislative problems of the nation is that Congress is more involved in the budget process than it was in the past. This increased involvement in the annual housekeeping of government came in the wake of the Nixon administration and Congress's resolve to take a more active role in setting the parameters of the whole budget rather than just individual pieces of it. The first step was for Congress to push back the beginning of each fiscal year from July to October, thus giving the members three additional months for careful consideration of each year's expenditures. Even so, Congress could not meet the new deadline and routinely began pushing the date back to December and relying on emergency resolutions to fill the gap. Still the members could not quite finish the task on time. When the date arrived to vote on the budget for the fiscal year 1982, they were still working on

266 / TRIBES ON THE HILL

the budget for 1981, which was half over. Never too concerned about such matters, Congress then tackled both budgets at once.

Why doesn't Congress work? With so much power concentrated in its hands, with all the daily control of the bureaucracy centered in its clans, and without any dangerous threat posed to it by the voters, the President, or any other institution in the society, why can't Congress get on with its job of running the nation? The answer is often attributed to the seniority system, entrenched interests, regional rivalries, an antiquated political system, the lack of strong parties, or the abuse of the filibuster and obstructionist tactics. Periodically each of these becomes the focus of a concerted effort to reform and modernize Congress, but just as quickly the idea is lost somewhere in the process of due consideration. These elements of the political process, however, have always been around and have not seriously impaired the course of politics in the past. It is quite possible that people have focused too much on these essentially normal, if not convenient, parts of the system as the cause, when in fact it is something else entirely.

Congress's paralysis results not from the political elements in its composition, but from the increasingly complex web of needless ritual and ceremony in which it has become ensnared. The greatest deliberative body in the world has become the greatest ceremonial body in the world, and the talents of its members are devoted less to deciding the matters of national policy than to arranging and considering the minute points of ceremony. When they should be working out the budget, they are too busy issuing press releases about it. When they should be looking at tax reform, the two houses are arguing over who should begin which part of the bill first and how far the conference room should be from the Senate office building or the House office building. Instead of overseeing government spending, they are fighting for a new office with a chandelier and more impressive view of the Mall. When they should be working on energy policy, they are jogging for the newspaper photographers. And instead of looking seriously at the needs of the military, they commit a public relations spectacle by riding in a new tank or launching a ship. Instead of working on foreign policy, they are on a state visit to the Caribbean or posing for a picture with the Pope.

Every society known to anthropology has some form of ritual and ceremony. But in most of the small-scale societies these rituals are incorporated into daily activities in a way that helps to make the drudgeries of practical work easier and to lessen the anxieties of the insecure. A festival may be a reward for the difficult tasks of harvesting, hunting, or fishing. An evening dance around the campfire may help to calm fears of the unknown. Even in the New Guinea ritual *Moka,* with all its fancy dress and feathers, its ritual speeches and ceremony, the basic task is still the very practical redistribution of pigs and yams from those people who have an excess to those who need.

Ritual in large-scale, settled cultures, on the other hand, often has a way of running amok. The ritual complex nourished in Congress has no parallel among the Shavante, Yanomamo, or Watutsi. For comparisons we must turn to groups such as the Aztecs, the Byzantines, Persians, or the French court at Versailles. There, at the center of the nation and far away from the tedium of normal work, empty ritual grew to play an ever-increasing role in the daily lives of the empire's leaders.

It is easy for us today to see the pernicious effects that ritual had on those societies, to see how they became entrapped in their escalating rounds of ceremony. It is much harder to discover similar trends in institutions closer to home, and separate out the essentials from the superfluous in our own political arenas. The Americans reward with reelection that politician who can best blow-dry his tinted hair and bat his curly eyelashes, rather than the one who is at his desk working on the details of the disarmament treaty. They applaud the one who most frequently struts and frets across their television screen, but ignore the one who has hammered out a policy on nuclear non-proliferation. The politician who can most passionately deliver an enraged diatribe in the committee room and who knows how to exploit the pauses in the question and answer session receives more attention than the one who has dealt thoroughly but less dramatically with the real issue.

Like Athenian politicians in the waning of that city's independence and democracy, American politicians are rewarded for their public image, their oratory, their sophisticated rhetoric, and even the cut of their garments, more than for the effectiveness of their work. These politicians, like their counterparts in the closing days of Greece, rarely even bother to write their own speeches, leaving such mundane technical matters to subordinates while they concentrate on what counts—the performance.

Just as politics and theater merged in ancient Greece, both being performed on different days in the same public arenas, so too in the United States have the two merged in the spectacle of television. Under such circumstances, it is hardly surprising that an actor finally won the highest political office in the United States with a former actress as his First Lady. When politicians become actors, actors also become politicians. At least the actor is a professional capable of making the performance *look* genuine.

The Carter administration probably failed because of its inability to help Congress bolster its rituals and performances, as much as for any other reason. The folk wisdom of Capitol Hill maintains that the failure of his administration was assured when his office refused to give extra tickets to the inauguration to Tip O'Neill. Symbolically, that casual approach to the important ceremonial concerns of Congress represented the reluctance of Carter, in congressional eyes, to cooperate with them in what was really important—appearances. Reagan, however, with his professional attention to the details of the performance, did not fall victim to that lack of concern. He played upon the susceptibility of Congress to the glory of pomp and circumstance. There was some grumbling in the lower congressional ranks about the new dress standards and the extra cost of all the extravagant public spectacles, but by and large the Reagan administration hit upon a receptive note in Congress. The politician who must play one of the polyester people back home while looking for votes appreciates being treated in Washington with the decorum and dignity he feels befit his high status in life. His act comes alive amid the black ties, uniformed guards, blaring bugles, and other accoutrements accorded to an actor on the stage of world events.

In most civilizations in which the leaders of the nation were more involved with pageantry and ritual than with the affairs of the nation, power temporarily passed into the hands of those "servants" around them. The decisions of government were exercised by eunuchs, by palace guards, slaves, the women of the harem, the Curia, or, as in the case of the modern Congress, by staff aides. As a temporary solution to the power vacuum, assistants can keep the machinery of state functioning in a piecemeal fashion while the leaders attend to their public appearances, their wigs, hair dryers, banquets, and official portraits. Gradually, however, the system grinds to a halt, the nation continues to deteriorate, and the system implodes under the weight of its own rituals. Power then passes elsewhere. It may go to the former subordinates, who, like the eunuchs of the Byzantine court, took over the government. It may flow into the streets, as it did with the Revolution in France, or the empire may fall to an outside power, as did Greece and Persia to the new vitality of the Macedonians. In any event, an institution so laden with ritual and so devoid of work and substance cannot long endure.

It is Congress's own culture that is its greatest threat to continued existence. It may be safe for a while, but if it continues to pay more attention to the appearances of its facade than to the real problems of the country, then its future as an institution is endangered, as is the prosperity and vitality of the nation as a whole.

CAN CONGRESS BE SAVED FROM ITSELF?

April Fool's Day of 1989 will mark the two hundredth anniversary of the first meeting of Congress. That occasion provides an opportunity to reassess what has been done by Congress and where it is going. The people in Congress have thus far been reluctant to question their own *modus operandi*. They quickly point to external origins for the evils in American society. The finger of guilt jerks from the Soviet Union to the oil cartel, from Japanese imports to world terrorism. Even when looking inward at our own society, members of Congress only want to blame factors far from Washington. One politician blames big business, the next the immoral minority; one looks at pollution, the other at the loss of the work ethic among laborers. Only when on the campaign trail do they point the blame back at Washington. It is always easy to blame some group of people or some visible entity, but it is difficult to step back and examine one's own social and cultural organization. But the Greeks knew (though they failed to act upon it) that the fate of human beings, their institutions, and even whole nations, often rests on small follies, little quirks in men's natures, which pull the world down around them.

America today, however, has one important tool which the past civilizations and endangered tribes of history all lacked. It is not something from our formidable arsenal of weapons nor an ingenious invention from the science lab. What we have behind us is the failed experiences of all those other peoples, the accumulated knowledge of thousands of years and hundreds of different cultures, preserved in cuneiform tables, Hebrew scrolls, broken potsherds, Latin manuscripts, Mayan hieroglyphics, Chinese engravings, and Greek texts. We have more knowledge about the total range of diversity in which human social life and culture can be found than any other people known to history. Most societies in this human history have had only their own experiences to learn from, as well as possibly those of one or two neighboring groups. The consequences of their actions were discovered only after the act was completed. But Americans today have the unique opportunity to anticipate the actions of their society by looking at the fates of others. They have the means to perform the arduous task of viewing themselves and their institutions through strange eyes and thereby accomplishing that elusive quest to understand themselves and their own culture.

If this knowledge of other people is put to proper use, there is no reason why the United States cannot continue as a vital nation with a strong political core. It can rejuvenate its institutions and keep the democratic arena alive as a place where problems are faced and decisions made rather than as a mere stage for the ritual performance of politics. There is no law of nature that civilizations and cultures must decline, be conquered, or collapse. That is merely a tradition which, with extreme care and study, may be avoided. Only the Congress can save itself from itself. Only Americans can save themselves and keep from being confined to the dustbin of museum relics as just one more interesting culture, which arose and then mysteriously withered away.

NOTES

Chapter 1: On a Hill Faraway

page

5 Henry Fleet, 1631; Robert L. Humphrey and Mary Elizabeth Chambers, 1977; William Henry Holmes, "Stone Implements of the Potomac-Chesapeake Tidewater Provinces," *Fifteenth Annual Report of Bureau of Ethnology,* Washington, D.C., 1897.

6 U.S. Department of the Interior, Geological Survey, *Building Stones of Our Nation's Capital,* Washington, D.C., 1975.

6 Aristotle, *The Politics,* Book IV, Chapter 14.

11 Henry Fleet quoted in Edward D. Neill (ed.), 1871, p. 228.

13 Humphrey and Chambers, *op. cit.,* p. 4.

19 Woodrow Wilson, 1885 (rev. ed. 1956), p. 59.

20 *Congressional Directory,* published annually by U.S. Government Printing Office, Washington, D.C.

PART I. CLIMBING THE POWER PYRAMID

Chapter 2: Coming of Age in Congress

page

28 David Maybury-Lewis, 1974.

30 *Congressional Quarterly,* January 20, 1979, 94.

34 Transcripts of Donald Riegle's lovemaking appeared in the Detroit *News*, beginning October 17, 1976. Riegle's own account of his early years in Congress may be found in his book *O Congress*, 1972.

35 William "Fishbait" Miller, 1977. "vagina instead . . ."

35 James M. Perry, "How Not to Win Reelection," *The Wall Street Journal*, October 19, 1980.

37 The alignment of classes and the seniority pyramid change slightly during the congressional session because of deaths and retirements. During 1981, for example, David Stockman left Congress to become Director of the Office of Budget and Management; a special election was called to fill the seat of Gladys Noon Spellman when illness prevented her from attending Congress; and a special election filled the seat of Ron Hinson after his arrest on a morals charge.

38 Dennis Farney, "House Panel Chairmen, Their Powers Reduced, Use Guile, Persuasion," *The Wall Street Journal*, May 3, 1979.

39 Alan Goodman, "What Happened to the Class of '74?", *Roll Call*, November 2, 1978.

40 Alvin M. Josephy, 1979, pp. 317–340. Re: Roosevelt election.

41 Walter J. Oleszek, 1978. Re: changing procedure in House.

42 Richard E. Cohen, "Freshmen in the Senate Being Seen— And Heard," *National Journal*, March 17, 1979, 439.

Chapter 3: Gathering a Clan

page

45 Andrew Strathen, 1979; Douglas Oliver, 1955; H. Ian Hogbin, 1964; Bronislaw Malinowski, 1922; also Bronislaw Malinowski, "War and Weapons Among the Natives of the Trobriand Islands," *Man*, 20:10–12, 1920.

46 "Slayers of Pigs and Men": Oliver, *op. cit.*, *passim*.

47 The "Big Man" phenomenon is found in numerous different societies in the New Guinea area. Frequently, however, these men are not warriors at all, concentrating their activities around civil duties, particularly as they relate to the redistribution of food and economic goods.

48 Harrison W. Fox, Jr., and Susan Webb Hammond, 1977.

50 Cox family: Jack Anderson, 1979.

50 Josephy, Jr., p. 348; William Miller, 1977, pp. 255–266.

51 Fox, Jr., and Hammond, *op. cit.*, pp. 22–28.

51 F. G. Bailey, 1969.

51 Plutarch's *Life of Gaius Marius.*
52 *Gravel* v. *United States,* 408 U.S. 606.
61 Stephen Isaacs, *The Washington Post,* February 16, 1975.
62 Jones and Woll, *op. cit.,* p. 128.

Chapter 4: Extending the Clan

page
67 Although Kennedy has not successfully sponsored a major piece of legislation, he did play a major role in the issue of airline deregulation, and some observers credit him with the resulting act. Details are available in Jones and Woll.
68 *Congressional Quarterly,* "Kennedy and Rodino: How Two Very Different Chairmen Run Their Panels," February 2, 1980, 267.
Steven V. Roberts, "Big Staff Reflects Kennedy Influence," *The New York Times,* May 4, 1979.
70 Carla Hill, "The Politician as Media Master and Life of the Party," *The Washington Post,* July 30, 1979.
73 John Stennis quoted in U.S. Senate, Hearings of the Rules Committee, 1977.

PART II. POLITICS IN WONDERLAND

Chapter 5: Conquering the Bureaucracy

page
88 James Bryce, 1921, p. 160.
88 In the anthropological literature, the tribe is usually referred to as "Tutsi" and occasionally as "Tussi." The prefix "Ba" or "Wa" is added to mean roughly "of the Tutsi people." Here Watutsi is used with the prefix and Hutu without it.
Jacques Maquet, 1961, 1971, 1972; Lucy Mair, 1974; Elliot P. Skinner (ed.), 1973.
Helen Codere, "Power in Rwanda," *Anthropologica,* IV:1, 1962.
René Lemarchand, "Power and Stratification in Rwanda," *Cahiers d'Études Africaines,* 6:4, 1966.
92 John Randolph quoted in Wilson, *op. cit.,* p. 117.
92 Memo of Patricia Harris, August 16, 1979, quoted in *Congressional Record,* October 23, 1979.
Lawrence Feinberg, "HEW Order to Employes Assailed by Congressman,"*The Washington Post,* October 24, 1979.
94 Wilson, *op. cit.,* p. 180.

94   Demosthenes, *On the Liberty of Rhodes,* Paragraph 1.

95   Fox, Jr., and Hammond, *op. cit.,* p. 119.

97   Aristotle, *The Politics,* Book III, Chapter 11.

98   Livingston Biddle, Jr., *The Washington Post,* May 15, 1980.

102   Morris P. Fiorina, 1977, p. 3.

103   *Congressional Record,* September 9, 1980, S12272-S12285.
ENR: McGraw-Hill's Construction Weekly, "Army Auditors Fault Corps," April 27, 1978; "Tenn-Tom Traps Corps in Political Web," February 8, 1979.
Johnny Green, "Southern Gothic: The Corps of Engineers Digs In Again," Los Angeles *Times,* June 10, 1979, V3.
James J. Kilpatrick, "Why This $3-Billion Boondoggle," Washington *Star,* July 29, 1980.
Wayne King, "Army Engineers Under Attack," The *New York Times,* February 4, 1979, 4E.
Ward Sinclair, "Stennis Advice Kills Hearing on Waterway," *The Washington Post,* May 12, 1980.
U.S. Army Corps of Engineers in Alabama, *Water Resources Development,* January 1977.

105   Mike Gravel quoted in *The Washington Post,* May 12, 1980.

110   Michael Psellus, *Chronographia,* Book VII, Paragraph 52.

Chapter 6: Domesticating the Lobbies

page

113   Marc J. Swartz and David K. Jordan, 1976, pp. 51–52.

116   James Madison, *The Federalist,* Paper #10.

116   Daniel Webster quoted in Josephy, Jr., *op. cit.,* p. 154.

116   John Quincy Adams quoted in ibid., p. 189.

117   Alexis de Tocqueville, 1945, Vol. I, p. 211.

118   John F. Kennedy, "To Keep the Lobbyist Within Bounds," *New York Times Magazine,* February 19, 1956, 42.

119   "how to be . . . effective": quoted from *Congressional Quarterly,* May 17, 1980, 1346.

119   Allard Lowenstein quoted in Mark J. Green, 1975, pp. 30–31.

120   Frank Moss quoted in *Congressional Quarterly,* July 12, 1979.

120   Robert Bates, Jr., "Big Oil Can't Always Get What It Wants," *The Washington Post,* May 20, 1979.

121   David Broder, "Mobil Executive, Foe of Restraints, to Aid Kennedy," *The Washington Post,* November 20, 1979.

122   F. G. Bailey, 1971, *passim.*

122 Marcel Mauss, 1975.
123 Marvin Caplan, "The Zing and Glamor of a Lobbyist's Life," *The Washington Post,* August 12, 1979.
123 Green, *op. cit.,* p. 33. "Senator Hollings . . ."
126 Art Harris, "Ambition That Sprouted in Georgia Thrived in D.C.", *The Washington Post,* May 28, 1979.
      Mary McCory, "Peers' Reluctance to Judge Is Talmadge's Strong Card," *The Washington Post,* May 1, 1979; "Minchew a Man of 'Blind Allegiance'?", *The Washington Post,* May 22, 1979.
127 Charles Peters, 1980, p. 6.
129 Don Oberdorfer, "British Say Helms Aides Hurt Talks," *The Washington Post,* September 20, 1979.
      Kathy Sawyer, "Two Helms Point Men," *The Washington Post,* November 27, 1979.
      Richard Whittle, "Helms Aides Run 4 Tax-Exempt Groups," *The Washington Post,* September 22, 1979.
130 *Congressional Quarterly,* May 17, 1980, 1345.
131 *Congressional Quarterly,* February 3, 1979, 183.
      Science, March 30, 1979, 1319–1322.

Chapter 7: Recycling Congress

page
141 Herbert C. Pell, unpublished oral history, Columbia University, 1951.
144 Margaret Chase Smith quoted in Hope Chamberlin, 1973, p. 146.
150 William S. White, 1968, *passim.*
158 Jones and Woll, *op. cit.,* pp. 114–122.

PART III. THE CONGRESSIONAL MYSTIQUE

Chapter 8: The Ritual of Legislation

page
164 Bernal Díaz, 1963.
166 Peter Farb, 1978, p. 191.
167 Fisher Ames quoted in Josephy, Jr., *op. cit.,* p. 45.
167 Fisher Ames quoted in George B. Galloway, 1969, p. 12.
172 James Sterling Young, 1966, p. 72. "Major debates and contests . . ."

173 Josiah Quincy and Roger Griswold quoted in Galloway, *op. cit.*, p. 130.

174 Alexander Borisovich Lakier, 1979, p. 252.

174 Bryce, *op. cit.*, pp. 120–121, 147.

176 Wilson, *op. cit.*, p. 69.

176 Lakier, *op. cit.*, p. 252.

177 Woodrow Wilson quoted in speech of Rep. Sydney Anderson, *Congressional Record*, September 11, 1913.

178 Georges Balandier, 1970, p. 41.

178 George Hoar quoted in Wilson, *op. cit.*, p. 83.

180 J. Parnell Thomas quoted in Anderson, *op. cit.*, p. 112.

183 James Hamilton, 1976. Regarding Butterfield testimony.

Chapter 9: Tower of Babel

page

188 Díaz, *op. cit.*, pp. 240 and 138.

188 Andres de Tapia quoted in Marvin Harris, 1977, pp. 159, 164.

189 Matthew Neely quoted in Donald R. Matthews, 1973, p. 243.

190 Lyndon Johnson, *Congressional Record*, April 4, 1956, 6148.

191 Abraham Kazen, Jr., Robert Bauman, and Eldon Rudd, *Congressional Record*, April 24, 1980, H2916.

192 Lewis Henry Morgan, 1851, p. 66.

193 "the living symbol": carved on the west front of the Dirksen Senate office building.

194 Joseph Cannon quoted in Warren Weaver, Jr., 1972, p. 30.

194 Barry Goldwater, *Congressional Record*, September 29, 1979, S13761.

196 United States Constitution. Article II, Section 5, Paragraph 3.

196 *Millar* v. *Taylor.* Quoted in Howard N. Mantel, "The Congressional Record." *The Western Political Quarterly*, Vol. XII, 4, 1959, p. 987.

197 Cicero (trans. Michael Grant), *In Defense of Aulus Cluentius Habitus*, pp. 50, 139.

198 Suetonius (trans. Robert Graves), *Julius Caesar*, 20; *Augustus*, 36.

199 Joseph Clark, *Congressional Record*, February 19, 1963.

201 Richard Neuberger, "The Congressional Record Is *Not* a Record," *New York Times*, April 20, 1958, 6–14.

201 Anderson, *op. cit.*, p. 29.

201 Weaver, Jr., *op. cit.*, p. 22.

202 Hale Boggs, *Congressional Record*, October 18, 1972.

202 Clarence Cannon, *Cannon's Procedure in the House of Representatives*, p. 125. Washington GPO. 1953.

202 Speaker Champ Clark quoted in Weaver, *op. cit.*, p. 22.

203 *Congressional Record*, April 24, 1980.

203 David Quadro quoted in *Congressional Record*, July 11, 1978, E3677.

203 Howard E. McCurdy, 1977, p. 86.

204 Jones and Woll, *op. cit.*, p. 163.

205 Select Committee on Improper Activities in the Labor Management Field, U.S. Senate, quoted in Hamilton, *op. cit.*, p. 10.

206 Budget estimates quoted from *Congressional Quarterly*, November 24, 1979, 2652.

Chapter 10: Choreographing the Congress

page
215 Josephy, Jr., *op. cit.*, p. 87.

216 W. A. Peffer, "The United States Senate: Its Origin, Personnel and Organization," *North American Review*, Vol. 167, 1898.

216 Aristotle, *The Politics*, Book II, Chapter 3.

217 John F. Bibby, Thomas E. Mann, and Norman J. Ornstein, 1980, pp. 82–94.

218 Herman Talmadge, *Congressional Record*, June 9, 1975, S10131.

218 Bryce, *op. cit.*, p. 149.

221 Wilson, *op. cit.*, pp. 194–195.

221 Ralph Nader Congress Project, Ted Siff and Alan Weil, Directors, 1977, pp. 26–52.

222 Mendel Rivers, *Congressional Record*, March 3, 1970, H5710.

223 Kenneth Bradshaw and David Pring, 1973, p. 68.

224 Charles Mathias, *Congressional Record*, January 30, 1980, S648.

224 Weaver, Jr., *op. cit.*, p. 185.

225 Margaret Boone, "Committee Work in Congress," *Practicing Anthropology*, Vol. 1, 3, February 1979, 6.

225 James Reston, "The Hidden Legislature," Washington *Star*, December 1, 1979.

225   John Warner, *Congressional Record,* December 20, 1979.

225   Morris Udall interview in the film *A House Divided,* Gateway Films, 1978.

225   Hollings's quote. Senate Appropriations Committee, *Hearings of the Subcommittee on the Legislative Branch,* April 21, 1975.

226   Mike Mansfield, *Congressional Record,* February 19, 1963.

226   Bradshaw and Pring, *op. cit.,* pp. 244–247.

227   Irwin B. Arieff, "Growing Staff System on Hill Forcing Changes in Congress," *Congressional Quarterly,* November 24, 1979, 2631–2646.
      Larry Light, "General Accounting Office," *Congressional Quarterly,* November 24, 1979, 2647–2652.
      Gail Gregg, "Congressional Budget Experts," *Congressional Quarterly,* November 24, 1979, 2653–2654.

Chapter 11: Battling Guerrillas and Swatting Gadflies

page
229   Napoleon A. Chagnon, 1977; Napoleon A. Chagnon, "Social Organization and Warfare," in Morton Fried et al. (eds.), *War,* 1968, pp. 109–159.

232   *Congressional Record,* April 9, 1979, and April 10, 1979.

233   *Congressional Record,* April 9, 1979, S4146.

234   Jesse Helms, Live Broadcast of the Senate Confirmation Hearings of Alexander Haig to be Secretary of State, Senate Foreign Relations Committee. Interview with Nina Totenberg, January 14, 1981.

235   Irwin B. Arieff, "House Freshmen Republicans Seek Role as Power Brokers," *Congressional Quarterly,* July 7, 1979, 1339–1348.
      Mary Russell, "Bob Bauman, Modern House Watchdog," *The Washington Post,* May 14, 1979, A3.

238   Morton Minz, "Election '80 Was Record Year for PACs," *The Washington Post,* January 27, 1981, A4.

240   Bryce, *op. cit.,* p. 188.

242   "Among the Accused," *Time,* February 18, 1980, 14.
      Michael Barone et al., 1979, pp. 181–182.

243   Fort Worth *Star Telegram* quoted in Green, *op. cit.,* p. 169.
      Barone et al., *op. cit.,* p. 889.

248   "The Senate heard two speeches today": quoted in Green, *op. cit.,* p. 247.

253   Chamberlin, *op. cit., passim.*
      Geraldine Ferraro, "Women as Candidates," *Harvard Political Review,* Spring 1979.

CONCLUSION

Chapter 12: Clan, Culture, and Nation

page
258 "The Great Congressional Power Grab," *Business Week*, September 11, 1978.
265 Bryce, *op. cit.*, p. 228.

BIBLIOGRAPHY

Anderson, Jack, with James Boyd. *Confessions of a Muckraker.* New York: Random House, 1979.

Aristotle, *The Politics,* translated by Thomas A. Sinclair. Middlesex, England: Penguin Books, 1962.

Bailey, F. G. *Tribe Caste and Nation.* Manchester, England: Manchester University Press, 1960.
Stratagems and Spoils: A Social Anthropology of Politics. Oxford: Basil Blackwell, 1970.
(ed.). *Gifts and Poison.* Oxford: Basil Blackwell, 1971.
Morality and Expediency. Oxford: Basil Blackwell, 1977.

Baker, Ross K. *Friend and Foe in the U.S. Senate.* New York: The Free Press, 1980.

Balandier, Georges. *Political Anthropology,* London: Allen Lane, 1971.

Barone, Michael, Grant Ujifusa, and Douglas Matthews. *The Almanac of American Politics 1980.* New York: E. P. Dutton, 1979.

Bibby, John F., Thomas E. Mann, and Norman J. Ornstein. *Vital Statistics of Congress, 1980.* Washington, D.C.: American Enterprise Institute for Public Policy Research, 1980.

Bloch, Maurice (ed.). *Political Language and Oratory in Traditional Society.* London: Academic Press, 1975.

Bradshaw, Kenneth and David Pring. *Parliament and Congress.* London: Quartet, 1973.

Bryce, Lord James. *The American Commonwealth* (originally published 1888). New York: Macmillan, 1921.

Chagnon, Napoleon A. *Yanomamo: The Fierce People,* 2nd ed. New York: Holt, Rinehart & Winston, 1977.

Chamberlin, Hope. *A Minority of Members: Women in the U.S. Congress.* New York: Praeger, 1973.

Cicero, *Murder Trials,* translated by Michael Grant. Middlesex, England: Penguin Books, 1973.

Clausen, Aage R. *How Congressmen Decide.* New York: St. Martin's, 1973.

Cohen, Abner. *Custom and Politics in Urban Africa.* Berkeley, Calif.: University of California Press, 1969.

Two-Dimensional Man. Berkeley, Calif.: University of California Press, 1974.

The Politics of Elite Culture: Explorations in the Dramaturgy of Power in a Modern African Society. Berkeley, Calif.: University of California Press, 1981.

Congressional Quarterly Press, *Origins and Development of Congress.* Washington, D.C., 1976.

The Washington Lobby, 3rd ed. Washington, D.C., 1979.

Inside Congress. Washington, D.C., 1979.

Demosthenes, selected speeches in *Greek Political Oratory,* translated by A. N. W. Saunders. Middlesex, England: Penguin Books, 1970.

Díaz, Bernal. *The Conquest of New Spain,* translated by J. M. Cohen. Middlesex, England: Penguin Books, 1963.

Drew, Elizabeth. *Senator.* New York: Simon & Schuster, 1979.

Dumont, Louis. *Homo Hierarchicus.* Paris: Gallimard, 1966.

Evans-Pritchard, E. E. *The Nuer.* Oxford: Clarendon Press, 1940.

Farb, Peter. *Man's Rise to Civilization: The Cultural Ascent of the Indians of North America.* 2nd ed. New York: Bantam Books, 1978.

Fenno, Richard F., Jr. *Congressmen in Committees.* Boston: Little, Brown, 1973.

Home Style. Boston: Little, Brown, 1978.

Fiorina, Morris P. *Congress: Keystone of the Washington Establishment.* New Haven, Conn.: Yale University Press, 1977.

Fleet, Henry. "A Brief Journal of the Voyage made in the Bark 'Warwick' to Virginia and other parts of the Continent of America" (original published in 1631). Reprinted in *The English Colonization of America During the Seventeenth Century,* Edward D. Neil (ed.). London: Strahan & Co., 1871.

Fox, Harrison W., Jr., and Susan Webb Hammond. *Congressional Staffs: The Invisible Force in American Lawmaking.* New York: The Free Press, 1977.

Fried, Morton, Marvin Harris, and Robert Murphy (eds.). *War: The Anthropology of Armed Conflict and Aggression.* Garden City, N.Y.: Natural History Press, 1968.

Galloway, George B. *History of the House of Representatives,* New York: Crowell, 1969.

Giraldo, Z. I. *Public Policy and the Family.* Lexington, Mass.: D. C. Heath, 1980.

Gluckman, Max (ed.). *Essays on the Ritual of Social Relations.* Manchester, England: Manchester University Press, 1962.
Custom and Conflict in Africa. Oxford: Basil Blackwell, 1963.
Order and Rebellion in African Tribal Society. London: Cohen and West, 1963.

Green, Mark J. (with Bruce Rosenthal and Lynn Darling). *Who Runs Congress?* New York: Bantam Books, 1975.

Groennings, Sven and Jonathan P. Hawley (eds.). *To Be a Congressman: The Promise and the Power.* Washington, D.C.: Acropolis Books, 1973.

Hamilton, James. *The Power to Probe: A Study of Congressional Investigations.* New York: Random House, 1976.

Harris, Marvin. *Anthropological Theory: A History of Theories of Culture.* New York: Thomas Y. Crowell, 1968.
Cannibals and Kings: The Origins of Culture. New York: Random House, 1977.

Hocart, Arthur Maurice, *Kingship.* Oxford: Clarendon Press, 1927.

Hogbin, H. Ian. *A Guadalcanal Society: The Kaoka Speakers.* New York: Holt, Rinehart & Winston, 1964.

Humphrey, Robert L. and Mary Elizabeth Chambers, *Ancient Washington: American Indian Cultures of the Potomac.* George Washington University Studies, No. 6, Washington, D.C.: George Washington University, 1977.

Jones, Rochelle and Peter Woll, *The Private World of Congress.* New York: The Free Press, 1979.

Josephy, Alvin M., Jr. *On the Hill: A History of the American Congress.* New York: Simon & Schuster, 1979.

Kiefer, Thomas M. *The Tausug: Violence and Law in a Philippine Moslem Society.* New York: Holt, Rinehart & Winston, 1972.

King, Larry L. *Of Outlaws, Con Men, Whores, Politicians, and Other Artists.* Middlesex, England: Penguin Books, 1981.

Kingdon, John W. *Congressmen's Voting Decisions.* New York: Harper & Row, 1973.

Kofmehl, Kenneth. *Professional Staffs of Congress.* West Lafayette, Ind.: Purdue University Press, 1962.

Lakier, Alexander Borisovich. *A Russian Looks at America: A Journal of Alexander Borisovich Lakier in 1857,* translated by Arnold Schrier and Joyce Story. Chicago: University of Chicago Press, 1979.

Madison, James, Alexander Hamilton, and John Jay. *The Federalist,* edited and introduced by Edward Meade Earle. New York: Random House, 1937.

Malinowski, Bronislaw. *Argonauts of the Western Pacific.* New York: E. P. Dutton, 1922.

Mair, Lucy. *African Societies.* Cambridge, England: Cambridge University Press, 1974.

Malbin, Michael J. *Unelected Representatives: Congressional Staff and the Future of Representative Government.* New York: Basic Books, 1979.

Maquet, Jacques. *The Premise of Inequality in Ruanda.* London: Oxford University Press, 1961.
Power and Society in Africa. London: Oxford University Press, 1971.
Civilizations of Black Africa. London: Oxford University Press, 1972.

Matthews, Donald R. *U.S. Senators and Their World.* Chapel Hill, N.C.: University of North Carolina Press, 1960; 2nd ed. New York: Norton, 1973.

Mauss, Marcel. *The Gift,* translated by Ian Cunnison. London: Cohen & West, 1975.

Maybury-Lewis, David. *Akwe-Shavante Society.* London: Oxford University Press, 1974.

McCurdy, Howard E. *The Insider's Guide to the Capitol.* Washington, D.C.: College of Public Affairs, American University, 1977.

Mead, Margaret. *Coming of Age in Samoa.* New York: William Morrow, 1928.

Miller, William. *Fishbait: The Memoirs of the Congressional Doorkeeper,* as told to Frances Spatz Leighton. New York: Warner Books, 1977.

Morgan, Lewis Henry. *League of the Iroquois.* Rochester, N.Y.: Sage & Brothers, 1851. Reprinted with introduction by William N. Fenton, Secaucus, N.J.: The Citadel Press, 1962.

Neill, Edward D. (ed.). *The English Colonization of America During the Seventeenth Century.* London: Strahan & Co., 1871.

Oleszek, Walter J. *Congressional Procedures and the Policy Process.* Washington, D.C.: Congressional Quarterly Press, 1978.

Oliver, Douglas. *A Solomon Island Society: Kinship and Leadership Among the Siuai of Bougainville.* Cambridge, Mass.: Harvard University Press, 1955.

Orfield, Gary. *Congressional Power: Congress and Social Change.* New York: Harcourt Brace Jovanovich, 1975.

Ornstein, Norman J. (ed.). *Congress in Change: Evolution and Reform.* New York: Praeger, 1975.
Interest Groups, Lobbying, and Policymaking. Washington, D.C.: Congressional Quarterly Press, 1977.

Peters, Charles. *How Washington Really Works.* Reading, Mass.: Addison-Wesley Publishing Co., 1980.

and Taylor Branch. *Blowing the Whistle: Dissent in Public Interest.* New York: Praeger, 1972.

and Michael Nelson. *The Culture of Bureaucracy.* New York: Holt, Rinehart & Winston, 1979.

Plutarch, *Fall of the Roman Republic,* translated by Rex Warner. Middlesex, England: Penguin Books, 1958.

Price, David. *Who Makes the Laws?* Cambridge, Mass.: Schenkman, 1972.

Psellus, Michael. *Fourteen Byzantine Rulers,* translated by E. R. A. Sewter. Middlesex, England: Penguin Books, 1966.

Ralph Nader Congress Project, *The Judiciary Committees,* Peter H. Schuck, Director. New York: Grossman Publishers, 1975.

Ruling Congress: How the House and Senate Rules Govern the Legislative Process, Ted Siff and Alan Weil, Directors. Middlesex, England: Penguin Books, 1977.

Redman, Eric. *The Dance of Legislation.* New York: Simon & Schuster, 1973.

Reid, T. R. *Congressional Odyssey: The Saga of a Senate Bill.* San Francisco, Calif.: W. H. Freeman & Co., 1980.

Reining, Priscilla Copeland and Barbara Lenkerd. *Village Viability in Contemporary Society,* AAAS Selected Symposium Vol. 34. Boulder, Col.: Westview Press, 1980.

Richards, Audrey and Adam Kuper. *Councils in Action.* Cambridge, England: Cambridge University Press, 1971.

Riegle, Donald with Trevor Armbrister. *O Congress.* New York: CBS Publications, Popular Library, 1972.

Ripley, Randall B. and Grace A. Franklin. *Congress, the Bureaucracy, and Public Policy.* Homewood, Ill.: Dorsey, 1976.

Congress: Process and Policy. New York: Norton, 1975.

Shack, William A. and Percy S. Cohen. *Politics in Leadership: Comparative Perspective.* Oxford: Clarendon Press, 1979.

Skinner, Elliot P. (ed.). *Peoples and Cultures of Africa.* New York: Doubleday, 1973.

Strathen, Andrew. *Ongka: A Self-Account by a New Guinea Big-Man.* New York: St. Martin's Press, 1979.

Suetonius, *The Twelve Caesars,* translated by Robert Graves, revised by Michael Grant. Middlesex, England: Penguin Books, 1979.

Swartz, Marc J., Victor W. Turner, and Arthur Tuden. *Political Anthropology.* Chicago: Aldine, 1966.

Swartz, Marc J. and David K. Jordan. *Anthropology: Perspective on Humanity.* New York: John Wiley & Sons, 1976.

Taylor, J. M. *Eva Perón: The Myths of a Woman.* Chicago: University of Chicago Press, 1980.

/ BIBLIOGRAPHY

ODY:

Tocqueville, Alexis de. *Democracy in America*, 2 vols., translated by Henry Reeve, revised by Francis Bowen. New York: Random House, 1945.

Trigger, Bruce G. (ed.). *Handbook of North American Indians*, Vol. 15: Northeast. Washington, D.C.: Smithsonian Institution, 1978.

Turner, Victor W. *Schism and Continuity in an African Society: A Study of Ndembu Village Life.* Manchester, England: Manchester University, 1957.

The Forest of Symbols. Ithaca, N.Y.: Cornell University Press, 1967.

U.S. Congress, *Legislative Activity Sourcebook: The United States Senate,* Commission on the Operation of the Senate, 1976.

The United States Senate: A Historical Bibliography. 1977.

Committees and Senate Procedures, Commission on the Operation of the Senate, 1977.

Senate Communications with the Public, Commission on the Operation of the Senate, 1977.

Senators: Offices, Ethics, and Pressures, Commission on the Operation of the Senate, 1977.

Studies Dealing with Budgetary, Staffing and Administrative Activities of the U.S. House of Representatives, 1947–1978. Commission on House Administration, 1978.

The Capitol, 7th ed. Washington, D.C.: GPO, 1979.

Weaver, Warren, Jr. *Both Your Houses: The Truth About Congress.* New York: Praeger, 1972.

White, William S. *Home Place: The Story of the U.S. House of Representatives.* Boston, Mass.: Houghton, Mifflin Co., 1965.

Citadel: The Story of the U.S. Senate. Boston, Mass.: Houghton Mifflin, 1968.

Wilson, Woodrow. *Congressional Government: A Study in American Politics* (originally published 1885). Cleveland, Ohio: World Publishing Co., 1956.

Woll, Peter. *American Bureaucracy*, 2nd ed. New York: Norton, 1977.

Young, James Sterling. *The Washington Community, 1800–1828.* New York: Columbia University Press, 1966.

INDEX

Caesar, Julius, 156, 198, 264
Calhoun, John C., 15, 174
Caligula, 198
Campaign contributions, 130, 131
Cannon, Joseph, 77, 194
Cannon Building, 31, 37
Capitol Building, 5, 14–18,
  178–179
  artwork in, 15
  cornerstone, 16
  dome, 14, 15
  underground complex, 16, 179
Capitol Hill, 14
  name origin, 5
Caplan, Marvin, 122, 123
Carter, Jimmy, 68, 80, 87, 105,
  107, 109, 110, 120, 143,
  153, 154, 230, 245, 264
Carter, Rosalyn, 183
Carter Administration, 262, 268
Carter Library, 211
Caucus, 18, 19, 22, 173, 174, 199
  word origin, 6
Cayuga Indians, 192
Central America, 11, 128
Central Intelligence Agency (CIA),
  152
Centre for a Free Society, 128
Ceremony. *See* Ritual
Chagnon, Napoleon, 228
Chambers, Mary, 13
Chaplains, 20
Charles II, King of England, 11
Cheney, Richard, 203
Cherokee Indians, 11
Chiles, Lawton, 81
Chowder and Marching Band, 20
Chrysler Corporation, 248
Church, Frank, 78–82, 146, 263
Churches, 258
Cicero, 197, 198
Civil Rights Act, 49, 251
Civil service laws, 99
Civil War, 93, 174, 175, 178, 199
Claiborne, William, 141
Clark, Bethine, 78
Clark, Champ, 202

Clark, Chase A., 78
Clark, Dick, 82
Clark, Joseph, 199
Clausewitz, Karl von, 90
Clay, Henry, 174
Clerical lawyers, 218
Clerk of the House, 214, 222, 223
Clerks, 48, 214, 215, 218, 221, 222,
  223
Coats, Daniel, 149
Cochran, Thad, 57, 149
Cohen, Bill, 148, 149
Collins, Cardiss, 139
Committee system, 18, 55, 58–63,
  73, 173–179, 184, 185, 215
  appropriations and authoriza-
    tions, 59, 72
  chairmanships, 55–58
  and congressional reorganiza-
    tion, 59–60
  of Continental Congress, 91
  open hearings, 179, 199, 216,
    218
  titles of, 57
Communism, 69, 140, 150
Comprehensive Employment and
  Training Act (CETA), 101
Conferences, 18, 184, 185, 199
Congress:
  1st, 166, 168, 172
  2nd, 172
  3rd, 171, 172
  4th, 172
  78th, 37
  80th, 217
  82nd, 188
  94th, 75, 217
  95th, 58, 82–83
  96th, 58, 131, 193
  97th, 37, 39, 72, 139, 142
  class of 1932, 40, 43
  class of 1974, 42, 43
  class of 1976, 42
  class of 1978, 42
  eighteenth and nineteenth cen-
    tury, 91–94, 166–178
  floor activity, 176, 221–227